Virtuous Policing

Bridging America's Gulf
Between Police and Populace

Virtuous Policing

Bridging America's Gulf
Between Police and Populace

David G. Bolgiano
L. Morgan Banks, III
James M. Patterson

CRC Press
Taylor & Francis Group
Boca Raton London New York

CRC Press is an imprint of the
Taylor & Francis Group, an **informa** business

CRC Press
Taylor & Francis Group
6000 Broken Sound Parkway NW, Suite 300
Boca Raton, FL 33487-2742

© 2016 by Taylor & Francis Group, LLC
CRC Press is an imprint of Taylor & Francis Group, an Informa business

No claim to original U.S. Government works

Printed on acid-free paper
Version Date: 20150617

International Standard Book Number-13: 978-1-4987-2350-3 (Paperback)

Visit the Taylor & Francis Web site at
http://www.taylorandfrancis.com

and the CRC Press Web site at
http://www.crcpress.com

Contents

Foreword

It is always an honor to be invited to write a foreword for a new book, but this one is special to me. I have known the authors for the better part of 20 years, and have been in their company at military and law enforcement conferences and training functions throughout the United States. I have been enlightened by their knowledge and experience, and inspired by their passion and commitment to the police officers and warriors of our country. This book is an expression of that passion and commitment. But it is far more than that—it is a labor of love, by three tried and true warriors, who are self-confessed "cop and warrior lovers." Only they could write this book. But it is not for the faint-hearted. It pulls no punches, shuns no controversial topic, and glosses over no issues or problems that beset America's law enforcement community in our day. They do not spare the rod for the ill informed or the ill intentioned—those terms are not mutually exclusive—who stand on the sidelines and cast stones at those who willingly risk their lives to protect their right to do so. Nor do they make excuses for those within the ranks of the cops and warriors—particularly those in leadership positions—who too often betray their oaths and duties by confusing risk avoidance with risk management.

Some may disagree with the authors' conclusions, and some may be shocked by their candor. But I think that most readers—particularly that "vast majority of the good cops" described by the authors—will be inspired and encouraged to honestly and objectively survey the scene in search of real problems and effective solutions. During my 32 years of service as an FBI special agent, I had the privilege to meet and interact with literally thousands of America's law enforcement officers. I have marveled at the number who selflessly left better-paying jobs and opportunities for a dangerous career of service, and I often wondered why. In fact, I've put that question to many whom I have met. As might be expected, the answers were as varied as the number of officers queried, and yet, there was a "golden thread" that ran through them that can best be described by these phrases, which I heard repeatedly: "I wanted to do something important," "I wanted to make a difference," "I wanted to give something back to my country and my community," and "I wanted to help people."

These statements, coupled with my personal observations of the officers' performances in the real world, encourage me to share the authors' high regard for the high aspirations of that vast majority of good cops. Too often those high aspirations are put to the test, as their job compels them to confront human nature at its worst. It would be unrealistic to think that none would become hardened or cynical as a consequence. The authors are not unrealistic. They neither ignore these realities nor exaggerate their effects. Most importantly, they strive to identify the causes—particularly those within the law enforcement community itself—and suggest solutions. Indeed, they honestly and courageously acknowledge the truth that not all cops and warriors are virtuous, and they candidly identify specific trends and friction points that work to separate the peacemakers from the communities they have sworn to protect and serve.

For those who may be prone to suspect the motives of these self-confessed lovers of cops and warriors, the title of this book—*Virtuous Policing: Bridging America's Gulf Between Police and Populace*—should be sufficient to allay such concerns. Knowing the authors as I do, I'm sure that they have no delusions about the obstacles to achieving this lofty goal, but being the warriors that I know them to be, I'm equally sure that they will not shrink before the challenges. If, as Winston Churchill once wrote, "virtuous motives, trammeled by inertia and timidity, are no match for armed and resolute wickedness," then it follows logically that armed and resolute wickedness are no match for virtue that is untrammeled by inertia and timidity. Clearly, the authors of this book are not trammeled by either inertia or timidity. God bless them!

John C. Hall
Supervisory Special Agent
Federal Bureau of Investigation (Retired)

Preface

In his gracious foreword to one of the authors' earlier works, *Combat Self-Defense*, Lieutenant Colonel Dave Grossman set forth his now-famous sheep, wolves, sheepdogs paradigm, in which law enforcement officers are cast as sheepdogs: the heroic societal shield between the flock and its predators. While police officers are indebted to Colonel Grossman for this, as well as for his body of work examining the behavioral dynamics of humans under combat conditions, the paradigm itself has been perverted to mean something never intended—that law enforcement officers are separate and apart from society or the flock. The sheepdog must *always* remain part of the flock; otherwise, a dangerous "us-versus-them" dynamic develops that is unhealthy to all good people and to society.

Recent events, such as the rioting, looting, and protesting that were the aftermath of the officer-involved shooting in Ferguson, Missouri, are too often driven by ignorance and emotion. While acknowledging that both ignorance and emotions are inseparable from the human condition, we will nevertheless endeavor to focus on tactical realities, legal principles, and well-settled ethical considerations in an effort to reach some ultimate truths about such cases. Right reason—not raw emotions—should drive any serious inquiry into these penultimate police–populace friction points.

In order to better understand these friction points, we will critically examine some specific fault lines and rifts between police and the populace. Our worst scenario is for the us-versus-them mindset to develop into an actual internecine warfare, as warned of in John Ross's 1996 prophetic tome *Unintended Consequences*. Or worse, where Ferguson becomes the new norm and police are forced to militarize themselves in order to survive. With the ubiquity of information—true and untrue—found on the Internet, technologies that have substantially diminished personal privacy interests, and omnipresent and sometimes overly intrusive laws, the friction points between heretofore law-abiding citizens and their police forces are in danger of increasing in number and magnitude.

Since it is doubtful that civilization could or would desire to turn back the clock of technology in a self-imposed curtailment of its wrath, the only things we *can* control are our laws and societal rules on how the police and the populace interact. Most of the law enforcement policies, procedures, and leadership methods we analyze will be done through the overarching lens of the cardinal virtues: self-control, justice, competency, and moral courage. Using case studies of some famous and not-so-famous police–populace interactions, we pick at them solely with the intent of our society collectively and sincerely learning from its mistakes. If we keep sticking our face into the same chainsaw—a simple definition of insanity—we risk falling off the cliff into either anarchy or a police state.

The authors are self-admitted cop and warrior lovers. We have spent the better part of our professional lives working as law enforcement officers, serving as soldiers, training with both of them, or as prosecutors in the military and civilian courts. The "average" law enforcement officer swears an oath, pins on a badge, and places his or her life in jeopardy by agreeing to be that part of the flock that must deal with life's unpleasant underbelly: murders, rapes, armed robberies, suicides, burglaries, petty thefts, prostitution, and drug dealings. As such, society owes them a degree of respect and deference.

But we also recognize that society places a great deal of trust in that average police officer. The powers to detain, investigate, and if necessary, take a life, are immense. All of this authority comes with concomitant responsibility. Most officers shoulder this admirably on a daily basis. It is for the vast majority of the good cops that we write this book. Having done so, we also acknowledge that it takes only a small minority of bad cops—especially in leadership positions—to spoil the lot. The evil minority of toxic police officers are either willfully ignorant or too pusillanimous by nature to be rehabilitated or made trusted members of the flock. Either way, they must be confronted by the collective good of our society with courage, justice, competency, and self-control. This must never be done with rage or vindictiveness. If ever our passions override our reason within these pages, we ask forgiveness. But, more importantly, we ask the reader to read beyond these errors in an effort to seek the greater truths possibly contained herein.

STYLE AND TERMINOLOGY

In order to keep this book readable and concise, we used the terms *police officer*, *cop*, and *law enforcement officer* to apply to all those sworn officers who protect the public, including policemen and women, sheriffs, deputies, corrections officers, and military police. Additionally, we often used the word *he* or *man* for ease of reading and certainly intend no offense to those dedicated female officers who serve. Similarly, we used the term *soldier* to include all those military officers, warrant officers, noncommissioned officers, and enlisted personnel who serve in all of our services, including the Army, Navy, Marine Corps, and Air Force.

Acknowledgments

We owe a personal debt of gratitude to some of the very best that law enforcement and the military have to offer in terms of leaders. Too large a group to single out everyone, we feel it is important to acknowledge those who have positively impacted our careers personally and have honorably and courageously served our great republic: Supervisory Special Agents John C. Hall, Urey Patrick, and Tom Petrowski of the FBI; Major General Gary L. Harrell, U.S. Army; former Navy SEAL, Maryland state trooper, and Secret Service agent Frank Larkin, now serving as a sergeant-at-arms, United States; Majors Jeffrey Rosen and Frank Melcavage, Baltimore Police Department; a host of fine operators from the military and law enforcement worlds, to include G. John Taylor, W. Hays Parks, Jason "Doc" Mark, Command Sergeant Major Mark Berry, Guy "Buddy" Johnson, George "Butch" Rogers, and Frank Barile of the Baltimore County Police Department; Jeff Kirkham, Mark Royka, Frank Short, and Jim Hicks at the Department of Defense and Drug Enforcement Administration; Gary Greco, Mike Braun, Tom Sheperd, Randy Watt, Tom Samples, and Bill Lewinski, Scott Burhmaster, and Patricia Thiem: the core team at Force Science Institute and all of that organization's instructional staff of experts; the late Dr. Richard Ward at the University of New Haven; and Chief Dean Esserman of the New Haven Police Department. Last, all the terrific officers in southeastern New Mexico with whom we have worked intimately over the past few years. These persons individually and collectively epitomize the selfless qualities needed to make virtuous policing and leadership a reality. We wish to sincerely thank our publisher, Carolyn Spence, and the Taylor & Francis production team. Their patience, diligence, and suggestions made our book a better product. We, the authors, are responsible for any error, omission, or poor wording. None of these individuals, except where specifically cited, are responsible for any of the content of this book. That is the sole responsibility of the authors. We also wish to express our undying love and gratitude to our families for enduring our time away from them both on missions for our country and in writing this book.

About the Authors

David "Bo" Bolgiano, JD, MSS, is a retired military officer and former Baltimore police officer with more than 34 years of combined service. He has served in multiple combat deployments with Special Operations Forces and in the 82nd Airborne Division in Iraq and Afghanistan. He last served as a faculty member at the U.S. Army War College. Bolgiano is the author of *Combat Self-Defense: Saving America's Warriors From Risk Averse Commanders and Their Lawyers* and coauthor, with Jim Patterson, of *Fighting Today's Wars: How America's Leaders Have Failed Our Warriors.* Bolgiano currently trains, lectures, and testifies as a recognized use-of-force expert for police and military clients and audiences.

Morgan Banks, PhD, is a psychologist and retired colonel in the United States Army. With more than 37 years of service, most of them spent as an operational psychologist, he helped establish the Army's Survival, Evasion, Resistance, and Escape Program, the psychological screening program for Army Special Forces personnel, and, prior to his retirement, was the Army's and USSOCOM's senior psychologist. Dr. Banks has worked extensively in the field of counterterrorism and has been deployed to both Afghanistan and Iraq. He has often written and lectured on the use and ethics of operational psychology.

James M. Patterson, JD, LLM, is a retired Special Forces–qualified Army Colonel with more than 36 years of service. He previously served with the 82nd Airborne Division, the 7th Special Forces Group, and the Asymmetric Warfare Group. He was also Command Judge Advocate for the 1st Special Forces Operational Detachment-Delta. A multiple-tour combat veteran of the Global War on Terror, Patterson also has experience as a sworn law enforcement officer in the American Southwest. He has written and lectured extensively in the fields of international law, use of deadly force, and operational law.

1

Introduction

Over the past two decades, we have had the honor to represent, treat medically and psychologically, or provide expert testimony on behalf of individuals charged criminally as the result of using deadly force in the line of duty. These young men and women—either law enforcement officers or warriors in the military—represent some of the finest human beings our republic produces. Full of courage, good intentions, and a desire to fight on the side of good against evil, they are also very human. Some are full of vim and vigor, possessing that bravado that many type-A alpha males and females exhibit. Others are quiet, patient, and even shy. Through the fault of others, they are thrust into an often negative limelight—sometimes even facing criminal charges for doing what society asks of them and for which society itself lacks the stomach or courage. These are men and women that respond when something "goes bump in the night." Instead of cowering under the sheets, calling the police, and praying nothing goes wrong, these folks volunteer to investigate that "bump," often to their physical peril.

After the dust settles, the bullets stop flying, and the last vestiges of the news media clear out, these police and military members' real troubles often begin. Almost immediately, whether it is after a shoot-out with suspected insurgents in Iraq or a police officer's use of force against a violent suspect in urban America, the second-guessers, naysayers, politicians, and others too afraid to physically try to "free those in Tibet" begin their chattering nincompoopery: "Why did the officer have to shoot that poor young man? He was only armed with a knife!" "Why didn't they swarm the suspect?" "The police should have used minimum force." "He was unarmed and surrendering." The list could go on and on. But all of these postincident commentaries fail for two major reasons: They ignore the tactical dynamics of a close deadly force encounter, and they fail to take the side of the good guys.

Winston Churchill once stated, "I utterly refuse to remain neutral between the fire brigade and the fire." Too often, those judging the actions of our young police officers and warriors expect or demand that it should be a fair fight. This is the definition of insanity. For if one refuses to acknowledge there are good guys, then why fight at all?

Time and time again, prosecutors, judge advocates, mayors, and even chiefs of police or military commanders—often themselves unskilled in the realities of a deadly force encounter and ignorant of the actual laws surrounding such encounters—superimpose their own notions of reasonableness onto a case after the fact. This is something our courts have often said:

> We must avoid substituting our personal notions of proper police proce-
> dure for the instantaneous decision of the officer at the scene. We must
> never allow the theoretical, sanitized world of our imagination to replace
> the dangerous and complex world that policemen face every day. What
> constitutes "reasonable" action may seem quite different to someone facing
> a possible assailant than to someone analyzing the question at leisure.[*]

Sometimes, political pressures, from either an angry civil rights group or a foreign government, compound this woeful ignorance or otherwise wrongly influence our system of justice. Either way, the least powerful person in the equation is sacrificed: the young warrior or police officer at the tip of the spear. If a general officer, or even the president of the United States, is not held legally accountable for the thousands of civilian, noncombatant deaths they cause when they order a Joint Direct Attack Munition (JDAM) bombing or Hellfire missile strike from an unmanned aerial vehicle, then how in good conscience can they hold young warriors responsible for unintended deaths resulting from split-second decisions of close-quarters combat?

This issue goes unnoticed by most in the press, who assume—wrongfully—that the military chain of command or civilian prosecutors know enough about the subject to make a wise and just determination when exercising their prosecutorial discretion. The fact remains that they do not. The press also often has an agenda other than seeking the truth: Titillating stories of a "rogue" cop or soldier sell more copies than the truth. But, especially in urban areas, all this does is widen the chasm

---

[*] *Smith v. Freland*, 954 F.2d 343, 347 (6th Cir. 1992).

between citizens and police. We, as a society, should collectively cringe and shame the media for repeating the irrelevant matter of an officer's or suspect's skin color. Absent some showing of a premeditated racial animus on either party, people simply do not have time to discern skin color during a violent encounter. Yet, all sides of the political spectrum of news outlets constantly strum the racial chord: "Unarmed *Black* Male Shot by *White* Officer."

One of the unfortunate but predictable results of this is a breakdown of the trust between the warrior and his or her leaders. When this happens, we often will see an increase in actual inappropriate behavior by the warrior. In other words, if the soldier or cop believes that he is "on his own," he will most likely still do what he thinks is right, but then he will cover it up, or he will act in a manner that increases the gap between himself and his leadership. When he believes that he is being asked to put his life at risk without the support of his leadership, he will find ways to justify actions that no one could question. Or, as a police officer, he or she will simply stop policing. And, in neighborhoods like Ferguson, where crime is a recurrent problem, it will be the citizens that suffer the most by this reduced enforcement.

When this lack of trust then extends to the population they serve, the social contract between the police or warrior and the people is destroyed. The result of this is most apparent in some of our large inner cities, where the police are not trusted, but only feared or hated. It is also readily apparent in modern combat zones where soldiers, even when shooting with provocation at a suspected jihadist insurgent, feel compelled to plant additional evidence at the scene. This is emblematic of the lack of trust between both warrior and leader, and warrior and the society in which he operates.

This is not to say that young police officers or soldiers do not have a clear duty and responsibility to act virtuously and within the scope of their lawful authority. If a soldier or cop randomly or carelessly shoots innocent civilians or noncombatants—essentially using force without lawful authority—then, he would be guilty of murder, manslaughter, or negligent homicide and should be fully prosecuted.

But, the overwhelming majority of our young men and women who volunteer to put on the uniform are not sociopaths. They do not wake up in the morning thinking, "I hope I get to kill someone today" (unless, of course, that someone is an Osama bin Laden-type terrorist). We expect virtue in our police and military ranks.

Therefore, a section of this book is devoted to what it means to be a virtuous leader and person. We must maintain the moral high ground, but unfortunately, the notion that such virtues are capable of being defined has been lost to a generation inculcated with the ridiculous idea that there is no right or wrong or everyone's opinion is of equal value. Multiculturalism trumps reason. In other words, so long as you're not offending someone, you are okay. This is moral, intellectual, and spiritual hogwash. Society should demand that its police and military are men and women of strong virtues. This character trait, rather than diversity of sexual preference or other irrelevancies, needs to be addressed in both the selection and retention of young warriors and officers. In other words, it is far more important that a person has a virtuous character, regardless of whatever immutable characteristic they may otherwise possess.

The tactical skills, laws, and leadership principles between the soldier and a law enforcement officer are nearly identical. For purposes of understanding the subject matters covered herein, the terms *warrior, cop,* and *law enforcement officer* will be used interchangeably. Where differences exist, they will be clearly spelled out. The specific audience of this book is comprised of military and law enforcement leaders and aspiring leaders. But, the general audience is the citizenry of our republic who pay taxes and typically are supportive of their police and military communities. This trust—between leaders and subordinates and between communities and their warriors—is an important two-way street, the boundaries and lawful expectations of which this book will hopefully clarify. Too much noise—noise of racial hatred, emotional hyperbole, or just plain ignorance—is clouding the important public discourse surrounding these topics. We attempt to rise above such rhetoric and take a serious, tough look at what works and what does not in these relationships.

The United States was established as a constitutional republic, not a democracy. For this we should be most grateful. The tyranny of the majority or the mob that concerned the founders should *rarely* prevail over the constitutional protections and rights of the individual. In order for this form of governance to succeed, a social contract, a bond of trust, must exist between society and its warriors, law enforcement and military. When this bond is broken, the risk of anarchy (as has happened in some of our inner cities and, recently, in Ferguson) or totalitarianism as a response increases dramatically. Moreover, our Bill of Rights merely acknowledges the preexisting God-given rights of the individual in order to maintain that bond. One key point here is that these are rights of individuals, not some collective right of our government.

This fundamental concept—that the state's authority emanates from the individual, not the opposite—is lost on many otherwise bright Americans. Recently, an Army officer, as a part of his War College thesis, wrote the following disturbing words: "Individual self-defense is not an inherent right, but rather flows from public authority delegated by the sovereign." That a military officer, sworn to uphold and defend the Constitution, would possess such a perverted understanding of our republic is troubling. That this individual is an attorney and advisor to our military's senior-most leaders is even more disturbing. The sovereign derives all its power from the people—not the reverse. This concept is why these United States were founded and why throughout the past centuries men and women have risked their lives defending true freedom.

There are limits on the authority of our government to exercise only that authority that we grant it. And that we retain God-given rights that should not be abridged. Among these rights are free speech, freedom of religious practice, the ability to defend ourselves from those who would do us harm, and specific protections against the ability of our government to use our legal system against us, for example, through an unlawful search and seizure or self-incrimination. This book is dedicated to the proposition that these notions are not quaint, antiquated ideas that are somehow irrelevant to our modern society. Human nature—human operating system version 1.0—has not and will not change. If we think that we are immune to the horrors of a coercive central government, we are perilously mistaken.

Similarly, if we believe that we are immune from the opposite danger, that of an anarchic existence that exists in many war-torn countries today, we are also mistaken. Therefore, we—the citizenry, the police, and the military—must be extremely careful about upsetting the balance between the legitimate authority we bestow upon our government, executed by human beings, and the individual autonomy that our Bill of Rights codifies. After all, we, the individual people of the United States, are ultimately responsible for our own safety and security, as well as the health and welfare of our families, our communities, and individual persons.

Essentially, all of the above revolve around the concept of true community policing. Mike Masterson, chief of police from Boise, Idaho, wrote a compelling article in the *FBI Law Enforcement Bulletin* that sets forth the importance of strengthening the police–populace bond. In the first paragraph, Chief Masterson states:

Law enforcement agencies devote much time and energy to the tangible things that can be improved—better-equipped squad cars, more efficient technology systems, new police headquarters and firearms ranges, ballistic shields, energy-conducted weapons, and handgun and rifle rotations. These projects often take away the focus from equally important intangibles, such as how police officers treat others. How they regard people, from coworkers and citizens to the individuals they arrest, is crucial to law enforcement's reputation and corresponds to officer safety.[*]

In many urban settings, it is very difficult for law enforcement not to develop an attitude of superiority when much of the community they police (1) throws trash on the ground, including in their own backyards; (2) urinates and defecates in public housing common areas; (3) has no concept of private property rights and the notion of ownership; and (4) routinely lies to the police even when the police are trying to help them. This is the sad reality in much of urban America. Think of the really blighted areas of Detroit, East or West Baltimore, or Newark.

There are a multitude of factors that have led to this result, including poor education, lack of meaningful employment, cultural perceptions of right and wrong, and a growing reliance on our elected government to fix essentially community issues that are not resolvable by elected officials. Addressing those problems is well beyond the scope of this book, and would take an act of God of Noah's flood proportions to remedy.

But, that does not mean we should throw our hands into the air and await a "zombie apocalypse." That may sell survival equipment and food, but it is not the adult and moral voice for our greater society. So, increasing the police–populace gulf found in such blighted areas is unthinkable and avoidable. Even in the most blighted areas, we can endeavor to fix urban America one department or neighborhood at a time. It takes a plan, patience, and hard work. This plan, our hope, goal, and belief in writing this book, will reverse the downward spiral that we see every day on the news.

Problems that police address are often merely the symptoms of far greater and more intractable societal issues. Crime is high among young Black men? Is that a police issue? In part, yes, but all a police department can do is put a Band-Aid on a sucking chest wound and tell the patient to take two Tylenol and call again if needed. Standard policing only deals with symptoms and not root causes.

---

[*] Masterson, Mike, "Improving Officer Safety and Citizen Support: Solving the Puzzle," *FBI Law Enforcement Bulletin*, May 2014.

A genuine community policing program, coupled with a departmental attitude evidencing a genuine community policing approach, focuses the department on addressing in an innovative and productive manner the underlying causes that drive crime, such as the high crime rate among young Black men. Now the cynic might claim that they are beyond hope and help and redemption. All one can do is lock them up. We don't agree with that because we have seen meaningful community policing approaches work. Moreover, ethically, it is the only right choice for our civilization. Each author has spent substantial portions of their lives in countries where there is no law and order—Iraq, Afghanistan, and other places—and we do not want to see American society trend in that direction. Too many Americans are in prison already.

2

Human Operating System 1.0

There are several themes that run throughout this book. None of them are particularly original, but we think it is helpful to set them forth here as overarching concepts in order to explain why we are who we are as human beings and how we got there. Good policing is about the art of persuasion. A police officer can use diplomacy, as in "Do you fellas think it is a good idea to keep drinking at this bar?" Or, an officer can use coercive force, such as "If you do not leave this bar immediately, I am going to lock you up!" Societally, it is better for all involved if officers learn how fellow human beings think and act—human operating system 1.0—so that diplomacy is used more often than coercion.

First, people are learning creatures. We are constantly changing our behavior, based on our environment, biological makeup, and genetics. Because biology is very difficult to change, and our genetic makeup is fundamentally immutable, for the purposes of this book we will focus on how the environment changes our behavior. It is no surprise that people generally do more of what is rewarded and less of that which is punished. Punishment can also produce reactive consequences that are not desired, making it more challenging to utilize than reward. In fact, these observations are true of all organisms. What makes humans unique in this regard is the sheer complexity of the amount of information that influences us. Our brain organizes and utilizes a tremendous amount of data, shifting and combining those inputs, focusing on one thing while ignoring another, and changes our behaviors, often without any awareness on our part. This basic fact of psychology is remarkably easy to forget and overlook when analyzing human behavior.

As a simple relevant example, a teenager who is struggling to find his future may steal something minor from a store. If he has virtuous parents, who have taught him right from wrong, he may feel guilty about the act.

Even so, he may steal for a variety of reasons, perhaps just to see how easy it is, perhaps to impress someone else, or just on a whim. Again, if his parents are strong role models for virtuous behavior, and they find out that he has committed a crime, it is highly likely that their reaction will decrease the likelihood of another such incident. Their influence on him will likely supersede both the encouragement of his "friends" who prompted him to steal in the first place and the immediate pleasure he got from possessing the item. On the other hand, if he does not have good role models for parents, or if his social group has encouraged him to demonstrate his "manliness" or identity by stealing, he will be repetitively rewarded for the act. Only if the likelihood of getting caught increases might this balance change. And, if the odds are small that he will get caught the first time, he will also learn from that fact. He will also learn (accurate or not) that he can continue to steal routinely, getting rewarded each and every time, and never get caught. It might take several years of his stealing (being rewarded by the approval of his peers each time) before he is caught. In the off chance that he then goes to court and is convicted of a crime, he will most likely receive minimal punishment, since he would be a first-time offender, although he would now have a permanent criminal record.

In turn, this criminal record makes it much harder for him to get a job; but on the other hand, he has learned that he can cope with being caught. The likelihood of his continued criminal activity has just increased. The factors, then, that have turned our judicial system on its head are these: a significant lapse between the time someone commits a criminal act (the first stealing event) and the punishment, and the minimal punishment that occurs. This is compounded by the fact that the punishment, while easy for the young man to cope with in the short term, will have a very significant negative long-term effect on his ability to be a productive member of society. He may also, based on his previous experiences, see the punishment as unfair. And, since it may be minimal in the short term, he may take pride in having coped with it. He has learned what his environment taught him. Stealing is cool, and the only negative repercussions are ones with which he can easily cope. By the time he realizes the hugely negative impact his behavior has had on his future, it is too late.

As we will discuss later in the book, there are some areas of our country that have much higher rates of crime than others. They are generally the more urbanized areas, and we believe that one major reason for this is the number of dysfunctional families that are raising children. Worldwide, young males commit most violent crime. Part of this is certainly biology.

There are many hormonal and developmental factors that are at play as boys turn into men. But, the way those factors are expressed are hugely impacted by the role models that young men are exposed to while developing. Again, there is nothing particularly novel in this concept, but the result in many of our country's urban areas is devastating, not only to the majority of people who are good solid citizens who have to cope with a higher rate of crime, but also, and more importantly, to the young men whose lives are ruined by it. Good—even great—police work cannot prevent this, but it is critical for those policing in such areas to understand the factors that are at play if we are to have any success in reducing crime and minimizing the gulf between police and populace. Given all these factors, however, the behavior of our police can only affect a very small part of the environment that results in these outcomes. Only if the laws are just, the judicial system responsive and timely, and our police rewarded for using good judgment will they be able to have any long-lasting, positive effect.

Most people, even in the most devastated urban centers (think of today's Detroit), are good people who are trying to live their lives to the best of their ability. Unfortunately, most policemen are disproportionately exposed to a small section of the population, most often under conditions that do not bring out the best in people. Good policemen learn from their experiences too. If they are patrolling a high-crime area, and individuals of one race conduct most of the criminal activity, then they will modify their behavior based on that learning. If they have reasonably felt more threatened when apprehending certain types of suspects (whether based on race, age, dress, or other objectively observable behaviors), they will learn that similar suspects should be approached with more caution in the future. Sometimes we change our behavior in a conscious way, learning from our experiences and integrating them into our behavior. Learning how to exit a vehicle and how to approach a potentially violent suspect are two examples. But much of what we learn is not conscious. Our brain does not consciously tell us all of the actions it is taking to protect us. We may just get a "sixth sense" feeling that something is wrong, or we may unconsciously feel comfortable taking a certain action. This feeling is based on our experiences, whether we are overtly aware of it or not. Sometimes this learned behavior keeps us alive. Any experienced cop will pick up on subtle cues to danger that he cannot specifically articulate.

But, we cannot forget that the brain is not immune from mistakes. Our brains are inherently lazy. If our experience has been that most young Black males with whom we interact are dangerous, we will learn that young Black males are dangerous. It is an easily statistically demonstrable fact that this is *not* generally true, even in high-crime urban areas. However, data will not easily change our expectations, because one is based on experience, and the other on dry research and demographic statistics on arrests. The fact that the learning that has occurred is biased is not relevant to the officer trying to best integrate his life experiences into his work. And, officers of all races learn these same errors: In other words, Black officers in a high-crime urban area will treat young Black male suspects with the same degree of suspicion as do White officers.

We have a saying in the military that "perception is reality." If I perceive something as dangerous, my body will react as if I am under threat, regardless of whether the threat is real. As mentioned above, police, especially in urban areas, are going to be exposed to a disproportionately high criminal percentage of the population. To survive, they will learn from this experience, and they will begin to act consistent with their experiences. Their perception of danger is real, regardless of the actual threat. A policeman can make two types of mistakes in this area. On the one hand, he can overestimate the dangerousness of an individual, in which case he may damage his relationship with the individual, and leave a bad taste in the mouth of an honest citizen. On the other hand, he can underestimate the dangerousness of an individual, in which case he can end up seriously injured or killed. It should not, then, be surprising that police are accused of being overly aggressive at times.

The huge social unrest and public outcry over the shooting of Michael Brown in Ferguson, Missouri, is an example of how powerful perceptions can be. Succinctly put, the police and judicial system apparently believe (perceive) that Michael Brown was attacking Officer Wilson, and that there was reasonable justification for Officer Wilson to use deadly force to stop him. Many of the people who live in Ferguson believe (perceive) that Officer Wilson shot an unarmed Black man. They also believe that Michael Brown's body was left for several hours uncovered in a degrading manner. Every one of the previous statements may be accurate, but the interpretation and the perceptions of what they mean are vastly different, depending on who perceives them. While the facts of the incident can be studied, the two dramatically different perceptions of the events of that day are both real, and are driving a huge wedge between the police and the population they serve. The factors that would have minimized this wedge did not and still do not exist in the relationship between the police and the citizens of Ferguson. It is to these factors that we write.

Much of what we have discussed here is not easily changed. In fact, we view many of these factors as persistent given the current environment in which we live. Impoverished inner cities will not spontaneously develop a new abundance of good role models for young men. Police will not develop a magical method of determining what someone is actually thinking, or of predicting without error who is willing to hurt them in order to prevent arrest. These are simply the fundamental human factors that exist, and they have existed as long as we have had a civilization that utilizes policemen to enforce our laws.

This leads to the second point we want to make: Humans are still using operating system 1.0. What we mean by this is that we have not had an upgrade to our fundamental operating system for at least 10,000 years, and there is no upgrade currently planned or anticipated. If you want to understand human behavior, you can look around you, but you also need to look at history. People operate the same way they have since the invention of writing and, of course, earlier. The same dilemmas and challenges that men and women faced 2,000 years ago challenge us today. Technology has changed, and cultures (our collective norms) continuously change, but the basic fundamentals of human behavior have not and will not change. Just like there will never be an end to war as long as there are people left on earth, there will always be people who violate our cultural norms and laws. And in any police force, there will always be a few bullies who abuse their position and power. The huge majority of people in this country, regardless of where they live, wish to live in a peaceable manner. The vast majority of police in this country are great Americans who wish to make life safer for their fellow citizens. But, just as there are those who commit violent crimes against other citizens, policemen are people too, with the same challenges as the rest of us. They are just as susceptible to cultural norms, and if those norms are insular, and an "us-versus-them" mentality develops, there can be predictable negative second-order effects. To this also, we write.

The last major theme we want to discuss is the natural progression of humans to always want to improve our lot. Whether it is the drive to develop better medicine or the push for better nutrition, or just the simple desire for more money and things, our operating system functions to push us in the direction of never being satisfied with what we have. No great leader ever said, "I left this organization exactly as I found it." Our nature is to strive for a better life. This is a fundamental part of human nature. Part of our need to improve things results in a greater and greater number of laws to control behavior and make us safer. Few politicians get elected by claiming, "I will prevent new laws from passing." No rational person believes that controls on human behavior are not needed. One can argue that establishing controls is the first hallmark of a civilization. Laws save us from the tyrannies of anarchy and the mob. The Code of Hammurabi is still studied because he established written laws that would apply to all. But, there are always costs to such controls. As we will explain, few laws exist without some negative second-order effects. This is true in society as well as in police departments.

"Never give an order that won't be followed!" That concept is fundamental to good military leadership, and the authors argue for all good leadership. Any good military leader knows that giving such orders works to destroy their credibility and undermine their authority. It also teaches subordinates that not all orders need to be followed. Remember that learning is always occurring. What happens when a law is passed that is not followed? The 55 miles per hour speed limit and its effects on safety is a good example of such ineffective arbitrariness. Another example might be the law making it illegal for anyone under the age of 21 to consume alcohol. The authors can attest that plenty of 19- and 20-year-old soldiers drink alcohol, and since they cannot drink in common settings, there are predictable negative second-order effects. It may be that the positive effects outweigh the negative effects in this law, but this is not always the case.

There is a great example in the news as of this writing. Eric Garner was selling individual cigarettes (loosies) on the sidewalk in New York City. (Making the selling of individual cigarettes illegal versus selling packs of cigarettes in a store may have some positive societal effects, although the authors have a hard time figuring out what those might be.) He was arrested, but apparently he resisted arrest and died during the resulting altercation. What is missed by much of the coverage of the event is the absurdity of the criminal charge. It was basically a charge of evading the tax on cigarettes. A law taxing cigarettes, a known cancer-causing and highly addictive item, makes plenty of sense. The tax will predictably reduce the use of cigarettes, and the tax can be used for plenty of positive social benefits. Unfortunately, the rather predictable second-order effects of passing such a tax are often ignored. Not only will there be a significant financial incentive created to break the law, but police can only enforce all laws, including this one, with the potential use of deadly force as an outcome. Even tax laws can only be enforced if society agrees that the police can, under extreme circumstances, use deadly force to enforce the law.

Otherwise, how can we enforce any law? If a person decides he will not follow the law, any law, and refuses to comply with those sent to enforce the law, what options are available? Eventually, deadly force must be in the repertoire of the officers. If a perception develops among the population that a law is not fair—that it is not an honest part of the social contract between the population and the police—bad outcomes are inevitable.

Simple math tells us that more laws mean more lawbreakers. More lawbreakers means more destroyed lives and costs to society. But as we discussed above, humans always want more laws. This is an inherent part of the human condition, and our police have the job of trying to make the best of it, and to help make it result in an overall positive outcome. It is a very challenging dilemma, to say the least. But, too much of the discussion in the media concerning Eric Garner's death focuses on the split seconds leading up to his death. We believe that more discussion ought to focus on the relationship between the government and the governed—and how to create an environment where such coercive interactions are lessened, not increased.

There are some things that can make that environment worse, though. If police were rewarded for making arrests, then we would expect them to make more arrests. This may be good, or we may just end up with more young men in jail at a huge societal cost. If the same police were rewarded for getting to know their local community, then that could be a huge help for community policing and actually lead to less crime. But, how does a department (and society) actually reward our policemen for something as nonmetric as this? This is the real challenge. It is very hard to put into a comparative statistics (COMSTAT) briefing how well our officers know and understand a local community. It takes hard work, patient leadership, and an affirmation of good community policing to crack this code. It can be done, though. In Chapter 18, we discuss one department, New Haven, Connecticut, under the leadership of Chief Dean Esserman, where this type of hard work is proving fruitful.

Most of the laws passed in our country are written in a sincere attempt to help our citizens, but often without thinking of second-order effects and unintended consequences. A great example of the predictable second-order effects of such well-meaning laws comes from *Car and Driver* magazine. Laws to prohibit impaired driving are designed to prevent accidents, and cell phone use as an impairment is certainly a significant cause of modern driving accidents. But, poorly written laws combined with poor law enforcement judgment lead to absurdity.

Evening rush hour in Fresno, California, can get ugly. On January 5, 2012, Steven Spriggs was stuck in it, fully stopped in his 2006 Toyota Highlander on the construction clogged Route 41. Waiting as darkness fell, he looked for a route around the congestion on his iPhone 4's navigation app. A California Highway Patrol motorcycle officer saw the phone's glow light up Spriggs's face, and Spriggs was soon staring at a $165 fine for violating California Vehicle Code section 23123(a).

Enacted in 2008, the law reads, "A person shall not drive a motor vehicle while using a wireless telephone unless that telephone is designed and configured to allow hands-free listening and talking, and is used in that manner while driving."

As the article points out, it is legal for a driver to pull out and unfold a map while driving, but not to look at his phone. While initially unsuccessful in challenging his ticket, Spriggs eventually succeeded when the California Fifth District Court of Appeals reversed the previous decisions.

The question the authors have is, what was learned by Spriggs? It would not take very many examples like this for the people of California to develop a very different image of the California Highway Patrol, and it would not be one that would strengthen the social contract between police and the populace.

A more outrageous example is one from New Jersey. The authors cannot state it better than Randy Balko in *The Washington Post*:

Last October, Shaneen Allen, 27, was pulled over in Atlantic County, N.J. The officer who pulled her over says she made an unsafe lane change. During the stop, Allen informed the officer that she was a resident of Pennsylvania and had a concealed carry permit in her home state. She also had a handgun in her car. Had she been in Pennsylvania, having the gun in the car would have been perfectly legal. But Allen was pulled over in New Jersey, home to some of the strictest gun control laws in the United States.

Allen is a black single mother. She has two kids. She has no prior criminal record. Before her arrest, she worked as a phlebotomist. After she was robbed two times in the span of about a year, she purchased the gun to protect herself and her family. There is zero evidence that Allen intended to use the gun for any other purpose. Yet Allen was arrested. She spent 40 days in jail before she was released on bail. She's now facing a felony charge that, if convicted, would bring a three-year mandatory minimum prison term.

Amazingly, what should have resulted in a quick education by the officer, telling Allen to unload and place her firearm in the trunk of her car, turned into a nightmare for a good, law-abiding mother of two. Part of the problem is that police leadership—because they do not trust their subordinates—have taken away much of the individual officer discretion that peace officers used to possess. We will discuss this further, as it is an integral problem in police–community relations. But, perhaps even more amazingly, the Atlantic County prosecutor Jim McClain decided to prosecute Allen to the fullest extent of the law, seeking a conviction and imprisonment. Eventually, after huge public pressure and a change in statewide guidance by the New Jersey attorney general, the prosecutor reversed his decision. Later, Governor Christie pardoned Allen. One news outlet noted that Allen's arrest "shocked the conscience" of a broad range of Americans.* It is an understatement to say that this action caused major damage to the social contract between police and the people they serve. Who would now trust the New Jersey police and judicial system to do the right thing? This is an example of a bad law enforced by the poor judgment of both the police officer and the prosecutor. Policing is about people, not zero-tolerance policies and agendas. Every case is different from the next, and police need to have the education, understanding, empathy, and authority to exercise appropriate discretion.

To recap the themes we are presenting:

1. People are always learning from their experiences. Rewarded behavior increases in likelihood, while punished behavior decreases. Punishment can also have a variety of hard-to-predict reactive consequences, making its use, while potentially very effective, challenging in execution.
2. Laws are essential for civilization, and the creation of new laws is an inherent part of the human condition. These laws and their enforcement form a bond, a social contract between the population and their police forces. The perception of this contact is often more important than the facts.
3. More laws inevitably equal more lawbreakers. Passing any law will result in some negative effects. The real question is whether the positive effects outweigh the negative ones.

---

* *The Daily Caller*, September 28, 2014, http://dailycaller.com/2014/09/28/shaneen-allen-to-avoid-prison-as-new-jersey-ag-revises-sentencing-guidance-for-gun-law-violations/.

4. Careful crafting of our laws (rarely done), along with a responsive and timely judicial system (grossly overburdened and slow at present), is essential to maintaining that bond.
5. Good policing, using good judgment by individual officers, is the best our police can do to maximize benefit and minimize the cost of the human condition.

3

How America Treats Her Warriors and the Cults of Tribalism and Victimology

Since 2001, America has focused on its military's deployments and concomitant use of force throughout the world or—as the warriors themselves call it—downrange. Arguments may be posited, pro and con, as to the utility of what has collectively come to be known as the rules of engagement (ROE) for the application of force in foreign countries. These rules attempt to create an operational link between the nation's overarching strategic goals and the tactical application of force at the pointy end of the spear. For instance, the United States could rapidly eliminate enemy resistance within a walled city by simply executing a Rolling Thunder–type solution: wave after wave of bombers indiscriminately killing every remnant of human life within that battle space. Would this serve to accomplish our national interests? On the one hand, yes. It would indeed remove the immediate threat posed by an entrenched enemy behind the city walls. However, from the perspectives of both international law and our long-term strategic interests, it would expose us to the world as barbaric monsters: perhaps no better than the radical jihadist terrorists we are supposed to be fighting.

But, lost in all of these debates is how we prepare our warriors physically and psychologically for their task at hand. In debating how we choose to portray ourselves to the world in the context of the ROE/use-of-force paradigms, we have lost the ability to critically assess our motives, objectives, and methodology on how we actually intend to fight and win the war. We thrash about trying to ingratiate ourselves to the third world community, all the while offering our warriors little to no choice as to how they are to conduct themselves in the harsh realities of the war into which they have been thrust. In nearly 14 long years of one deployment after another; of gearing up and training to go downrange; of multiple engagements in close-quarters combat, stability operations, counterinsurgency (COIN), or whatever currently in-vogue terminology our politicians toss about as we try to figure out what the hell we are doing, soldiers, sailors, airmen, and Marines (and their families) are getting ground to bits. And, opposite of what occurred in World War II, a very small percentage of America's population is shouldering this burden. To most, it provides "predator porn" on YouTube or subject matter experts for the next generation of video games like *Call of Duty*.

Since the advent of our modern, all-volunteer military in the 1970s, only 0.47 of 1% of our citizenry has taken up the sword and shield to defend this great country. Many of these youngsters leave the military but continue serving their communities, towns, and cities as firefighters, paramedics, policemen, and the like. For many, half of their life has been an amorphous blur of trying to do the right thing at the individual level, while at the collective community level we wrestle about in a futile attempt to define just what it is they are supposed to accomplish. The sad saga of District Heights, Maryland, police sergeant Johnnie Riley, set forth later in Chapter 12, is a prime example: a 20-year "good guy" that his community threw under the bus for a mistake made while arresting and detaining a violent recidivist criminal. So, the frustration, confusion, and lack of trust infused within these warriors by the national collective voice in combat follow them to the community township level. We choose to ignore the philosophical underpinnings of just what it means to be an American at the national level, and we are surprised when we see a struggle for identity on the part of our officers in the modern-day era of community policing.

This isn't all that hard to understand. We are what we model. Philosophers for thousands of years have admonished us to model ourselves after the virtuous man, the ethical person, the rational being. But, if we as a community refuse to acknowledge just what are our core values and beliefs (in fact, if we refute the very notion of virtue), then how can we expect our young to exhibit appropriate behavior at the lower strata of community? Again, Ferguson, Missouri, is a prime example of this problem. The police and the community are operating on two different social norms and planes: communication between the two devolves to shouting, violence, and more confusion.

The first rule of action when you find yourself in a hole is to quit digging. As a nation, we seem to have lost the ability to grasp this commonsense concept. We must lose the rhetoric, vitriol, and false flags of race in order to rationally identify the problems extant. Then, it will be possible to assess the underlying causes of such problems and develop and implement appropriate remediation measures. This book is intended to be an ethical guide for law enforcement in today's postmodern era. We have tried to strip away the false flags and red herrings of racial animosity and hatred in order to more clearly identify problems and map out just how we got to where we are. All of this is necessary in order to rationally suggest measures to get us back on the path of a virtuous society wherein we are not controlled by a separate Praetorian Guard of law enforcement officers, but protected and guarded by our fellow citizens who just happen to be peace officers.

First, we have to recognize that there is indeed a problem. One need look no further than to two local and apparently isolated incidents that occurred nearly 20 years apart to ascertain that we have a seemingly unbridgeable gulf between our citizenry and those that are hired to police it. In 1992, there was the Rodney King case wherein the LA Police acted out on an individual who refused to abide by society's agreed-upon principles. Instead of peaceably being interviewed or even detained, King acted in a hostile and threatening manner, disregarded the rules of civilized conduct, and placed many other citizens at risk due to his behavior. Upon capture, the police administered some old-fashioned street justice to a recalcitrant King. Was this right? No. But surprising? Hardly. The officers involved, however, were subsequently prosecuted and acquitted of criminal wrongdoing.

But the resulting violent riotous rampaging came as a surprise to even the most ardent cynics. Something within the very fabric of police–community relations had changed. We are not suggesting that police officers should administer street justice to anyone. Such actions quickly cross the line to criminal behavior. We simply set this case out as a turning point in the continuum of police–community relations. It made America aware that large metropolitan police officers might act differently from how they did on the 1960s TV series *Adam-12*. The Rodney King case was a watershed moment for police–populace relations in America.

Fast-forward 22 years to the bracketing incident in Ferguson, Missouri, where a 6-foot 3-inch, 290-pound suspect punched an armed uniformed police officer in the face and then attempted to grab the officer's sidearm. The officer shot Michael Brown, who then fled on foot. In hot pursuit, the officer was then confronted with a noncompliant suspect who again charged the officer. This incident ended with Mike Brown lying dead in the street. Surprising is the outcome of this incident: Rather than rally around the policeman for putting his life at risk, the very citizens whom that officer swore to protect turned into a riotous mob. The crowd went on to loot, vandalize, commit arson, and further erode the bonds holding the community together. After a grand jury, comprised of Black and White citizens, heard eyewitness testimony from mostly Black witnesses and refused to indict Officer Wilson, the riots erupted again. Had it not been for unseasonably cold weather throughout the country, the violence could have been much worse. Vitriol and seething rage replaced right reason.

What changed in the intervening years between Rodney King and Mike Brown is a culture fostered and numbed by frenetic intemperance and unrelenting images and stories from an unfocused warfare overseas—the numbing effect of a 24/7 news cycle beaming into our living rooms with the latest casualty figures and alleged outrages perpetrated by our citizen soldiers—and a sad assault upon race relations fostered and engineered by political hacks and quarterbacked by a legion of outside forces not concerned with the welfare of the citizens of Ferguson, but rather with their own political messaging. Rather, these forces, along with a compliant media, are focused merely upon lining their pockets, fomenting unrest, and continuing their quest for raw political power.

But, what has happened to our society? Why do certain elements of this society fear and distrust the police sworn to protect them? And why do police in many areas not see themselves as a part of the community they serve? Have we degraded into an ungovernable rabble of "us-versus-them"? Many within the political sphere would argue that we are well on our way toward becoming a Balkanized country wherein we are too different, too diverse, and too philosophically divergent to be governed by our fellow citizens. We are rapidly falling prey to the voices of tribalism and away from what it is to simply be an American. Today, there are "hyphenated Americans" who refuse to identify and assimilate into a homogenous culture, identity, or community. This trend must stop if we are to reverse the downward plunge into anarchy and further development of victim classes without hope of meaningful participation in what is the greatest country on earth. All three authors have spent multiple combat deployments in Iraq and Afghanistan, where tribe trumps society, and we do not want that to happen to our once-great republic. But, it appears as if Samuel P. Huntington's clash of civilizations has come home to roost.*

---

* The clash of civilizations is a theory that people's cultural and religious identities will be the primary source of conflict in the post–Cold War world. The theory was first introduced by political scientist Samuel P. Huntington in a 1992 lecture at the American Enterprise Institute, which was then developed in a 1993 *Foreign Affairs* article titled "The Clash of Civilizations."

When a person takes an oath as president of the United States to uphold and defend the Constitution of the United States, that oath should apply to all Americans. Sadly, the country is more racially divided than it was six years ago and the police are trending toward an us-versus-them militarization rather than returning to being peace officers who are part of our communities. This must be reversed.

America used to be better educated by the media. By way of example, for 33 years, 1966–1999, William F. Buckley Jr. hosted the television series *Firing Line*. He had truly diverse guests, including darlings of the left, such as Timothy Leary, Allen Ginsburg, Norman Mailer, William Sloane Coffin, Gore Vidal, John Kenneth Galbraith, and even Saul Alinsky, as well as conservatives and religious leaders, to include Mother Teresa, Malcolm Muggeridge, Ronald Reagan, and Margaret Thatcher. The hour-long talk show was sheer intellectual entertainment and a shining example of what the First Amendment was all about: informing the voter. Despite differences of opinion between host and guests, the exchange of views was almost always polite. Guests were given time to answer at length and not talked over or interrupted by whomever shouted loudest to occupy the bully pulpit. Nowadays, if an issue takes more than 45 seconds of airtime, America yawns. But, these are important issues, and we best take notice of what is being changed. Our very freedoms are at stake.

If left unchecked, such tribalism may be the unraveling of our republic. To first identify with a tribe rather than a nation is akin to what Afghans do. In fact, most see themselves as Pashtuns, Tajiks, or 1 of 30 other diverse tribesmen more than they do as Afghans. If America goes down that route, where individuals see themselves as part of hyphenated tribes, then our future may be as bleak as Afghanistan's. And, not surprisingly, this is exactly what our radical Islamic adversaries desire. To them, there is no constitutional separation of church and state, no god but Allah, and no sense of community policing other than one imposed by crazed *Mutaween* Sharia police.

If we are no longer a nation of workers endeavoring to better our lives and improve the lives and future of our children, we will become a divided smorgasbord of identity groups rather than a melting pot. Those groups may be social, cultural, ethnic, political, economic, or religious. The common theme of tribalism is to refuse to acculturate into those esteemed norms that have held the West together: the cardinal virtues, thrift, patriotism, and self-imposed faith. Rather, we have nearly succumbed to this "great society" wherein there is no need to be concerned with the welfare of others, only one's personal entitlements.

We are creating a culture totally devoid of value, virtue, relative worth, and meaningful pursuits. We have created a very large dependency class devoid of most of its civilized bonding mechanisms. And, when a politician points to this 47% figure—very close to the tipping point—he is vilified for stating the obvious. The result is rampant street violence, misogynistic and profanity-laced lyrics, and seething hatred and envy against other tribes. After all, it is the values we share that make us strong.

The very concept of "isms" and such tribalism has become fodder for pseudointellectuals within our colleges and universities. While China, India, and other near-peer competitors focus on mathematics, physics, chemistry, and the classics, American education appears focused on creating victims. As a result, producing anything of value to the community is beyond the entrenched and embattled worldview of these purveyors of victimhood. They have denigrated the reality of the American dream into a myth made up by corporate oppressors. Our parents would be ashamed. Today's culture knows no shame.

Now embittered by the hollowness of their own entitlements, they further poison the minds of our youth with the tired old adage that our country is unfair and a danger to the world. This mantra dovetails nicely with the trash being put out by the racists and poverty pimps further poisoning the minds of the citizenry within our cities. How often do you hear Americans being referred to as simply American? Why is it necessary to hyphenate our lineage to identify with a particular tribe? Why is a tribe more important than our identity as American? This is not hyperbole. As recently as Thanksgiving 2014, at Morgan State University in Baltimore—a part of Maryland's state-funded university system—Louis Farrakhan was a guest speaker. Farrakhan stated in his speech that mob violence was justified in response to the decision not to indict officer Darren Wilson in Ferguson, and peaceful protests are only in the interest of "White folks."[*]

"We going [sic] to die anyway. Let's die for something," he told the crowd to roaring applause. He even said the parents of teenagers should teach their kids how to throw Molotov cocktails. "Teach your baby how to throw the bottle if they can. Fight," he advised, and then imitated throwing the explosive device. Farrakhan further argued that the "law of retaliation"

---

[*] Greer, Scott, "Farrakhan on Ferguson," *The Daily Caller*, November 29, 2014; Donovan, Doug, "Speaking at Morgan, Farrakhan predicts violence in Ferguson," *The Baltimore Sun*, November 22, 2014.

justified violence, claiming such authority is sound in both the Bible and the Koran. This is not a pot-smoking hippie antiwar gathering of the 1960s, but a 21st-century America under the putative leadership of an African American. Tribalism is selling well, it seems.

Tribalism also fosters a climate of exclusion versus inclusion. If you are a member of the tribe, you have community only so far as the boundary of that tribe. All else is considered suspect and potential enemies. These thoughts fly in the face of our founding fathers' dream of creating a homogenous community where all are included and treasured as parts of the greater whole community. They also fly in the face of the historical assimilation of many other tribes: Irish Americans (who overcame employment signs that read "Irish Need Not Apply") or Jewish Americans (who fought the anti-Semitism so brilliantly depicted in the movie *Gentleman's Agreement*). That greater community should be encouraged as it brings out the better angels of our nature. It encourages acts of mercy, goodwill, and community. Tribalism fosters distrust, fear, and envy. Look at Ferguson and Farrakhan's speech in Baltimore to see tribalism at its worst. We need to have that discussion on race, but in an intelligent and rational forum.

There is also a corollary to tribalism with regard to trust within those chosen to protect the community. Police themselves can devolve into an incestuous and dangerous tribe. There must be a baseline level of competence, virtue, magnanimity, humility, and values instilled within those entrusted to care for our society. Otherwise, the failure of these traits will show the "protectors" to be no better than those who lack these traits and characteristics. Thus, the link between the protectors and the protected will disappear, and chaos will reign. Truly, the foxes will be guarding the henhouse. Instead, as Dave Grossman rightly points out in the foreword to *Combat Self-Defense,*[*] the sheepdogs should be guarding the flock. But, it takes a morally fit and courageous person to be a sheepdog. Otherwise, he becomes a mere predator.

This distinction is a difficult concept to implement, as many choose to believe that within our military or within our townships, those that are chosen to be protectors must mirror the behavior and values of that community. The authors disagree. The values and mores of those chosen to be protectors must be *above* the mean level of those within the community. Police must be above reproach, tribes, and petty resentments.

---

[*] Bolgiano, David G., *Combat Self-Defense: Saving America's Warriors from Risk-Averse Commanders and Their Lawyers*, Little White Wolf Books, Severna Park, pp. 1–5, 2007.

•

To allow our protectors to mirror the behavior of those they protect will eviscerate our civilized society. One needs look no further than New Orleans post–Hurricane Katrina to see the effect of a community-modeled police force. Many of the guarantors of a secure society within that exigency in New Orleans violated the trust of those they protected. They failed in the very mission they were hired to accomplish. Trust is a pivotal concept between those that protect and those that are protected. Once trust is lost, the consent of the governed is lost, and consequently, autonomy and the ability to self-regulate will soon also be lost.

How do we bridge the gulf between the governed and the governing in matters of trust? How did we get to this juncture? Is this a general theme throughout the communities of America, or is it limited to select communities? Hopefully, and this is the major thesis of this book, our republic will trend away from post-Katrina New Orleans and Ferguson, Missouri, events and the static states of East Baltimore, Detroit, and dozens of other ghettos littered about our country. To the authors, it is a sin that certain neighborhoods in America are "no-go areas," just as the French have allowed to happen in certain jihadist-controlled precincts of Paris. We need to study, understand, and fix this quickly. It will take time to reverse these trends, but time is of the essence for us to make the effort.

As a starting point, we can learn from history. Any study of governance and morality must include a discussion of Aristotelian principles. Aristotle understood the danger of an uninformed populace: those that respond to life's challenges with greed and avarice rather than virtue and magnanimity, those that refuse to enter into the civil contract to give in order to get. Aristotle tried to explain this in his wonderful work *Nicomachean Ethics*. Aristotle attempted to answer these difficult questions in a series of lectures dedicated to his son, Nicomachus. In these lectures he attempted to explain the bonds between our citizens and their protectors. Contrary to those who would ignorantly lump Aristotle with all those other "dead old White men," Aristotle is an important and relevant voice in our discussion as to the underpinnings of a civil society.

Thomas Hobbes and, to some extent, Machiavelli tried to interpret Aristotle via realist, existential means. Like today's pop philosophers or media pundits, these two philosophers often embraced smashmouth commentary and brutal street tactics in attempts to explain the rational contemporaneous world of the moment. However, they were unable to deconstruct the central notions of Aristotle and his theory of virtuous governance. In fact, Hobbes himself acknowledged the importance of civil governance by imagining what would happen without it:

> In such condition, there is no place for industry; because the fruit thereof is uncertain: and consequently no culture of the earth; no navigation, nor use of the commodities that may be imported by sea; no commodious building; no instruments of moving, and removing, such things as require much force; no knowledge of the face of the earth; no account of time; no arts; no letters; no society; and which is worst of all, continual fear, and danger of violent death; and the life of man, solitary, poor, nasty, brutish, and short.*

Whereas Hobbes and Machiavelli more often concerned themselves with the challenges of the moment, Aristotle looked outward toward the governing roots of citizenry. It is the realpolitik of a Rahm Emmanuel versus virtuous leadership as envisioned by the drafters of our Constitution. We urgently implore Americans to dismiss the strident, loud, and brutal voices of tribalism and realpolitik, and embrace the glory and fineness of a truly virtuous society. Angry, loud voices breed discontent and envy. Virtue sows peace and harmony. We strongly urge the latter.

This is not an impossible dream, because much of Aristotle's emphasis was on education. Aristotle advocates society to "model thyself after the virtuous man."† This raises an important question in today's world: How should one even recognize virtue in our modern society that rewards sloth, evilness, objectivism of sex, and instant gratification? The answer, again, according to Aristotle, is education. Through a proper classical education, he argued, one could recognize virtue and its associated benefits. The virtue of a good education must be habituated within the community at an early stage. Habituation must occur to become a habit. Habits eventually become rote behavior and ingrained character. These notions are bearing fruit in

---

* Hobbes, Thomas, "Of Man, Being the First Part of Leviathan," Chapter XIII, *The Harvard Classics*, edited by Charles W. Eliot, p. 9, 1909–14.

† Aristotle, *Nicomachean Ethics*, Book X, Chapter 8. See also Hartman, Edwin M., "Can We Teach Character: An Aristotelian Answer," *Academy of Management Learning & Education*, Rutgers University, vol. 5, no. 1, 68–81, 2006. "Aristotle holds that your character is a matter of what you enjoy doing (NE II 3: 1104b5ff.): good things if you are a good person, bad things if you are a bad one. Good character is therefore a matter not only of doing the right thing but also of having the right desires and emotions (NE X 8:1178a9–24, etc.). You should be grateful for kindnesses, angry if and only if you are seriously wronged, sympathetic toward the wretched. If you do the right thing while gritting your teeth, you are not really a person of good character, and virtuous action is not in your best interests. The person of good character has an enjoyable life, acting rationally and doing good things, unless misfortune intervenes."

privately funded and run charter schools such as the Ignatius Academy in Baltimore and the Willows Academy in Chicago's North Side.

Otherwise, Aristotle argues that when young people are not properly instructed in the virtues, they fail to understand and experience the highest forms of pleasure. Since they understand neither the good educational benefits nor the rewards of the highest forms of pleasure, they succumb to the easiest ones, that is, the cheapest and most base and vile of pleasures. Banality, sinfulness, and lecherous behavior become the norm. Instead of virtues that provided a societal cloak of modesty, we are left with a rudderless ship. This is what teachers are faced with in many public schools where chaos reigns: Students roam the hallways, assault teachers and fellow students, openly use hard drugs, and seethingly ejaculate whatever primitive thoughts erupt in their underdeveloped cerebral cortex. This is best described by an anonymous young graduate student frustrated by the fraud, waste, and abuse of her experience in the Teach for America (TFA) program:

> The city where I taught lives and dies by a lowest-common-denominator standardized test, used primarily as a way to make everyone (administration, faculty, students) miserable. "We aren't teaching to the test," our administrators lied, "we are simply helping students do *their very best.*" *The material was lackluster, and despite my best attempts to jazz it up, students were apathetic at best. I couldn't blame them for that.*
>
> I *could*, however, blame them for starting a fire in the back of my classroom. For piercing their own lips and ears as I attempted to simultaneously explain my slides on personification, and confiscate their makeshift awls. I could blame them for vandalizing my classroom. For breaking the door to my room, throwing objects at my head, and instructing me to "shut the fuck up, bitch" so often that I started playing a grim version of Teacher Bingo. I won if I heard it more than twice per period.[*]

In stark contrast, Johns Hopkins University neurosurgeon Ben Carson, a child of poverty who worked his way to the height of his profession, understood the importance of an educated, virtuous populace:

> The Roman Empire was very, very much like us. They lost their moral core, their sense of values in terms of who they were. And after all of those things converged together, they just went right down the tubes very quickly.

---

[*] Anonymous, "Teach for America Burned Me Out," September 26, 2012, http://thebillfold.com/2012/09/teach-for-america-burned-me-out.

Quite frankly, having an uninformed populace works extremely well, particularly when you have a media that doesn't understand its responsibility and feels more like it's an arm of a political party. They can really take advantage of an uninformed populace.[*]

How is this relevant in today's society? A society that treasures good education will reap its benefits. For instance, in many Asian cultures, wherein education, honor, and reverence of their elders are followed, their members are rewarded by very high academic performance and success in business endeavors. Yet, they have also become acculturated to Western society as voters and supporters of our shared constitutional freedoms. No other ethnic group appears to be able to match the emphasis placed upon education and honor as much as Asians collectively have done of late. Consequently, they achieve success in society and enjoy a relatively crime-free existence in their own neighborhoods.

Education is not venerated within many poor Black[†] communities, and young aspirants to the American dream are oft castigated and insulted as not being Black enough or acting too White. Is this true in all poor Black communities? Of course not. To think otherwise would be both bigoted and racist. But, why is it often such a problem in the racially segregated Black communities? Is it that these citizens don't aspire to have their children achieve success? To want their children to be happy and inherit the American dream? Like Shylock in Shakespeare's *Merchant of Venice*, do they not bleed? Most parents of any background want their children to succeed. Then, where have we gone wrong? Why is it we are called a "nation of cowards" by the U.S. attorney general for not discussing this discrepancy, yet when we do discuss it, we are called racists for trying to assess the facts and the foundational environment of how this all came about?

For instance, St. Louis is 44% White and 49% Black, but statistics show a racial imbalance in crime. Based on the city's official crime data for 2012—the most recent year for which data are readily available—97.6% of those arrested for murder were Black and 2.4% were White. More than 82% of those arrested for serious crimes like murder, aggravated assault, and larceny were Black, while just 17.5% arrested were White. An honest

---

[*] "Ben Carson: U.S. Like Ancient Rome; Obama Not My Target," Newsmax, February 8, 2013, http://www.newsmax.com/Newsfront/Ben-Carson-Prayer-Obama/2013/02/08/id/489602/#ixzz3wz35EAJe.

[†] The authors use the term *Black* rather than *African American* because we do not support breaking Americans into hyphenated culture groups, and we wish to work toward a time when the character of a person's heart is more important than his or her ancestral heritage.

discussion of this problem first needs to occur in order to find a sustainable, lasting cure to a diseased society.

The cultural divide between the governed and the governing appears to be largest within the Black communities. Why is it that the Black urban community distrusts the police and the police distrust the community? Of course it is not because the color of their skin. Again, Aristotle points to education as the remedy for these communities. Education will help in the communities where the laws are inadequate or no good, and parents need to create the "right habits" in young people themselves with the right help from lawmakers. This requires more hard work and less vitriol. If we can bridge this gulf within these communities, we will be well on our way toward healing our nation and attaining a much higher level of community policing—one wherein police and the policed are mutually supportive and intertwined.

And, lest anyone accuse us of focusing on minority communities, the most base, vile behavior is celebrated by mostly White Hollywood. It heaps wealth and fame upon the very persons vectoring our society toward its destruction. Kim Kardashian, "Snooki," Paris Hilton, and Pamela Lee-Anderson have eclipsed whatever little talent they may have at one time possessed and harvested fortune and fame by publishing the most vile videos of themselves engaged in acts that should be at once private and sacred within the bounds of matrimony. In 1964, Associate Justice Potter Stewart of the U.S. Supreme Court famously stated, "I shall not today attempt further to define the kinds of material I understand to be embraced within that shorthand description [hard-core pornography], and perhaps I could never succeed in intelligibly doing so. But *I know it when I see it*."* A mere 50 years later, we submit that Justice Stewart would be shocked at what is now shown over primetime network television. This is not progress.

It is never too late for anyone to convert to a more virtuous life. One famous former agnostic, British author Malcolm Muggeridge, wrote *A Third Testament*, in which he profiles seven spiritual thinkers, whom he called God's Spies, who influenced his life: Augustine of Hippo, William Blake, Blaise Pascal, Leo Tolstoy, Fyodor Dostoevsky, Dietrich Bonhoeffer, and Søren Kierkegaard. Muggeridge also famously quipped: "I wrote in a mood of anger, which I find rather absurd now: not so much because the anger was, in itself, unjustified, as because getting angry about human affairs is as ridiculous as losing one's temper when an air flight is delayed."

---

* *Jacobellis v. Ohio*, 378 U.S. 184 (1964).

Accordingly, we three do not write in a mood of anger. We firmly quote the Order of the Garter, "Evil to he who finds evil here." Anger was not intended, only stark truths for discussions in order to cleanse the wounds of hatred. That cleansing may be painful, but it is being done with purity of heart.

America needs to renew her commitment to virtuous living. Doing so will enhance the peacefulness of all our neighborhoods, help restore policing to the status of peace officers, and shrink the currently widening gulf between police and populace. It is not a quick fix, but one worth the fight. And, we need to start that fight immediately if we are to save America from itself.

So, with that as a background to some of the hurdles we face, the remainder of this book will more narrowly focus on what society can do within the confines of its police–populace relationship. We will examine some specific friction points, symptoms, and cases of where that relationship was strained or broken. Then, we will provide some recommendations and case studies on what improves that relationship.

4

Virtuous Leadership for Law Enforcement

Everything in which we poor men have a part—even holiness—is a fabric of small trifles which, depending upon one's intention, can form a magnificent tapestry of heroism or of degradation, of virtues or of sins. The epic legends always relate extraordinary adventures, but never fail to mix them with homely details about the hero. May you always attach great importance to the little things.

—**St. Josemaría Escrivá**, *The Way* (1902–1975)

Leaders are magnanimous, high-minded, and conscious of their potential for greatness. Their dream is to conquer the summit of professional achievement and personal excellence. The classical definition of magnanimity is *extensio animi ad magna*—the striving of the spirit towards great things. The Latin word *magnanimitas* derives from the Greek *megalopsychía*. Its opposite is *micropsychía*, which means pusillanimity or small-mindedness. Small-minded men cannot even conceive of greatness. The notion that life has a high purpose is foreign to them. Ivanoff, the central character in Anton Chekhov's play of the same name, gives advice to a friend that anyone who dreams of being magnanimous would be well advised to ignore: "My dear friend, you left college last year, and you are still young and brave. Being thirty-five years old I have the right to advise you.... Choose some nice, commonplace girl without any strange and startling points in her character. Plan your life for quiet; the grayer and more monotonous you can make the background, the better.... That is the pleasant, honest, healthy way to live."

—**Alexandre Havard**, *Virtuous Leadership*

America's law enforcement agencies need people of good virtue to lead and man them. Herodotus's commentary "to ride well, shoot straight, and speak the truth"* recognizes that there are absolute truths and an internal moral compass that warriors should follow. The legislative, executive, and judicial branches of government, as well as the court of popular opinion, are constantly militating for us to "leave our fond medieval illusions behind and join the existentially-ambiguous, every-man-a-magisterium chaos of our liberal, individualistic, postmodern world."† This must not happen if we want to keep our society in proper balance. Any person or group that lacks in one or more of the cardinal virtues is doomed to failure. As William Penn, the founder and namesake of Pennsylvania, said:

> Governments, like clocks, go from the motion men give them; and as governments are made and moved by men, so by them they are ruined too.... Let men be good and the government cannot be bad.... But if men be bad, let the government be never so good, they will endeavor to warp and spoil it to their turn.‡

It is time to reexamine the importance of the cardinal virtues, specifically as they relate to law enforcement, and to defend them against a vocal minority attempting to extinguish their eternal guiding flames. In his outstanding books, *Virtuous Leadership* and *Created for Greatness: The Power of Magnanimity*, ethicist and author Alexandre Havard sets forth the foundations of what makes a leader magnanimous instead of pusillanimous. Books well worth reading in their totality, Havard's key concepts derive from the cardinal virtues: courage, justice, competence, and self-control. Police leaders should then strive to cement these virtues within their agencies with an organizational sense of unit humility and magnanimity. Once an organization's culture adopts such an ethos, it can survive life's vicissitudes much more harmoniously.

This cultural understanding that virtue and fundamental truths should guide our daily actions is under insidious assault by those that allege such beliefs are antiquated or even unconstitutional. Such efforts must be soundly repulsed. To remain accountable to both the Constitution and

---

* Davis, William Stearns, *Readings in Ancient History: Illustrative Extracts from the Sources*, Vol. 2: *Greece and the East* (Boston: Allyn and Bacon, 1912), pp. 58–61.

† Douthat, Ross, "Why I Am Catholic," *New York Times*, October 28, 2014.

‡ Clarkson, Thomas, *Memoirs of the Private and Public Life of William Penn*, Vol. I (London: Richard Taylor and Co., 1813), p. 303.

the public they serve, police officers' moral compass must be immune to the fluky trends of modernity. Living pursuant to the cardinal virtues can inoculate them against the self-absorbed, licentious behaviors one routinely observes in Hollywood and professional sports leagues. Unfortunately, there are those trying to change that very culture by marginalizing the voices of virtue within polite society.

If law enforcement is to remain a true and just guardian of our populace, it must not proceed under the false belief that aspiring to live virtuously is somehow irrelevant in a postmodern world. The first obstacle posited by those who object to infusing virtue's lessons into policy is that doing so violates the First Amendment's Establishment Clause,* which proscribes a formal church–state relationship. Such an objection is a canard that is predicated on ignorance of history and the law.

Historically, the importance of the cardinal virtues is acknowledged in all of the world's major religions, but also in classical literature and philosophy. Legally, those that bristle against any open religious activity in government seem to ignore the Free Exercise Clause of that very same amendment. Sadly, these voices have found traction of late, especially within the current executive branch.

Our nation's founders, like William Penn above, recognized the importance of the goodness and virtues engendered by the free exercise of religion. Accordingly, they never intended to cordon off such wisdom from polite and practical society. For these reasons, or if only to protect others' God-given right to exercise their religious freedoms, senior police leaders need to remain vigilant against extreme progressive voices who wish to diminish such rights. Without abiding by the cardinal virtues, leaders and the force become susceptible to corruption, imprudence, and all other temptations of unbridled power.

COURAGE

Courage does not necessarily mean physical courage. Most who volunteer to wear the uniform of either a police officer or a military warrior possess some degree of physical courage: Who else goes toward the sound of guns instead of running from them? This courage is what Lieutenant Colonel

---

* U.S. Constitution, First Amendment.

Dave Grossman[*] refers to in his wonderful essays about the sheep, wolves, and sheepdogs. But, the courage to which Havard refers is a moral courage: an internal courage that resists toxic leadership, seeking the easy way out or leadership techniques that lack critical thinking.

Scripture speaks to those who "are willingly ignorant."[†] It is one thing to be unaware of the truth; it is altogether different when people know what is true, yet ignore it out of cowardice or political expediency.

A few examples of this from both the law enforcement and military worlds are in order. While the authors recognize that in the United States, police functions are typically not performed by the military, the organizational leadership principles for one are equally valid for the other:

- Statistical tools are used by organizations to track their performance in a consistent, open manner. Two of these, comparative statistics (COMSTAT) in law enforcement agencies and quarterly training briefs (QTBs) in the military, can be effective ways to identify areas or requirements that need more of the organization's assets. For instance, as it was envisioned, COMSTAT would identify high-crime areas or neighborhoods that might need to be flooded with law enforcement tactical units in order to catch the truly dangerous criminals. Like any tool, statistics like this can be misused. One common mistake is to assume that a high rate of crime is the result of poor police work. In other words, the police commander in charge of that area or neighborhood, rather than the criminal element, was somehow in charge of the spike in crime. Does an increase in the rate of arrests indicate a rise in crime, a rise in enforcement, or simply a temporary change in priorities? For example, an increase in DUI arrests might be the result of an increase in drinking while driving among the public, an increase in enforcement of the law, or a temporary establishment of DUI checkpoints. If the leadership of a police department uses the rate of DUI arrests to evaluate the performance of their officers, a number of second-order effects might occur, not all of which are positive. Also, toxic leaders will often simply use raw COMSTAT numbers as a whipping post to publicly humiliate subordinates at staff meetings. This routinely occurred in the Baltimore Police Department under

---

[*] Bolgiano, David G., *Combat Self-Defense: Saving America's Warriors from Risk-Averse Commanders and Their Lawyers* (Severna Park: Little White Wolf Books, 2007), pp. 1–5.

[†] 2 Peter 3:5.

the regime of a former commissioner, who has since been fired and convicted of a federal felony. District commanders came to despise COMSTAT meetings because of this.

- Similarly, so that commanders can accurately gauge the readiness of their subordinate battalions, QTBs are conducted to brief them on the readiness of their units. The QTB is simply supposed to be a reporting tool. It is also supposed to be a forum where the readiness status and statistics of a unit can be openly discussed, and it allows a good commander to understand the nuances that directly impact his ability to fight. However, there is a very high risk, given the competitive nature of military command, that a commander will focus on the numbers, the metrics, and not on an overall understanding of readiness, of which numbers are only one indicator. For example, it is not uncommon for some commanders to manipulate the metrics in a manner that would put them in the best light, even if that light were fundamentally inaccurate. The essential competitiveness of military command will lead less-than-courageous leaders to dissemble on their readiness, and potentially to berate and bully their subordinates to provide the best possible numbers. In some cases, this may help the subordinate to work harder for success, but more often, it leads to inaccurate data being used, in order to placate the higher command.

As an example, a maintenance unit may be required to present how quickly it is repairing or replacing equipment that has been broken by the combat units. The rate of how fast the equipment is being repaired is important information for a commander to know. However, this number is affected by several factors, including how efficient the maintenance unit is, how badly damaged the equipment was, and the availability of repair parts. It is easy to hold the maintenance commander totally responsible for keeping the metric low, but much of this may be out of the hands of that commander. If the pressure to produce is too high, there is an increased likelihood of inaccurate data being presented. Another example is the number of soldiers involved in off-duty motorcycle accidents or DUIs. These incidents are often driven by a number of factors that are mostly well beyond the actions of a unit commander. Nevertheless, an ignorant and toxic division commander will use the QTB to publicly humiliate and punish subordinate commanders for events that are simply statistical anomalies. Hence, the statistical tools designed to enhance mission effectiveness become tools of poor leaders to berate their subordinates rather than force multipliers for those they are supposed to serve.

A last example is the suicide rate of soldiers. Not only is this an extremely difficult metric to compare to that of the nonmilitary population, but also the reasons for a change in the rate are multifold. Most factors are *not* within the ability or power of a subordinate commander to affect. Nevertheless, it is still quite common for many commanders to hold their subordinates responsible for the suicide of a member of their command, regardless of the underlying causes. Moral courage can be very difficult to exhibit when a leader's future is on the line. This is doubly true when the topic is the safety of soldiers. A commander's staff plays a key role by exhibiting the courage to give a commander their honest view of a situation. A good commander will ask for honest feedback, even though he may not agree with it. An insecure commander will not tolerate the presentation of alternate viewpoints. But, a weak staff will only magnify that bully commander's wrath and intolerance. Of course, a magnanimous organization would obviate this possibility, but magnanimity is a rare unit virtue. As defined by Alexandre Havard:

> *Magnanimity (greatness) and fraternal humility (service), which are principally virtues of the heart, constitute the essence of leadership.* Magnanimity is the habit of striving for great things. Leaders are magnanimous in their dreams, their visions and their sense of mission; also in their capacity to challenge themselves and those around them. Fraternal humility is the habit of serving others. It means pulling rather than pushing, teaching rather than ordering about, inspiring rather than berating. Thus, *leadership is less about displays of power than the empowerment of others.* To practice fraternal humility is to bring out the greatness in others, to give them the capacity to realize their human potential. In this sense leaders are always teachers and fathers/mothers. The followers of a leader are the people he serves. Magnanimity and fraternal humility are virtues *specific* to leaders; together they constitute the *essence* of leadership.[*]

Staff planning for an operation, big or small, needs officers that thoroughly examine all the planning factors involved with their eyes wide open. There is a military maxim that states "hope is not a plan," yet history is replete

---

[*] Havard, Alexandre, *Virtuous Leadership: An Agenda for Personal Excellence*, Second Edition (New York: Scepter Publishers, Inc., 2014).

with examples where hope and desire without proper planning and preparation have led to disastrous results. Enthusiasm and hope without competence, absent luck, nearly always produce disaster. Planning requires subordinates to not be afraid to ask the hard questions, and to verify and explicate assumptions. This can be extremely difficult to achieve in real life. When the staff does not have the moral courage to ask the hard questions, details can get glossed over, and assumptions may not be properly challenged. Military examples of this abound. This can be especially probable with a likeable commander that the staff wishes to please, or a commander intolerant of alternate viewpoints. Both can be deadly.

- After the successful campaign to remove the Taliban from power in Afghanistan and destroy Al Qaeda's logistic base, the United States invaded Iraq. The military was very supportive of the fight, and the justification was clear. Most of the world, including most of the Iraqi General Officer Corps, believed that Iraq had chemical weapons and was willing to use them. In hindsight, the usually thorough Army staff did not properly conduct the planning that was necessary for Phase IV military operations: Once we crush the Iraqi military, then what? That's a question that should have been answered sooner rather than later. Looking at the results now, it appears incredible that we did not do better planning. But in the moment, it can be very difficult to ask the hard questions.
- In law enforcement situations, poor planning can also result in a comedy of errors. Some, like Ferguson, are not comical at all. Disjointed responses from local, state, and federal agencies resulted in a chaotic orchestration of actions. Much of this may have had something to do with the political influence—politicians with no police experience superimposing their notions of reasonableness onto a volatile and quickly moving situation. Why, for instance, did the president of the United States feel compelled to go on live television right after the grand jury's announcement and deliver a disjointed statement at apparent odds with the prosecutor?

In another example, the United States strategically shifted from a limited and clearly defined operation in Afghanistan to remove the Taliban from power and destroy an Al Qaeda safe haven to an ill-defined mission to somehow transform Afghanistan into a more Western democratic nation. It is hard to imagine how a thorough staff analysis would have supported such a mission without planning on staying in the country for several decades. Again, in hindsight, it is clear that these examples were not properly planned, and led to predictable results. But at the time, few voices objecting to the plan were heard. In the military, we value loyalty, and some may see keeping quiet as loyalty to a commander. While one should do everything reasonable to support a virtuous commander, a soldier's true loyalty is to the nation. Understanding and preventing these types of mistakes should be every military staff officer's goal.

In law enforcement, the equivalent would be the decision to form and utilize Special Weapons and Tactics (SWAT) teams or emergency response teams (ERTs) without appropriate training and guidelines for their use. To properly train and utilize SWAT/ERT requires an assessment and selection screening process, followed by a long-term training commitment that is expensive in both time and money. This commitment is much more expensive than simply obtaining the weapons and equipment for the team.

This lack of continuous training can produce disastrous results. More insidiously, it results in often unnecessary and excessive use of force, further widening the gulf between police and populace. After spending large amounts of money on a resource, it is very difficult *not* to use it. In this particular case, there are very predictable negative second-order effects that will occur if SWAT teams are not used very sparingly. A courageous moral leader may be one who—against all the political pressures from higher headquarters and the desires of subordinates—decides *not* to employ a SWAT team, and instead uses more traditional but less "sexy" police tactics. We discuss this in detail in Chapter 9 and elsewhere.

JUSTICE

As discussed, below, prudence or competency is the *internal* focus of one's intellectual abilities: the application of reason to a given problem. Justice is more *outwardly* focused. It is that trait which seeks to give everyone his or her rightful due. While maintaining discipline in our society is very important to a safe and orderly state, and most people desire and expect malefactors to be brought to justice, the *virtue* of justice is much greater than the sum of what is set forth in the letter of the law. Good police commanders utilize justice as a positive motivator on the path toward a humble and magnanimous career for themselves, their subordinates, and society at large.

Members of successful police departments are more concerned with respecting the rights of others and giving them proper credit where credit is due. It has been said that Field Marshal William Slim, commander of the China–Burma–India Theater of Operations in World War II, never said *I*, rarely said *we*, and always said *you*.* Sam Damon, the protagonist in Anton Myrer's brilliant novel *Once an Eagle*,† further exemplifies such a person. Damon is a professional warrior who puts duty, honor, and the men he commands above self-interest. He justly earns his promotions. The book's antagonist, Courtney Massengale, is an unjust, self-absorbed bully who advances by political scheming and trampling upon subordinates and contemporaries. *Once an Eagle* should be mandatory reading for all those aspiring to be virtuous leaders. Its lessons apply to military, police, and civilian corporate leaders.

Justice also requires an acknowledgment and obeisance to the natural law or divinely inspired law. Absent such a framework, we are left with simply the subordinate laws and whims of man. We would be well served to remember that Adolf Hitler did nothing illegal under the laws of the Third Reich. The reason that Hitler's acts were so unspeakable is that they contravened divine or natural law.

A just leader respects both the natural rights of others (the right to be secure in life and limb, obligations to family and associates, fundamental property rights, and the right to practice one's religion and hold sacred beliefs) and the legal rights of others (the statutes and rules governing society, their agency's internal operating procedures, personal contract rights, and other rights and entitlements found under the law). If legal rights should ever come into conflict with natural rights, however, the latter take precedence. Hence, a police officer has both a right and an obligation to disobey clearly unlawful, unethical, or unconstitutional orders. Without an underlying concept of right or wrong—what is justice—how would that officer ever be able to discern this? Natural rights are not derived from the sovereign, but from our creator. Those that deny this—as did the Nazis—extinguish the leavening influences of the natural law.

---

* Fraser, George MacDonald, *Quartered Safe Out Here: A Harrowing Tale of World War II* (New York: Skyhorse Publishing, 2007).
† Myrer, Anton, *Once an Eagle* (New York: Harper Collins, 1968).

Fairness and doing the right thing are synonymous with the sense of justice for a leader. Not playing favorites, while rewarding competence and eliminating poor performers, is tough. Looking out for the welfare of others is critical, but so is not falling prey to the seemingly just zero-tolerance policies. Such policies are a poor substitute for command discretion and wisdom. Each case a leader faces is different. Good leaders understand this. An otherwise great warrior who makes one mistake should not be treated the same as a poor performer and malcontent who commits the same offense. One is salvageable, and the other is a burden on the system. Even a poor leader should be able to understand this. Yet, systemically, America keeps trending toward ridiculous zero-tolerance policies that touch upon every aspect of human conduct. This is how we end up with "dating contracts" and the state being involved in what should otherwise be the conduct of private and personal affairs. Similarly, a child who is playing cowboys and Indians in a schoolyard with toy pistols (or, simply, making a pistol with his hands) saying "bang, bang" is a far different matter than a young sociopath storing a real gun in his high school locker.

Police officers, as well as principals and teachers, are supposed to possess the common sense and judgment to distinguish between good and evil. Instead, zero-tolerance policies have led to the suspension of the former and toleration of the latter. The predictable second-order effect of such rules or laws is the accurate perception that leaders have no common sense. If the principal of a school cannot tell the difference between a loaded firearm in a student's locker and a pastry that is eaten into the shape of a handgun, any reasonable student at that school would assume the principal is an idiot, and should not be respected. The same is true of a commander who does not have the intelligence or wisdom to decide individual cases on the basis of the individual facts of the case. A leader is always in the public view of his subordinates. Every action he takes either adds to or detracts from his standing with his subordinates. This is true for school principals, military leaders at every level, and police chiefs.

A good leader in any profession must always be taking care of his or her subordinates. This certainly includes punishment when necessary, but also rewarding those who go above and beyond. This can be displayed in many ways, but if the subordinates believe that the leader is primarily out for himself or herself, not only will morale plummet, but so too will the effectiveness of the organization. The perks of rank, in both the military and law enforcement, are there only for the purpose of assisting the leader in his duties. If the leader forgets this fundamental fact, he will lose the respect of those he leads. How many of today's generals expect and receive royal treatment with special drinks and food, all served up by bootlicking subordinates?

The same can occur in law enforcement. It is one thing to accept a cup of coffee offered to a police officer in gratitude by a shop owner on a cold, rainy day. It is entirely something else when police officers expect that cup of coffee or "police discounts" from every merchant within their precinct. One of the authors, while a patrolman in Baltimore, routinely observed some district commanders sending subordinates out among the community to reap furniture, delicatessen foods, and electronics from cowed merchants throughout the jurisdiction. The unspoken compact was that the merchants would receive "special protections" in exchange for the tendered goods. This was nothing less than a uniformed Mafia shakedown.

SELF-CONTROL

Epistemologically, self-control or temperance demands control of one's animal desire for pleasure. We wring our hands and wonder why too many law enforcement officers commit acts of brutality and sexual assault, and how come so many senior law enforcement and military leaders commit other diverse acts of moral turpitude. Often, these acts are a failure to moderate desires in the face of temptation. Self-control is that virtue which attempts to overcome the human condition best stated as "the spirit indeed is willing, but the flesh is weak." But, if we have institutionally disavowed the notion that there are fundamental rights and wrongs, is it any wonder we are in this quandary?

However, self-control is much more than just tempering sexual desires. In the realm of virtuous leadership, self-control might mean that choleric personalities restrain their tempers, impatient persons exercise listening skills, tardiness is replaced by timeliness, or phlegmatic persons make an effort to be more outgoing. "Everything that grows begins small. It is by constant and progressive feeding that it gradually grows big."* This notion applies to seeding and growing virtue in organizations and individual lives. Taking such seemingly small steps can gradually build a command imbued with a sense of unit humility. It can truly help transform an organization from a dour, miserable place to work into a magnanimous command where people are excited and proud to serve.

---

* St. Mark the Hermit, *De lege spirituali*, 172.

Magnanimity is an underutilized and not frequently understood word. It is that "loftiness of spirit enabling one to bear trouble calmly, to disdain meanness and pettiness, and to display a noble generosity."* It is the essence of chivalry. A magnanimous person is the opposite of a pusillanimous or small-minded person. Every police officer, but especially police leaders, should strive to foster environments where magnanimity flourishes. Absent a deep understanding and practice of the cardinal virtues, however, such a goal is futile because the leader lacks the inherent capacity to foster unit humility and magnanimity. In other words, a person can be polite, politically correct, and yet still be a pusillanimous bastard.

Controlling personal behavior becomes more and more important as one gains rank and responsibility, and the accompanying scrutiny that always follows. It is easy for many military and senior law enforcement leaders to develop an expectation of entitlement that manifests itself in many ways. It starts with other people holding the door for them and carrying their bags and ends up with horrid and unseemly examples that are both Kubrick-esque and borderline sociopathic in their disregard for others, especially subordinates. A few examples:

- Mayor Bloomberg of New York City used his millions of dollars to get elected and promote his radical gun control and gun confiscation programs not only in his city, but also in other cities throughout the Union. But, just like the Hollywood elite and other champagne progressives that support gun control for the "rabble," Bloomberg had a coterie of armed police guards to protect himself: the devil with everyone else. Finally, in 2013, when Mayor Bloomberg left office, he hired a number of New York police officers to provide armed security—this from the same man who has spent millions of dollars attempting to prevent the average citizen, who themselves cannot afford armed guards, from having firearms to protect themselves. The arrogance of these people is seemingly without bounds.

- A senior general officer designated one of the elevators in the headquarters building as his personal elevator. While this may have had a real initial value in helping him do the job he is paid for, over time it produced a number of negative effects. His staff forbade subordinates to use it, even when the commander wasn't there. At one point, colonels were designated as "elevator guards" to keep those

---

* Stern, Julian, *The Spirit of School* (Great Britain: Continuum International Publishing Group, 2009), p. 125, citing *Encyclopedia Britannica*, 2008.

who needed the elevator from using it—an elevator paid for by the taxpayers. This pattern of behavior usually gets worse over time. In this case, this commander saw no ethical problem for his wife to travel with him—again, at taxpayers' expense—on "official" trips around the world. On one occasion, a foreign potentate gave the commander's wife boxes and boxes of expensive designer shoes: At nearly $2,000 a pair, this could be seen as nothing short of a bribe paid for favors. Amazingly, the commander's aide-de-camp was incredulous when a judge advocate attempted to prevent the general from accepting this "gift." Once a sense of entitlement begins, it will increase until disaster causes a change. Often, that change is in the form of a change of command, but by then the damage to reputation is already done.

- A former commander of the Army's famed 3rd Infantry Division forced his staff to sing "Dog Face Soldier" (the division song) before every staff meeting. He would have the chief of staff—a senior colonel—walk around the staff table to ensure each member was singing with equal and hearty enthusiasm. He then would demand that his coffee, water, and juice be set before him in the same sequential order. Heaven forbid if the juice were to the right of the coffee! Ostentatiously, he would hold his fingers up in a "V for victory" symbol as a signal for a cigar to be cut, lit, and placed into his hand by his aide-de-camp. This same leader—on the rare occasions he would venture outside the wire to visit troops—would alight from his command helicopter and stand, arms outstretched in a Christ-like pose, so his assembled subordinates could dress him in general's belt, vest, load-bearing equipment, and pistol belt. Not surprisingly, he was a shoot-the-messenger bully and a miserable commander who screamed at subordinates during daily battle update briefs (BUBs) and individual soldiers throughout his command. The Army rewarded such insanity by promoting him to his third star.

- A former judge advocate general (JAG), a service's highest-ranking legal advisor, actually advised his subordinates on how to be the perfect toady in order to be competitive for promotion. Career progression is certainly important, but is it more important than serving the nation? And, is being subservient to and coddling general officers the model of an effective officer? Is it any wonder that one Air Force JAG actually forced subordinate officers to hold an umbrella over his head while he played a round of golf in the rain? JAGs are supposed to be the leaders of the corps of officers designated as the "conscience of the command." How do officers, who presumably start out their careers as humble, good persons, devolve into such egotistical monsters? Lack of the virtue of self-control is a prime reason.

- A former Baltimore police commissioner would routinely scream at his subordinate district commanders during weekly COMSTAT briefings. Not only does this behavior violate the leadership principle of "praise in public, reprimand in private," but it also creates a hostile work environment that is not conducive to candor and productivity. Subordinates will simply "look busy" and give the numbers that the commissioner wants to hear. Not surprisingly, this same commissioner was later investigated for crimes of moral turpitude. After a night of drinking and carousing with his political buddies, he would routinely show up at crime scenes in the middle of the night and traipse through evidence and bellow orders to the real police investigating serious crimes. Subordinates despised him mainly because he lacked the self-control to override the bully cop instincts he likely learned early in his career in another major city.

COMPETENCY

As Francis Bacon noted,* one rarely finds a wise head on a young body. Hence, this virtue, like all the others, must be taught and learned. Aristotle defined prudence as *recta ratio agibilium*, meaning "right reason applied to practice."† In law enforcement, this is reflected in a shift commander who has mastered fundamental tasks so well that in the tense circumstance of a riot or natural disaster, these are enabling rather than distracting. At a purely tactical level, it is that SWAT/ERT member so intimate with his weapon systems that he can focus on potential threats, not on whether his weapon's selector switch is on safe or fire.

When a leader consistently makes wrong decisions—or makes rash decisions, right or wrong—then that individual is said to be imprudent. Due to the complexity and rigors of modern policing, it is easy to err in this fashion. Accordingly, competent leaders seek the counsel of others and

---

* Bacon, Francis, *Apophthegms*, No. 97 (1624): "Alonso of Aragon was wont to say in commendation of age, that age appears to be best in four things—old wood best to burn, old wine to drink, old friends to trust, and old authors to read."

† Pellegrino, Edmund D., *The Virtues in Medical Practice* (New York: Oxford University Press, 1993). For Aquinas, prudence was a *recta ratio agibilium*.

quickly learn to delegate responsibilities and authorities to trusted sub-ordinates. They also encourage freethinking among their subordinates. Those assigned to a dysfunctional unit, where the commander browbeats all those who disagree, will instantly recognize this lack of virtue in their boss. "Don't be the nail that sticks above the surface" is the unspoken advice in such organizations. Sadly, courageous subordinates are often crushed, while bootlickers, or those who simply remain silent, get promoted.

Competency is the result of practice. But, it also may require personal humility. Disregarding the advice or warnings of others whose judgment does not coincide with one's own may be a sign of imprudence. It is possible that the commander is right and his subordinates wrong, but the opposite may be true, especially if the commander is consistently disagreeing with those whose demonstrated judgment is sound. Absent a moral barometer, derived from either natural law or our collective religious catechisms, there is no measure of right reason. Accordingly, bad commanders will simply bully others to get their way. That is why assaults upon society's seemingly archaic moral code are so intrinsically dangerous. For he who believes in everything believes nothing and, consequently, lacks a com-pass by which to steer a true and straight course.

Learning and remaining competent in both the great and small things is essential for a virtuous leader. It would surprise most Americans that many senior military and law enforcement leaders are unskilled and fundamentally ignorant of the primary tool in their tool kit: small arms skills and the tactical dynamics of deadly force encounters. They simply are not "gun guys," and while they may be graduates of Harvard's School of Government or hold other advanced degrees, they are woe-fully inadequate in the knowledge, skills, and abilities they demand of their most junior subordinates. For the most part, their legal advisors are no better equipped to provide operationally and tactically savvy advice. A few examples follow:

- In both Iraq and Afghanistan, Army sniper teams routinely used 175-grain boat-tail hollow-point bullets. The small open tip in that round is designed to stabilize the bullet in flight, thereby maximiz-ing its accuracy at longer ranges—sometimes over 1,000 yards. In both theaters, certain judge advocates interpreted these as hollow points and opined that these rounds violated the law of armed con-flict because of that law's proscription of the use of dum-dum rounds designed to enhance suffering. This is simply contrary to current legal interpretations, as well as the Department of Defense's own legal analysis of that very round. As an independent observer would expect, this round, as well as all small arms rounds in the U.S. inventory, is lawful under the law of armed conflict.* But, the junior judge advocates, experts in their own minds because they attended a week-long course at the JAG school, were incompetent. This error had a primary effect of impeding combat operations and putting our warriors at unnecessary risk, and had a predictable secondary effect of undermining our warriors' confidence in their leadership. Their misunderstanding of the fundamentals unnecessarily exposed our warriors to danger because, temporarily, our snipers couldn't accurately engage the enemy at a distance.

- Operational commanders, due to their misapplying the strategic concept of minimum force to the tactical level, sometimes fail to provide adequate indirect and direct fires (artillery, mortar, Hellfire, or close air support) to subordinate troops in contact with the enemy. This is well evidenced by the travails of Medal of Honor recipient Dakota Meyers during the Battle of Ganjgal on September 8, 2009, in Kunar Province, Afghanistan. After inserting in the valley and approaching Ganjgal, Meyer's unit came under heavy machine gun, small arms, and rocket-propelled grenade (RPG) fire from approximately 100 Taliban fighters. Soon pinned down in a three-sided Taliban ambush and being taunted over open radio channels by Taliban fighters, the Americans called for artillery support. This request was rejected by the tactical operation center due to concern over new rules of engagement put in place by the commander of the International Security Assistance Force in an effort to reduce civilian casualties. Both an Army artillery noncommissioned officer and an Air Force joint terminal attack controller tried to take immediate action to provide the ambushed American unit with fire support, but their command overruled them. The coalition forces were taking increasing fire and could observe women and children shuttling fresh ammunition to Taliban fighting positions. By the time fire support was provided—hours into the firefight—three U.S. Marines, their Navy Corpsman, their Afghan interpreter, and several Afghan soldiers had been killed, and an Army soldier attached to the unit had sustained mortal wounds.

---

* See W. Hays Parks, "Part IX of the ICRC 'Direct Participation in Hostilities' Study: No Mandate, No Expertise, and Legally Incorrect," *New York University Journal of International Law & Politics,* Spring 2010.

Tactical directives or rules of engagement (ROE) should *never* preclude actions in self-defense. This is critically true of soldiers in combat under fire, as well as police officers. This is the legal equivalent of forcing a police officer to wait until he is actually attacked before calling for backup units. While it may be true that a counterinsurgency requires a more surgical application of violence, it does not mean that "U.S. forces may have to get shot first!"* To misunderstand this reality demonstrates a complete lack of competence in tactical warfare.

The following chapters are comprised of specific case studies during which one or more of the cardinal virtues have been lacking or compromised, and examples where good leadership made a difference. They also examine potential lapses in unit humility and magnanimity. For a unit, organization, or agency to operate most efficiently and happily, its leaders must strive to infuse a sense of mission, humility, and greatness in all things. When that happens, most members feel a sense of purpose that is beyond compensation. Not only is their work more rewarding, but also the work itself generates better products. Most of the authors' careers have been spent in such organizations, working with the finest men and women our country can produce, both military and law enforcement. On the other hand, most of us with any time in service—as either a cop or a military member—have had the misfortune of working under a pusillanimous or toxic leader. In those instances, the workday drags on interminably and there is no sense of purpose.

A former director of the Joint Improvised Explosive Device Defeat Organization (JIEDDO) Counter IED Integration Center (COIC) once explained that there are four sliding scales he uses in discerning whether to accept a new job:

- Meaningful nature of the work
- Fiscal compensation
- Flexibility of hours vis-à-vis his family's needs
- Can't work for dickheads

This was a somewhat coarse, but accurate, description of why it is important to have a humble and magnanimous leader and work environment. Police and military missions are dangerous and difficult enough. Cops

---

* Witnessed by students attending the Operational Law Course in 2013 and by students at the 3rd Infantry Division as taught by a mobile training team from the Army's Center for Law and Military Operations, Judge Advocate General's Legal Center and School, circa 2007.

and soldiers are not well compensated fiscally and typically do not have work hours conducive to a good family life. Therefore, at a minimum, they must derive meaning from their missions and should not have to work for dickheads, that is, micromanaging bullies who neither trust their subordinates nor value their knowledge.

While everyone comes into a leadership position with a unique set of strengths and vulnerabilities, a good leader understands where he is strong and where he is weak. He works to maximize his strengths and minimize his vulnerabilities. To know thyself may be the first and most important rule of leadership.

In the succeeding chapters, we will examine situations in both military and law enforcement settings whereby leaders failed or succeeded in extolling magnanimity. At the end, we will recommend some personal exercises and life choices that can positively effect leaders, their unit's mission, and hopefully, lessen the gap between warriors, police officers, and citizens. The sanctity and security of our free constitutional republic rests on such a good relationship. The worst thing to happen would be for all of America to continue the trend of tearing apart the social and political bond between our government and the people.

5

Virtuous Policing and Maryland's Own NSA

Early in January 2014, Floridian John Filippidis and his family were traveling home after visiting family in New Jersey. After passing through the Fort McHenry Tunnel on Interstate 95 in Baltimore, a Maryland Port Authority patrol car pulled over the Filippidis's SUV without any articulable reasonable suspicion (the minimum legal standard required for any police car stop). They were questioned about owning a gun, detained, and searched, their car contents were emptied—searched on the cold roadway—and after approximately 90 minutes to 2 hours of detention, they were released. What would prompt the Maryland Transportation Authority Police (MTAP) to randomly select their vehicle? The answer is alarming and chilling to any American concerned about his or her constitutional right to travel state to state without being detained, searched, and frisked by law enforcement officers.

John Filippidis—like tens of thousands of law-abiding citizens—possesses a concealed carry (CCW) permit issued by the state of Florida. This permit allows him to lawfully carry a concealed weapon in Florida and dozens of other states that offer reciprocity with Florida. Maryland, like many states in the Northeast, is not a right-to-carry state and has reciprocity with no other state on the concealed carry issue. Filippidis and other Florida concealed carry permit holders cannot carry a loaded firearm in Maryland. While transiting Maryland and other restrictive states, concealed carry holders must either (1) leave their firearm at home or (2) secure it, unloaded, in a locked compartment away from its ammunition and not easily accessible. Typically, this means locked in a trunk. This latter option is guaranteed by the Constitution and federal law, to wit, the 1986 amendment to the Gun Control Act of 1968. Regardless of this right, as he told the police from the beginning, Filippidis's pistol was safely at his home in Florida.

What happened is that Maryland state has a network of technical security databases, to include the Automatic License Plate Reader (ALPR), that access the databases of other states that coordinate with them. For states that do not willfully comply, or those that are not as technically capable, Maryland data-mines information from diverse systems, public and private. The state's innocuous-sounding intelligence fusion center that does all this is the Maryland Coordination and Analysis Center (MCAC) in Pikesville. This center has access to, and contains, Florida's concealed carry permit holders' names and mines all state database systems for vehicle plate numbers of the holders. These license plate numbers are then stored in a cross-referencing database within MCAC. Apparently, the system "flags" or alerts officers anytime a law-abiding concealed carry permit holder drives his or her car past one of these ALPR devices. Regardless of what one's opinion is concerning this Orwellian technology, the following is legally accurate: Mere possession of a concealed carry permit by a citizen does not give law enforcement officers carte blanche articulable reasonable suspicion to make a car stop or conduct a field interview of that citizen.

In our experience as law enforcement officers, combat veterans, and instructors on the ethical, legal and tactical dynamics of deadly force, we often review and testify on behalf of law enforcement officers who use force in the line of duty. Typically, so long as they were acting reasonably under the circumstances, officers are immune from lawsuit even if, in the clear vision of hindsight, they were wrong in their actions at the moment. This is because the Supreme Court, in its seminal case of *Graham v. Connor* in 1989, stated, "The calculus of reasonableness must embody allowance for the fact that police officers are often forced to make split-second judgments—in circumstances that are tense, uncertain, and rapidly evolving—about the amount of force that is necessary in a particular situation."

In the Filippidis's case, if all media reports are accurate (and Maryland has not denied it), then it is abundantly clear that the officers acted unreasonably. This was a calculated, preplanned action whereby law enforcement accessed confidential information about a law-abiding citizen and then used that information as a pretext for conducting a vehicle stop. This is exactly the type of police action that lends tremendous credence to pro-gun owners' concerns that gun registration leads to gun confiscation. The activities currently afoot in many northeastern states—secret gun confiscation task forces and seizing weapons from the estates of decedents not two weeks cold in the ground—reinforce this mistrust.

Even if the Maryland Port Authority Police had made a legitimate car stop based on some articulable reasonable suspicion, the fact that Filippidis had a Florida concealed carry permit is not relevant in Maryland. There is no presumption that an otherwise law-abiding citizen from another state is committing a felony in Maryland just because he possesses an out-of-state concealed carry permit. To the contrary, the fact that a citizen has undergone the strict background checks required for such a permit should indicate that this person is neither a felon nor a dangerous threat to the officer or society.

Most people, most of the time, both non-law enforcement and law enforcement, are not acting with criminal intent. For a free and safe society to exist, it requires common expectations of behavior from both law enforcement and the citizens they protect. Citizens have a right to expect that law enforcement will act in a reasonable, ethical, and professional manner. Simply put, since law enforcement officers possess the tremendous power to detain, to give lawful orders that will be followed, and the ability to arrest, cops must have the overall trust of the people they are hired to protect. If law enforcement loses the trust and confidence of the majority of their citizenry, then the social agreement that allows law enforcement to have police powers breaks down with potentially disastrous results.

This is what we believe has happened in many of our larger urban areas. The good citizens of the inner city do not trust the police, and the police do not trust them. This is a bad situation for all involved, and everyone should be working to patch and fix that social contract. The Filippidis's case demonstrates that, at least in Maryland, at least some of the time, the police have no intention of abiding by that good social contract. Treating everyone as "perps" has the corrosive effect of breaking down the relationship and trust between cops and those they protect and serve. We all have a civic responsibility to maintain societal trust. This case does not help buttress that trust. Unfortunately, the easy response from both sides is to blame the other. The police will blame the citizens, and the citizens will not trust the police to do what is right.

We hope that Maryland abandons this unlawful use of technology, and that other states aren't considering such clearly invasive and unconstitutional practices. Our republic cannot afford to slide further into an "us-versus-them" mentality between police and the law-abiding citizenry. Even in high-crime urban areas, the actual number of malefactors is very small. There are ways, such as the constructive use of comparative statistics (COMSTAT) in New Haven, Connecticut, that police can protect their citizenry without blanket rules and overreaching of their authority. It takes hard work and due diligence. Lazy policing is not rewarded by public trust.

Many police trainers set up a false dichotomy, whereby officer safety becomes the primary focus of their tactics, techniques, and procedures, and courtesy and politeness are presented as a weakness. While it is true that when confronted with an imminent threat of grievous bodily injury, politeness and etiquette should take a back seat to aggressively subduing the threat, the fact remains that too many officers create a hostile environment out of one that could have been settled without violence. In fact, living an ethical professional life based on the cardinal virtues can better ensure that police are more likely to kill people who warrant being killed and less likely to harass, or even kill, good folks like the Filippidises.

One of the authors was stopped by a state trooper for speeding in South Carolina several years ago. There was little question that he was moving faster than the posted limit. After stopping, the officer requested his license and registration. The driver paused and, before moving, told the officer that he had a firearm in the glove box, something that was allowed by South Carolina law even without a permit. The officer's response was remarkable, saying something to the effect of, "Of course you have a firearm in your glove box; after all, this is South Carolina." At no point was the officer agitated or disturbed by this event, and he continued to act in a very professional manner. One can only speculate what would have happened to Filippidis and his family in Maryland if he had forgotten to leave his firearm at home in Florida. This South Carolina example is a case of an officer who continued to maintain his ability to treat the driver with respect and trust as a fellow citizen, even while writing him a ticket. From an officer safety standpoint, the very fact that the driver notified the officer of his firearm was a clear indication that he would most likely comply with the officer's instructions. In too many other states, however, the driver would have had a gun shoved in his ear and then be placed spread eagle on the pavement.

Of the many police use-of-force cases that have gone viral on YouTube and other Internet sites, a recent case out of Southern California where at least three officers suffocated a homeless man is a perfect exemplar of police creating a confrontation out of what easily could have been handled peaceably. We discuss this case in detail in Chapter 7. But, as in so many other similar YouTube police–populace interactions, the officer is screaming profanities at a destitute homeless man. Perhaps silly television shows like *Cops* teach officers that it is appropriate to lower their vocabulary to the lowest common street denominator. Too often, police officers try to justify this by stating, "They don't listen unless you curse at them." We think this is a canard. People listen to polite lawful orders much more readily than screamed orders that challenge persons otherwise not inclined toward violence to become, at best, recalcitrant.

Another part of the problem is that law enforcement agencies have succumbed to measuring success by statistics. This barometer is incapable of measuring the abilities of a true peace officer—imbued with wise discretion—from the realm of the possible. While it is difficult to teach the wisdom gained by years of sound experience, it is possible to teach the foundational cornerstones upon which good, sound, and reasonable police judgments can be made.

In *Virtuous Leadership*,* Alexandre Havard writes about how the cardinal virtues of courage, self-control, competency, and justice can be taught. These principles, with a layering of unit humility and magnanimity, can create good leaders and healthy work environments. This is especially true in law enforcement agencies. From the basic police academy levels, through in-service training, all the way to top-tier leadership courses, these basic virtues need to be taught and emphasized. Training manuals and general orders need to reflect and reinforce the peace officer concept. Leadership by management, as seen by an overreliance on statistics and Lean Six Sigma (and other organizational management course) models, will result in officers that learn to game the system and avoid making discretionary judgments necessary for a civil and trustful society.

One symptom of that can be measured by looking at the way different jurisdictions view firearm ownership. As the lines of demarcation become more stark between right-to-carry states and those that do not recognize individuals' inherent right of self-defense, incidents like the Fillipidis's case will be on the upswing. All law-abiding firearms owners, as well as those who chose not to carry, should be alarmed by these incidents. Hopefully, by legislative or court action, such encroachments upon our individual liberties will be thwarted. In the meantime, there is an increasing belief among lawful firearms owners that a traveler cannot trust some

---

* Harvard, Alexandre, *Virtuous Leadership: An Agenda for Personal Excellence*, Second Edition (New York: Scepter Publishers, Inc., 2014).

law enforcement in jurisdictions such as Maryland, New Jersey, New York, the District of Columbia, Connecticut, and California. One need only look at how some New York police officers are unlawfully seizing firearms from travelers whose luggage has been misrouted by airlines into JFK or LaGuardia. This feeds into the cycle of mistrust between citizens and the select group of individuals who have sworn to uphold the law. If this cycle continues, it will not have a positive outcome for either group. We sincerely hope and pray that the rhetoric on both sides can be tamped down and America can return to being the free and peaceful republic that her founders intended.

•

6

In Defense of Self and Others in the Ghetto: Loss of Right

The following case is based on a true account, as are most exemplars in this book. The names and locations are sometimes changed to protect the innocence and anonymity of the participants. We picked this case because it demonstrates a failure of virtuous and discretionary policing, as well as the huge and ever-widening gap between the police, the criminal justice system, and the population they are both supposed to serve. It is a prime example of a zero-tolerance policy misapplied and gone awry. It also demonstrates a gross incompetency of a legal system as it relates to individuals' inherent right to defend themselves against imminent threats of grievous bodily injury or death in our blighted urban areas.

FACTS

On June 29, 2013, Tyrone Smith, a Black male, age 28, 5 feet 6 inches, 170 pounds, was walking with his girlfriend, Natalie Burrows, in the 600 block of Saratoga Street in Baltimore, Maryland. At approximately 11:40 p.m., the couple was confronted by Danika Lake, a Black female, age 20, 5 feet 9 inches, 135 pounds. Lake, just recently released from prison after serving a portion of her sentence for robbery, was Tyrone Smith's former girlfriend. Sometime during the short confrontation, Danika Lake pulled an edged weapon—a box cutter-type knife—and threatened to slash or stab Natalie Burrows with it. At the moment Lake brandished the edged weapon, she was within 3 feet of Burrows.

At this point, quickly thinking and acting quite bravely, Tyrone Smith picked up a piece of 2 × 4 wood that was in the street and struck Danika Lake once in the back of her head. This act instantly stopped her assault upon Natalie Burrows. Thinking the matter resolved, Natalie Burrows and Tyrone Smith left the area on foot. In response to a 911 telephone call, the Baltimore City Fire Department showed up and an ambulance transported Danika Lake to the University of Maryland Medical Center. There, she was treated for a two-suture cut on the back of her head. After further examination, to include a negative CT, she was released a few hours later in the early morning hours of June 30, 2013.

In response to a 911 call from the hospital, a police investigation was also initiated. A Baltimore Police Department detective was assigned to the case, and his investigation revealed the following additional facts: Prior to confronting Natalie Burrows and Tyrone Smith, Danika Lake told her friend and co-defendant in a robbery case, Brianna Arrows, that she was changing into her "fighting clothes" and was "going to fuck them up." Arrows also told police that Danika Lake was angry and armed herself with "a knife" prior to leaving on her search for Burrows and Smith.

Tyrone Smith, while presumably not aware of that conversation, was aware of Danika Lake's prior conviction and arrest record, as well as her propensity for violence. Despite this being a clear case of self-defense—in other words, this was not a mutual affray or a situation escalated or caused by either Natalie Burrows or Tyrone Smith—the Baltimore police detective sought and obtained a felony arrest warrant charging Tyrone Smith with aggravated assault and a deadly weapons charge. Danika Lake remained uncharged, as the investigating detective apparently lacked the virtue of *competence* in understanding the laws of self-defense. The detective also did not exercise any discretion based on common sense in applying the city's state attorney's office draconian zero-tolerance policy for domestic assaults.

This is problematic for factual reasons. Tyrone Smith and Danika Lake's previous relationship had ended. They were no longer living together—not even an "item"—yet the detective treated it as a run-of-the-mill domestic violence case. Such cases typically result in the arrest of the male party regardless of underlying facts or circumstances. As any cop knows, some female residents of the city have quickly learned how to play the game of crying "assault and battery" just to get their former boyfriend locked up. In this case, the detective didn't care. Rather than using a minimum level of thoughtfulness or common sense, the detective took the easy and wrong course of action that was in no manner based on the actual facts of the incident. Tyrone Smith was subsequently arrested and, because he could not make bail, spent nearly 12 months in pretrial confinement for doing nothing other than exercising his constitutionally guaranteed right of self-defense! Twelve months in jail for acting justly and objectively gallant.

DISCUSSION

30-Foot Rule Explained

It is common knowledge among trained law enforcement officers that a suspect armed with an edged weapon closer than 30 feet away presents a deadly threat. This is because an average suspect can close that distance in less than two seconds, while the officer will take nearly that amount of time to recognize danger, draw and point his weapon, and then press the trigger. Then, assuming everything works in the officer's favor—he accurately fires and hits the suspect, and the bullet strikes and immediately impairs the brain–nerve function—the edged weapon may still strike and cut the officer or an innocent other due to the suspect's momentum. In the case at hand, the threat was only 3 feet from her intended victim at the time Tyrone Smith struck the threat in the back of her head. Tyrone Smith did not have any other weapon, so he wisely used an improvised weapon found on the ground.

Reasonableness of Tyrone Smith's Use of Force in Defense of Others

Employing force—to include deadly force—is permissible when there is no safe alternative to using such force, and without it, the person using force in self-defense or in defense of innocent others would face imminent and grave danger. Often, those using defensive force in such situations are law enforcement officers. In this instance, it would have been perfectly reasonable for a law enforcement officer to employ a baton, Taser, or even a firearm in an attempt to stop Danika Lake's assault with an edged weapon upon Natalie Burrows. An officer is not required to place himself, another officer, a suspect, or the public in unreasonable danger of death or serious physical injury before using deadly force. Citizens acting in self-defense, or in defense of innocent others, are similarly not required to ponder or take lesser alternatives in the face of such a threat. As Supreme Court justice Oliver Wendell Holmes so eloquently stated in the 1921 case of *Brown v. United States*, 256 U.S. 335, "Detached reflection cannot be demanded in the presence of an uplifted knife."

To justify a use of deadly force, it must (1) be necessary to prevent or end (2) an imminent danger of death or serious injury that one has reason to believe exists and (3) that imperils self or others. *Necessary* means that no other means were reasonably available sufficient to the urgent purpose of defense of life or prevention of serious injury. It is the critical urgency of the threat of imminent serious injury that makes deadly force necessary because no other form of force has the reliable capacity to stop the threat with the speed and effectiveness essential to protect oneself or innocent others from harm. *Imminent* means simply that the danger could happen at any moment—it does not have to have happened or be happening yet, but could happen at any moment. *Probable cause* is a level of belief that is the constitutional standard of a "reason to believe," which in turn must arise from the perceptions, knowledge, experience, and reasonable inferences at the moment the decision is made to use deadly force.

Analysis of a decision to use deadly force must look at what the person employing force knew or reasonably believed at the moment the decision was made. The issue is whether one was reasonable in believing that there was an imminent danger of death or serious injury to self or others based on what was known, what was reasonably believed, and what could reasonably be inferred. This is an objective analysis independent of one's intents or motivations. In other words, could a reasonable person have believed imminent danger existed under the totality of the circumstances, and accordingly, would deadly force then be necessary to stop the threat? More simply, would it be reasonable for another person in the shoes of the defender to choose deadly force? Before answering that question, one must be schooled in the realities of deadly force encounters.

Many persons, untrained or ignorant of the tactical realities of deadly force encounters, often attempt to substitute their notions of reasonableness in the clear vision of 20/20 hindsight. This misunderstanding can often be found when law enforcement officers confront an individual armed with an edged weapon. Most people unskilled or uneducated in such matters become upset when a cop or group of cops shoots a suspect armed "only with a knife," and sometimes from seemingly safe distances. Almost invariably someone asks, "Why didn't the officers swarm the suspect—there were four cops and only one bad guy?" Ignoring the obvious question—who wants to be the first "swarmee"?—such Monday morning quarterbacking ignores the ability of an individual armed with an edged weapon to inflict death or grievous bodily injury on a group 30 feet away armed with firearms. Again, most hearken back to the image from the Indiana Jones movie where "Indy" shoots dead a scimitar-wielding assailant who only brought a knife to a gunfight. While a cute movie ploy, the scene inaccurately represents the true threat an individual with an edged weapon presents. In a real-world scenario, Indy would stand a very good chance of getting cut badly, if not killed, by the assailant, even after fatally shooting him. A fatal wound may take minutes to actually incapacitate the assailant.

Of extreme relevance is the Baltimore Police Department's own training guidelines, which state in pertinent part the following:

> Anyone can cause devastating injuries with an edged weapon. A person with a little practice can be almost unstoppable. An attacker with an edged weapon never has to reload, and usually does not miss. Serious injuries are easy to inflict. Pepper spray can be effective in most cases, but the spray does not disarm an armed attacker, nor does it have immediate stopping power. The baton can also be effective, but the officer will have to get within striking distance. Remember! If you can touch the suspect, the suspect can touch you! The most important action you can take when confronted with an attacker with an edged weapon is to CREATE DISTANCE!
>
> *Empty hand defense is last resort, not option.* (emphasis added)

So, if an *armed* police officer on the streets of Baltimore is warned and presumably aware of the danger posed by a knife-wielding assailant, why isn't the same deference given to an *unarmed* citizen? Perhaps the detective in this case was not familiar with his own department's guidance on edged weapons. More likely is the common problem that police officers presumed that they, and only they, possess the right of self-defense. They make the mistake—and we see this most often in the northeastern states—in believing that the right of self-defense emanates from the government. And then only they, as agents of that government, are capable or righteous enough to do so.

Such reasoning is faulty as a matter *de jure* and *de facto*. Inherent, God-given rights accrue to all free men and are guaranteed by the U.S. Constitution. We fought and won the Revolutionary War to break away from a system of governance where all rights derive from the sovereign. And, when one examines the true tactical capabilities of the average cop, it is at best a toss-up as to who is better prepared to successfully engage and win a fistfight or gunfight: citizen or cop.

Moreover, as discussed in detail in later chapters, the realities of wound ballistics, the psychological and physiological dynamics of reaction to a deadly threat, and the fact that law enforcement officers miss approximately 80% of the time during actual engagements will tilt the scales in favor of the assailant with an edged weapon. Such is the case here—magnified by the fact that Danika Lake was only three feet from her intended victim. Had Tyrone Smith attempted to tackle or physically restrain Danika Lake, her flailing arms possessing the box cutter could have easily caused severe and life-threatening wounds to her intended victim, Natalie Burrows, as well as Tyrone Smith. In fact, even after being struck by Tyrone Smith, Danika Lake maintained custody and control of the box cutter. Tackling an individual armed with an edged weapon is an extremely bad tactical option. Yet, that is exactly what the prosecuting attorney, ignorant on the dynamics of such an encounter, suggested when she was presented with the self-defense claim, asking, "Why didn't he just tackle her?"*

Even if a police officer on the scene were to fire multiple gunshots and get good center-of-mass hits with all of them, the suspect might still have enough oxygen in her brain and adrenaline in her system to keep attacking for an additional 5 to 10 seconds. So, using a baton or other impact weapon (other than shooting the assailant in the head at close range to immediately incapacitate her) may have been the best option under the circumstances.

Law enforcement officers—as well as Tyrone Smith in this scenario—are always in the position of having to react to the actions of those with whom they are dealing. They are further at risk by the fact that they cannot know for sure what a particular subject is going to do or exactly when he or she

---

* Even after this was explained to her as a bad option, she countered with, "Well, I am still charging this because it is a domestic violence case!" as if the fact that Tyrone Smith and Danika Lake were in a prior relationship (1) constituted a domestic case, and (2) even if it did, that somehow obviated an inherent right of self-defense.

will do it. They can only react to what the subject does, and what they can reasonably infer to be the subject's intent in the context of the situation, the subject, and the preceding actions. This illustrates the unavoidable necessity for law enforcement officers, and those acting in lawful self-defense or defense of others, to act despite a level of uncertainty that will always exist. The law enforcement officer is always in the position of having to react to the actions of others, trying to interpret those actions, and then trying to react quickly enough to overcome the lag time that has ensued. The same physical realities confronted Tyrone Smith in this instance.

While there is no indication that Tyrone Smith was aware of Danika Lake's previous enunciated intentions to "put on her fighting clothes," as witnessed by Brianna Arrows, he was aware of her arrest and conviction for previous violent crimes. He was also aware of her extraordinarily jealous nature and recent anger at his jilting her for another while she was incarcerated. Accordingly, when she angrily confronted him and his new girlfriend, and then pulled an edged weapon and threatened to cut and stab Natalie Burrows, it was reasonable—in fact, was an objectively valorous act—for him to intervene in the manner he did. It was the reckless and determined endangerment to others posed by Danika Lake's brandishing and threatening Natalie Burrows with a box cutter that induced Tyrone Smith to strike her once from behind. Lake went looking for trouble, arming herself with a dangerous and deadly weapon, but her battery upon Natalie Burrows was interrupted by the objectively reasonable use of force in defense of others that Tyrone Smith used to stop her.

Even in the clear vision of 20/20 hindsight, his was sound judgment and proper exercise of discretion. There were many other options available to Tyrone Smith—do nothing, run, attempt to tackle Danika Lake—but none would have as safely and effectively stopped the imminent threat posed by Danika Lake as the action of striking her with the improvised weapon at hand: the 2 × 4 stick Tyrone Smith found on the ground.

Use of force in defense of self and others against the imminent risk of death or serious injury is fraught with risks and chance. Deadly force is ideally used to preempt a reasonable risk of death or serious injury, thereby preventing an imminent risk of harm from becoming an actual danger of harm. If that risk of harm has gone beyond imminent and become an actual or real danger, then even the application of deadly force may not be sufficient to prevent death or injury to self or the innocent victim. The immutable physical realities of reaction times and wound ballistics make this so.

There is no ignoring the realities of reaction times. It is unreasonable to allow an attacker a fair chance to prevail through either greater skill or strength or the vagaries of mere chance. The attacker need only be lucky to succeed. One acting in lawful self-defense or in defense of innocent others does not have to gamble life or physical safety on sheer chance. Tyrone Smith did not have to gamble on the outcome by waiting to see if Danika Lake actually cut or stabbed Natalie Burrows with the box cutter, or waiting to see if he himself was actually cut or sliced by this vicious threat. He reasonably perceived a sudden, imminent risk of serious injury from Danika Lake's brandishing and threatening with an edged weapon a mere three feet away. His decision to think quickly and act under the circumstances was objectively reasonable.

An important aspect of the action-reaction cycle that cannot be overlooked is that all parties to the confrontation are acting, reacting, moving, and making decisions simultaneously and independently of each other. One cannot predict with certainty what an assailant might do: One can only react based on snap decisions made under situations that are tense, uncertain, and rapidly evolving. The investigating and arresting Baltimore police detective ought to have known all of this. Had he or a fellow officer shot Danika Lake at the time of her assault, it would have been ruled a good shoot! The prosecuting attorney should have been aware of these immutable realities as well. However, it seems that their rules didn't apply to Tyrone Smith: a mere civilian urban dweller. And police and prosecutors wonder why seething resentment and mistrust exist among that population. Perhaps Ferguson was not about Mike Brown, but rather about the double standard exemplified by this case in Baltimore. How many other Tyrone Smiths are sitting in prison for simply acting in self-defense. The Fillipidis's case made national news outlets because the victim there was a retired upper-middle-class White male from the suburbs. No press was there for Tyrone Smith.

The time factor is also integral to this incident. From start to finish, the critical moments of this confrontation lasted mere seconds. More precisely, at the moment of acute risk, when Danika Lake's actions suddenly induced Tyrone Smith's well-advised perception of an imminent threat to Natalie Burrows, he had fractions of a second to react to the implications of Lake's actions, assess the degree of danger created, and decide what to do to best protect both Burrows and himself. Fractions of a second is not a time frame conducive to reflective analysis and tranquil contemplation of factors and alternatives. Tyrone Smith's perception of danger was logical and real, corroborated by his knowledge of Lake's past violent propensities, recent release from prison, and personal experiences with her. The immediate need to react for his and Natalie Burrows's safety was imperative and abrupt. His decision to use deadly force in defense of himself and Burrows was warranted by the circumstances. In fact, fleeing from the scene and leaving Natalie Burrows to fend for herself would have been cowardly, not chivalrous, and even more dangerous, the knife-wielding attacker need only pursue, stabbing her victims in the back the whole way.

Since Tyrone Smith was otherwise unarmed, the only reasonable means he had at hand that had the potential to effectively stop or preempt the danger in time was to pick up the 2 × 4 stick and hit Danika Lake on the head. Just as in most justifiable law enforcement use of deadly force cases, this incident was a life-or-death situation.

After waiting nearly nine months in prison for his day in court—something that would never happen to a suburban or rural defendant[*]—his trial was postponed for an additional two months simply because there were no free courtrooms. And the authorities wonder why the urban residents don't trust the system! A case like this cannot help but make worse the divide between the citizens of a municipality and their cops. What lesson would an average citizen take from the actions of the detective and prosecutor?

Finally, after spending 12 months in pretrial confinement for a crime he didn't commit, Tyrone Smith accepted the terms of a plea agreement where he would accept a conviction, but his punishment would only be time served. The trial judge urged him to reject the plea and demand a jury trial. In the end, the system ground him down. He just wanted to be free, so he accepted the plea. The system failed him and the citizens of Baltimore in innumerable ways.

An innocent man now has a conviction, lessening his chance of getting meaningful employment. The system was weakened further by having one more mouth to shelter, guard, and feed for a year while Smith awaited trial. The community sees that the system or "the man" is not interested in justice, so why trust them? Any reasonable person would not.

All of this could have been avoided had the investigating detective recognized it as a self-defense case and closed it. But, with the extreme political pressure—much of it based on ballyhoo instead of fact—concerning

---

[*] Because (1) the police in those jurisdictions would have instantly recognized the self-defense nature of the acts, and (2) even if an arrest were made, reasonable terms of bail would have been set and a trial quickly held.

alleged sexual assaults, both law enforcement agencies and prosecuting officers are blindly prosecuting any case that has the slightest, albeit irrelevant, nexus to domestic violence. Fueled by such ridiculously inflammatory television shows like *Law & Order: SVU* and the like, young prosecutors and detectives see wife beaters behind every allegation or injury. The resultant zero-tolerance policies lead to cases such as this one. A peace officer, with the slightest degree of intellect and discretion, could have seen this for what it was and closed the case (unless the true victims, Smith and his girlfriend, wished to file assault charges against Lake for pulling the box cutter).

Self-defense is an inherent, God-given individual right that should not be surrendered to law enforcement. Regardless of one's personal religious beliefs, this concept was codified in our Constitution and reiterated by our Supreme Court. Relying on any external entity, especially the police, for one's personal security is a fool's errand. Cops have neither the capability nor the legal requirement to prevent most crimes. Only in the rarest of circumstances will an officer be able to stop a crime in progress, and only by increasing the likelihood of righteous arrests and prosecution will the police impact future criminal acts.

Individuals are always responsible for their own safety. They may rely on the assistance of others, but there should be no expectation or requirement that police protect an individual from all or even most criminal acts. Two recent incidents that made the headlines starkly make our point: (1) the citizens in Boston cowering in their basements after the Boston Marathon bombing and (2) the captain and crew of the *Maersk Alabama* cowering when attacked by Somali pirates in the Gulf of Aden. Why didn't the citizens of Boston arm and defend themselves, to say nothing of allowing police to search their homes without warrants? And, why were the crew of an American-flagged merchant vessel—transiting waters known to be occupied by pirates—not in possession of weapons to effectively defend themselves?

The answers to these two questions are seemingly complex. But it all comes down to the fact that many Americans have lost their sense of self-reliance and, in turn, believe that the government will be there to rescue them. Hollywood would have us believe that SEAL Team 6 or *24*'s Jack Bauer will always come to the rescue. We should never have forgotten how important it is to teach our sons and daughters to ride, shoot straight, and tell the truth.

DANE-GELD[*]

A.D. 980–1016

It is always a temptation to an armed and agile nation
To call upon a neighbour and to say: —
"We invaded you last night—we are quite prepared to fight,
Unless you pay us cash to go away."
And that is called asking for Dane-geld,
And the people who ask it explain
That you've only to pay 'em the Dane-geld
And then you'll get rid of the Dane!
It is always a temptation for a rich and lazy nation,
To puff and look important and to say: —
"Though we know we should defeat you, we have not the time
   to meet you.
We will therefore pay you cash to go away."
And that is called paying the Dane-geld;
But we've proved it again and again,
That if once you have paid him the Dane-geld
You never get rid of the Dane.
It is wrong to put temptation in the path of any nation,
For fear they should succumb and go astray;
So when you are requested to pay up or be molested,
You will find it better policy to say: —
"We never pay any-one Dane-geld,
No matter how trifling the cost;
For the end of that game is oppression and shame,
And the nation that pays it is lost!"

                                   —**Rudyard Kipling**

---

[*] Not coincidentally, Great Britain's 22nd Special Air Service (SAS) Regiment presented the U.S. Army's 1st Special Forces Operations Detachment-Delta (Delta Force) with a bronzed relief of this poem, and it is prominently displayed in that unit's headquarters.

7

Murder in Southern California (or Cops Emulating the TV Show Cops)

One of the worst things to happen to law enforcement is the ubiquity of so-called reality television shows like *Cops*, which often bring out and highlight the worst in police attitude and behavior. In law enforcement, we used to call it the John Wayne syndrome (which is unfair to "The Duke," as he was by all accounts a patriot in the truest sense of the word and a fair, just man). But the term refers to that point in young officers' careers whereby they begin to treat everyone with an "I'm in charge" bullying mentality. It is when they start wearing and using "sap" gloves or begin to look like Delta Force operators rather than peace officers. But more than appearances, it is an insidious, bullying attitude that is best exemplified by the following infamous case out of Fullerton, California: the brutal beating death of Kelly Thomas in July 2011.

On January 14, 2014, the former officers involved in this incident were both acquitted in their criminal trial. The facts, nevertheless, are demonstrative of just, fair, and competent policing gone wrong. Instead of behaving like peace officers, these cops appeared to act like roadhouse bullies in their stomping to death of an initially passive, helpless, homeless, and obviously mentally unstable young man. The officers' language alone was unnecessary and unprofessional.

The authors are most often sympathetic with police officers under nearly identical situations. Police are not paid to ignore society's problems; they are paid to investigate and interact with some of its most dangerous elements. When a mentally deranged suspect violently resists arrest, it is an extremely dangerous situation for all involved because there is always a weapon present, that being the arresting officer's sidearm, as well as the suspect's fists, knees, elbows, head, and teeth. The fact that the officers involved were acquitted of criminal misconduct in this case is not surprising, as the law does not judge cops on prearrest behavior or tactics, but rather by how a reasonable officer would act at the moment the arrest is made under situations that are tense, uncertain, and rapidly evolving.

But, in this case, the entire incident appears to have been provoked by an aggressive, mean-spirited cop. It would most likely never have escalated to a violent physical altercation had it not been for the disturbing attitude of the officer in his initial interactions with the suspect. His initial behavior in particular is the subject of this chapter.

FACTS

Kelly Thomas was a schizophrenic homeless man living on the street in Fullerton, California. The incident in question occurred on a sidewalk underneath a highway overpass. The police were called to the Fullerton Transportation Center in response to a 911 call made from the nearby Slidebar nightclub that someone was trying to break into cars outside the club. Investigators determined Thomas was not trying to break into cars when Officers Wolfe and Ramos confronted Thomas at the transportation center.

While Wolfe went through a backpack Thomas had with him—it is unclear what the probable cause was for this warrantless search or if it was done under the pretext of a Terry* cursory search for weapons—Ramos and Thomas engaged in a lengthy, often sarcastic and prickly, exchange. Thomas ran from the officers after Ramos held his fists up to him and ordered him to follow his instructions, police officials claimed. That touched off the skirmish that ultimately included six officers piling onto Thomas in an effort to restrain him. This is not uncommon, especially if officers are dealing with an individual experiencing excited delirium (ExD) syndrome or other mental illness. The probable cause necessary for an arrest has never been clearly established. But, ignoring a police officer's brutish behavior or commands is not always a crime. The command must be lawful and in furtherance of the public peace. In the minds of some

---

* *Terry v. Ohio*, 392 U.S. 1 (1968) is a U.S. Supreme Court decision that is often cited as the rule allowing officers to perform a cursory pat-down of a subject if they have articulable reasonable suspicion (ARS) the subject is armed. It is unclear whether such ARS existed in this instance.

police bullies, however, questioning by an individual or failure to immediately comply equates to a personal challenge or threat.

The incident began with Officer Ramos putting on gloves and announcing to Thomas that his fists were getting ready to "fuck him up," and ended with Thomas in an irreversible coma after being suffocated by six police officers in total: five of them coming to the aid of Ramos, who initiated the entire incident.

More than 30 years ago, one of the authors was working a uniformed patrol post as a police officer in Baltimore, Maryland. On his post was a restaurant–bar named Jimmy's that was frequented by a great number of Bethlehem Steel workers after their shift ended. These were strong men—muscles rippling their arms and backs—men with whom an officer would be wise not to tackle lightly. One evening, a police radio call came out for a disturbance at Jimmy's. The first officer on the scene entered the bar, approached the bartender, and inquired as to what was the problem. The bartender motioned to a huge man, sulking in the corner of the bar with an almost-finished beer in his big hand. It appeared that the bartender had just informed the large sulking patron that he had too much to drink and was "cut off." The bear of a man quietly informed the bartender that if he wasn't served by the time his glass was empty, he was going to "bust up the place."

Now, for a police officer, there are a number of ways to handle such a problem. One would involve an immediate show of force and ordering the drunken patron to leave—essentially, the "my way or the highway" line of reasoning. This approach leaves very little room for negotiation, humiliates the subject, and nearly always ends in violence and arrest. The other manner of handling it—a manner taught and learned by wiser and typically more experienced officers—is to apply logic and reason to the problem, giving the subject an honorable way out. It goes something like this:

Officer (sitting down next to the patron with gun side away from the potential threat): Hey, Sir, what seems to be the problem? (*An open-ended question that both gives the upset patron an opportunity to explain his side of the story and does not present a challenge*)

Inebriated patron: I've been buying beers here all evening, spending my hard-earned cash. *Now* this asshole of a bartender says I am not good enough to be served!

Officer: I completely understand how you feel, but here's my two cents. If some bartender was that rude to me, I'd rather spend my money elsewhere and not make him richer. Why not mosey on out to the county and drink at a friendlier establishment where they treat you better. In fact, I'd take a few of your friends with you—that would hurt the bartender even more.

At this point, the drunken steelworker has two choices: either assent to the officer's advice or dig his heels in and say, "Fuck you, I ain't leaving." Over 90% of the time, even drunk and belligerent steelworkers will leave peaceably. For the remaining 10% of the drunk and belligerent population, the cops are no worse off than had they come in all muscled up looking for a fight. Moreover, the brief discussion at the bar gives backup officers more time to arrive should the event go sideways.

To again paraphrase Francis Bacon, "You will rarely find wise heads on young bodies." But, one can teach young bodies how to behave with self-control and maturity. If they learn from the TV show *Cops* and their new side partners who say, "Kid, forget everything you learned at the academy," they will set off on a course of violence and failure exemplified by the Fullerton incident.

On most YouTube links to the 30-minute surveillance camera video of the Fullerton incident, it is interesting to note that the accompanying bloggers mostly tell the viewer to queue forward to the 15:00 minute mark, "where the action begins." This is misleading for a number of reasons. Primarily, the viewer will miss the entire first 15 minutes, wherein the police behavior is quintessentially bullying and *Cops*-like policing with an attitude. One officer, dealing with an obviously mentally challenged homeless person—someone whom should be treated with compassion and empathy—is rude, threatening, and discourteous, to the point whereby he divests himself of his authority under the color of law. If a cop speaks to any reasonable person that way, the cop deserves to have his face stomped into the ground. Unfortunately, the poor victim was incapable of defending himself against such a bully, and the cop and his buddies ended up killing this man—for what? Trying to just survive and sleep on the ground.

Moreover, the officer's instructions to Kelly Thomas would be difficult enough for a sane and sober person to understand. He shouts, "Put your hands on your knees and sit up!" What the heck does that mean? And, as clearly seen in the video, the subject even queries the officer, "What do you mean?" What follows next is sickening. The police officer loudly shouts more confusing orders, then uses Thomas's "noncompliance" as a pretext for physically wrestling Kelly Thomas to the ground. The beating, choking, and suffocation of the homeless man that follows should be chilling to any American with the slightest concern for civil rights and police integrity. The tortured screams and gasps of the 135-pound Thomas were unable to persuade the jury that the force used was excessive.[*]

The officers' defense team argued that any force that *might* have been excessive was predicated upon Thomas's supposedly violent resistance, but that seems a little unlikely for a number of reasons:

- The testimony of a medical expert that Thomas died of a "weakened heart" brought on by "years of meth abuse." While the authors are fully aware of the threats posed by an individual undergoing the rigors of ExD, there was little evidence of ExD on the video, especially in the initial 15 minutes of the encounter. From the beginning, the officers were not treating Thomas as a mentally disturbed citizen, but rather as a problem.
- The officer who initiated the attack and spent most of the incident on top of Kelly Thomas outweighed the homeless man by at least 100 pounds. Suddenly, this guy with a heart so weak he could have died "at any time" looks almost superhuman.
- But, the most damning evidence that these officers responded with excessive force is a comparison of postaltercation photos of Kelly Thomas and the initiating officer (Figures 7.1 and 7.2).

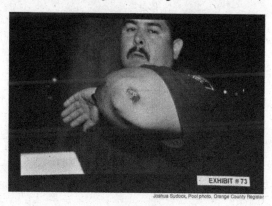

EXHIBIT # 73

Joshua Sudock, Pool photo, Orange County Register

FIGURE 7.1
Officer's injuries postincident.

---

[*] Cushing, Tim, "Jury Finds Two Officers Charged in Beating Death of Homeless Man Not Guilty," *Legal Issues*, January 14, 2014.

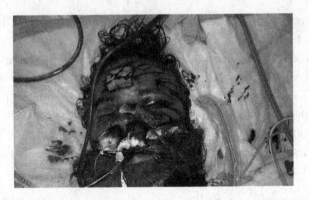

FIGURE 7.2
Kelly Thomas postincident.

Kelly Thomas was not a model citizen. In fact, he was generally a pain in the neck for beat cops in Fullerton. He had over 90 prior contacts with the police in the previous decade. But he was an American citizen due the same civil rights and dignity owed all of us. His beating death was the result of police officers who lacked virtue. If you do not want to compassionately deal with schizophrenic homeless persons, then you ought not to be a police officer.

Again, the authors are self-admitted cop lovers and defenders. But, that does not mean we tolerate or applaud police behavior that is vicious and completely bereft of the cardinal virtues. The Fullerton beating of Kelly Thomas is an unfortunate example of such shortcomings.

8

Officer Ray Bunn and Atlanta's Injustice System

This chapter concerns one case, in Atlanta, Georgia, whereby a brave, wholesome, good-hearted American was forced into a deadly force encounter at three in the morning. The relevant facts of this incident took less than three seconds from start to finish. The officer was investigated and cleared by three separate investigative entities: Atlanta Police Department's Homicide Division, the Internal Affairs Division, and the Georgia Bureau of Investigation (GBI).

Three and a half years later, due solely to the politic drum beating of an ill-intentioned and woefully ignorant civil rights group, a vile and racist radio personality, and a politically elected and cowardly Fulton County state's attorney, Officer Ray Bunn was *criminally* indicted and charged with murder for his line-of-duty shooting. Now fired from his job and bankrupt due to attorneys' fees and no income, Ray Bunn faced the fight of his life. This chapter details that fight and the fundamental flaws within our system. Ultimately, the Supreme Court of Georgia intervened and quashed the case. But, the damage was already done. If, after reading this chapter, one is not sickened by the gross abuse of authority displayed by those in power in Atlanta at that time, we have lost our battle for freedom from mob tyranny in that part of America.

On July 14, 2002, Atlanta Police Department (APD) officers Terry Mulkey and Raymond Bunn were patrolling in an unmarked APD car. They were driving north on Peachtree Road approaching East Shadowlawn Drive in the city's tony Buckhead neighborhood. At approximately 3:40 a.m. the officers heard the sound of glass breaking, followed by the sound of a car alarm. The officers looked in the direction of the sound and saw a black sedan in an adjacent parking lot, later identified as a Buick Grand

National. They saw a male suspect, who had been leaning in through the broken window of the Buick, running across the parking lot to the back lot area to the officers' right as they turned into the entryway. Officer Mulkey activated the emergency lights on their car and drove into the entrance of the parking lot toward the black Buick.

The APD car was positioned across the entryway/exit of the back parking lot area. Due to the width of the entrance/exit, it could not be blocked entirely, and there was enough room to the rear of the APD vehicle to allow the unimpeded passage of a vehicle. Both officers exited the APD car to pursue the subject, who was now running toward a light-colored SUV in the southeastern corner of the lot. Both officers were wearing their badges on chains about their necks (seen by witnesses) and were yelling, "Police! Stop!" Officer Bunn was also wearing a T-shirt with an APD badge image imprinted on the breast.

The SUV backed out of its parking position, turning so that it faced the APD officers and the exit of the lot. The suspect got into the SUV (later identified as a 2001 Chevrolet Tahoe), and it began to move forward toward the officers.

Officer Bunn was on foot between the Tahoe and the APD car. He began to move back toward the APD car, drawing his weapon as he did so. The Tahoe came to a sudden stop, and Officer Bunn reversed course to approach the car. As he did so, the Tahoe suddenly started forward, accelerating toward Officer Bunn. Officer Mulkey later estimated the Tahoe's speed at 25 to 30 miles per hour. He thought it was going to pass behind the APD vehicle in the entryway, but then it changed direction and came directly at the officers.

Officer Bunn estimated he was within 10 feet of the car when it advanced on him. His impression was probably influenced by a known visual phenomenon of looming. Looming creates an impression in an observer's mind that an object coming directly at oneself is both larger and moving faster than it actually is. He tried unsuccessfully to evade the car by moving back and to his right. He fired two shots at the driver of the Tahoe as he felt his left knee being struck by the vehicle; the impetus of the impact also spun him toward the SUV.

Officer Mulkey was on foot to Bunn's left when he saw the suspect Tahoe in motion toward them. He backed up to gain cover behind the APD vehicle and tripped over the curbing in front of it, falling behind the driver's side of the car. He did not see Officer Bunn hit by the Tahoe, but he did hear the shots fired by Bunn and a loud thump as the Tahoe passed.

The thump followed the shots almost simultaneously. Afterwards, he saw an injured Bunn crawling toward him on the pavement.

The driver of the Tahoe, later identified as Corey Ward, was hit by two of Officer Bunn's shots. One shot struck him in the left temple. The other shot inflicted a grazing wound across Ward's lower chin/right jaw and terminated in the door panel of the front passenger side door of the Tahoe. Ward died instantly and the Tahoe continued forward, passing across the front of the APD vehicle (within 1 foot of it), jumping over the curb in front of the APD vehicle, until it came to a rest against the parking lot's boundary curb bordering East Shadowlawn.

Officer Mulkey approached the Tahoe on foot and was ordering the five passengers inside out when Officer Thomas Munson, APD, arrived on the scene in response to Mulkey's radio calls—the first of many to respond. He also observed Officer Bunn on the ground in apparent pain holding his left knee.

A factor necessary for an application of deadly force to be justifiable is the reasonable perception that the individual or individuals involved posed a risk of imminent death or serious bodily harm to the officer or to others. Regardless of any postincident expressions of intent or the application of 20/20 hindsight to uncover facts unavailable to the officers involved, the only pertinent factor is the perception of imminent risk reasonably inferred by those observing and at risk from the actions of Corey Ward.

First, the initial decisions by Officers Mulkey and Bunn to investigate were proper and reasonable. Car vandalism and break-ins were a common problem in their patrol zone. Mulkey saw the suspect break the window on the Buick. Both officers had heard the glass breaking and the car alarm sounding from the Buick Grand National. They saw the suspect running across the parking lot and initiated a pursuit on foot. They did not know or anticipate that the subject would get into a car, but nevertheless positioned their vehicle with the intent of blocking egress from the back lot area.

Critics of the officers have suggested that they should have executed a tactically pure car stop where the officers could approach the suspect vehicle from behind. This criticism ignores the simple fact that they were on foot in pursuit of a subject on foot and had no reasonable expectation that the incident necessitated a car stop. Wishing that a different tactical scenario occurred cannot change the immutable facts as they actually occurred. Through no fault of their own, these two officers found themselves unexpectedly in front of the subject's car. To imply that they should have returned to their vehicle, somehow driven to the rear of the Tahoe, and then pursued a textbook car stop is a flight of fancy that ignores reality. It would have also likely invited the onset of a high-speed chase out of the parking lot and into the surrounding streets, imperiling pedestrians, other vehicles, and the officers.

When he saw the Tahoe in front of him and moving at him, as reported by David G. Brown, consulting engineer, in his reconstruction of the event, the exemplar Chevrolet Tahoe that he used was able to cover 20 feet in 1.5 seconds from a stop, attaining a speed of approximately 18 miles per hour.

In the best of circumstances, a human being will require 0.7 to 1.0 second to react to an external stimulus. That is, from the moment something is observed to the moment recognition occurs in the brain (whether conscious or reflexive) to the moment a physical reaction will initiate, 0.7 to 1.0 second of time is required, and that is under controlled circumstances with no unexpected external stimuli. There is no such thing as an instantaneous reaction to stimuli. Reaction time is significantly degraded in the presence of additional factors such as stress, fatigue, drugs or alcohol, age, and environmental conditions such as lack of light, loud noise, or surprise events. In the case at hand, it is certain that Officer Bunn did not react instantaneously to the sudden advance of Ward's vehicle at the 20-foot spot. His reaction would have required an elapse of time during which the Tahoe had significantly closed the gap between them. If he were 10 feet in front of the Tahoe, as he estimated, he would have had even less of a margin within which to react. In either case, the car would be upon him before he could evade it. The fact that he was struck by the Tahoe proves this beyond doubt.

Thus his reaction—moving back and to his right to evade the oncoming car—would have occurred concurrently with the car reaching him. Actions and consequent reactions all take time, and all occur independently and simultaneously. Officer Bunn had a maximum of 1.5 seconds to diagnose the situation and protect himself—and the bulk of that time would be used up in the process of observation, recognition, and initiation of the chosen response.

He had less time if he believed the vehicle might hit him, and he would need to try to stop it before he was struck. One witness in the Tahoe testified that he saw the officer in front of them and they continued to drive at him. Another said that they drove right at him. Corey Ward obviously did not intend to stop and made no attempt to do so. Officer Bunn had a window of time in which to act of approximately 0.5 second, in a best-case scenario.

The prosecution intended to use an expert video produced by the Kineti Corporation. This animated reconstruction was flawed and inaccurate to such a degree that it is entirely useless in assessing the reasonableness of Officer Bunn's actions. For the following reasons, it should never have been made or relied upon in the prosecution of Ray Bunn:

1. It unrealistically portrays the events from a bird's-eye view instead of from the relevant and meaningful perspective of a reasonable officer on the scene.
2. Its "stop action" technique strongly suggests that the officer had time to deliberate and carefully choose his shots. This ignores the tactical dynamic of action versus reaction as described by Urey Patrick, and adds an element of scienter that would not be extant in the rapidly evolving scenario of a use-of-force encounter.

The prosecution also ignored the fact that vehicles are a dangerous instrumentality. The entire focus of both the civil case against Officer Bunn and the subsequent criminal charge, failed to appreciate the fact that a motor vehicle, when driven at a law enforcement officer in the manner that occurred here, presents a dangerous instrumentality, and the appropriate tactical response is for a law enforcement officer to fire at the operator of such an instrumentality. As Urey Patrick has accurately stated, "The only round that has knockdown power is a Ford F-150."

Moreover, as opposed to any other profession, except perhaps soldiers in a combat setting, law enforcement officers are required to stand their ground and, in fact, seek out danger. It is therefore absurd to place any legal liability on an officer for doing his job or, in the clear vision of 20/20 hindsight, perhaps using less-than-optimal tactics. To suggest that Officer Bunn had a duty to somehow leap out of the way of the oncoming Chevrolet Tahoe driven by the decedent is sheer folly. First, the law doesn't require it, and second, the tactics may not have encouraged it. Officer Bunn was performing his duty: investigating a suspected felony in progress at 3:40 a.m.—that not much good is occurring after 2:00 a.m. is a law enforcement truism. While the death of a human is nearly always tragic, the decisions and actions that put this tragic event into play were on the part of the decedent and his associates, not Officer Bunn.

The legal standards and discretionary functions of a prosecutor vis-à-vis law enforcement officer shootings are tremendous. But, the law and logic should accrue in favor of the officer, absent some act of gross negligence or malice aforethought on behalf of the officer involved. Legally, the only *potentially* gray area in this case is whether Officer Bunn acted reasonably enough to avoid potential *civil* liability. After reading the investigation reports and all of the collateral documents in the file, we are more than perplexed as to how a prosecutor, in good faith, could ever had sought a *criminal* indictment in this case. This is especially true in light of Georgia's qualified immunity statute, which shields officers who act objectively reasonably from both civil and criminal liability.

First, it is nearly impossible for anyone who was not present on the early morning of July 14, 2002, to assess what constituted reasonableness. To do so runs the risk of judging from the detached reflection of an office setting the reasonableness of another's actions under duress. Often, such attempts result in reports unfair to the decision maker on scene. Moreover, to fully appreciate the propriety of Officer Bunn's actions on the morning of July 14, one must understand both the tactical circumstances and the written rule of law. Nevertheless, it is clear that Officer Bunn's actions were lawful and appropriate under the circumstances.

The only legal query is whether Officer Bunn's actions were reasonable under the circumstances. A reasonableness inquiry is an objective one: The question is whether his actions were objectively reasonable in light of the facts and circumstances confronting him, without regard to his underlying intent or motivation. As repeatedly enunciated by the U.S. Supreme Court, the reasonableness of a particular use of force must be judged from the perspective of a reasonable, similarly trained officer on the scene, rather than with the 20/20 vision of hindsight. The calculus of reasonableness must embody allowance for the fact that officers in a fire-fight or tactical situation are often forced to make split-second judgments in circumstances that are tense, uncertain, and rapidly evolving about the amount of force that is necessary in that particular situation.

It is abundantly clear that at least two eyewitnesses to the event—Officer Bunn himself and his partner, Officer Mulkey—observed the Tahoe starting forward and accelerating toward Officer Bunn. Officer Mulkey, in fact, later estimated the Tahoe's speed at 25 to 30 miles per hour. He thought that it was going to pass behind their police vehicle, but then it changed direction and came at the two officers. A vehicle traveling at 30 miles per hour is traveling at 44 feet per second. To allege, as the state attorney's office did in this case, that Officer Bunn had time to deliberately fire his weapon with malice is patently absurd.

Police officers are trained and on the lookout for what are known as preassaultive indicators. The number one preassaultive indicator is verbal noncompliance. When an armed and credentialed law enforcement officer points a weapon at an subject and orders him to halt or freeze, and the subject ignores the warning and continues at the officer, such actions by the suspect are key indicators of hostile intent. Whether the subject is armed with an edged weapon, firearm, or 6,000-pound vehicle is irrelevant: The officer must be prepared to defend himself and innocent others.

In this case, despite repeated verbal warning, visual displays of the officers' badges and credentials, and the presence of blue flashing police lights on the department vehicle, the decedent persisted with his attempt to first evade and then assault Officer Bunn and his partner with a danger- ous and deadly weapon.

Specific knowledge as to the subjective intent of the decedent suspect is ultimately irrelevant to the legal analysis at hand. The subject's ignoring the repeated warnings of openly armed law enforcement officers—along with all of the other signs of criminal mischief—is a clear indicator of hostile intent. This fact is well recognized in civilian law enforcement training scenarios. Whether the suspect actually intended to run over the officers or simply escape is legally and tactically irrelevant. This last point was lost on the prosecutor, as well as the trial judge at the initial motions hearing, who actually asked one of the authors, who was on the witness stand as an expert, "Isn't there some test to show what that young boy was actually thinking?" Really, Your Honor?

Lastly, it would be inappropriate to question what alternatives could have been taken by Officer Bunn. As so eloquently stated by the U.S. Supreme Court in the case of *Brown v. United States*, 256 U.S. 335 (1921),

> detached reflection cannot be demanded in the presence of an uplifted knife. Therefore in this Court, at least, it is not a condition of immunity that one in that situation should pause to consider whether a reasonable man might not think it possible to fly with safety or to disable his assailant [, or to consider other alternatives,] rather than to kill him.

Those who may not recognize a 6,000-pound vehicle driven at a law enforcement officer as an imminent threat are either untrained in the tactical arts or uneducable. Could Officer Bunn have successfully jumped out of the way of the oncoming vehicle? Perhaps. Was the dece- dent attempting to run the officers over or merely attempting to escape?

We do not know for sure. But, the law—and common sense—dictates that a sworn law enforcement officer in the performance of his duties does not have to gamble with his life once he reasonably believes that a hostile act threatening death or serious bodily injury is imminent. There was ample cause for Officer Bunn to so believe. Yet, a racially motivated, politically elected state's attorney felt otherwise. If Officer Bunn were Black and the suspect White, this case would have *never* been filed. This is a sad indictment of the circumstances as they existed in Fulton County, Georgia, at the time of the indictment.

That the skin color of either a suspect or officer would be a factor in determining the disposition of a case in 21st-century America is astounding. We hope and pray that such circumstances change and that the law is applied rationally and fairly regardless of one's color. Prosecutorial decisions such as this are an example of sheer tribalism: the Balkanization of America about which we are so worried. The race of Officer Ray Bunn and the race of the decedent in this case, just as in Ferguson, should be of no consequence. Yet, news media outlets, so-called civil rights leaders, and others that should know better continue to fuel the flames of racial discord. Mercifully, in Ray Bunn's case, the Supreme Court of Georgia stepped in and impartially applied the law to the facts.

9

The Overutilization of SWAT and the Militarization of Our Police Departments

In January 1973, one of the authors watched as the city of New Orleans was brought to a standstill by a single deranged man, who in the course of his rampage killed nine people, including five policemen. New Orleans had no dedicated element to face such a threat, and brave officers died while attempting to assault this man who was effectively barricaded in a downtown hotel.

Around the same time in the early 1970s, prompted by the emergence of domestic terror organizations such as the Symbionese Liberation Army (SLA), the group that kidnapped and brainwashed newspaper heiress Patricia Hearst, a few major metropolitan police forces developed tactical teams to effect hostage rescue and other dynamic entry situations. The Los Angeles Police Department's (LAPD) Special Weapons and Tactics (SWAT) became famous due to a TV series of the same name. Baltimore Police Department's Quick Response Team (QRT) and New York City's Emergency Service Unit (ESU) were some of the teams upon which other departments modeled their SWAT efforts. SWAT was intended to be used in extremely dangerous hostage rescue, violent felony arrest, and other situations where the threat to society and police was extreme. This capability was developed based on a very real need for a highly trained team that was prepared to take on the rare, but extremely dangerous, task of neutralizing these most dangerous threats to the community.

Performing this task successfully requires extensive training, which is even more important than the best equipment. After 9/11, however, the increase in the ubiquity of SWAT across the nation was astounding. Every small-town sheriff's office seemed to sprout SWAT teams to fight against our newest threat: terrorism. Leveraging monies from the fledgling Department of Homeland Security (DHS), military support of domestic law enforcement, and so-called asset forfeiture schemes, many in law enforcement began emulating these very specialized forces.[*]

It is important to understand that the authors are not advocating a return to the days of officers armed with six-shot revolvers, starched white shirts, and low-quarter shiny shoes. Police need to be tactically armed with at least the same level of firepower that street criminals have access to, dressed in uniforms that allow comfortable freedom of movement yet do not give an edge to their opponents in a gunfight, and possess, as Lieutenant Colonel Dave Grossman calls it, a "bulletproof mind." However, police also need to realize that they are part of the society, not at war against its members. There is a huge difference between modernizing the equipment of today's law enforcement officer and the intensive training and equipping of a highly specialized force. One unfortunate result of this is the blending of traditional law enforcement with these specialized elements. A SWAT element is not charged with traditional law enforcement duties. It is trained in specific tactical military skills that are used in a very aggressive and potentially lethal manner. The greater the occurrences of this type of police work, the greater the risk of a breakdown in trust between the police and the community they serve. Nowhere are these second-order effects as stark as in departments' use of SWAT to enforce minor offenses like gambling violations or simple possession of narcotics.

It is entirely appropriate to use SWAT to arrest a dangerous felon on the loose. The U.S. Marshal Service performs thousands of high-risk apprehensions of wanted, dangerous felons, including escaped convicts, utilizing highly trained tactical teams. This is an appropriate and expected use of SWAT and militarized tactics. Moreover, local, state, and federal SWAT teams and emergency response teams (ERTs) provide important response options to situations requiring high-risk entries: active shooter events, bank robberies turned into a hostage-taking event, and other truly dangerous tactical settings. We commend these officers and their

---

[*] As a somewhat humorous observation, too many of these officers had the fancy equipment, but lacked the physical skills and abilities to properly implement them. Their appearance as the proverbial 100 pounds of shit in a 50-pound sack was only outweighed by their lack of tactical skills. A real Delta Force operator once correctly stated, "Amateurs talk hardware, while professionals talk software" (the hardware being all the cool equipment and the software being the ever-important, yet perishable, mental and physical abilities to put that hardware to good use).

departments' and agencies' use of their skills. But, these cases and the utilization of SWAT should be the exception rather than the norm.

This chapter will examine two different cases where SWAT was misused, both with tragic and deadly consequences. We are not judging the reasonableness of the force used at the time that decision was made by the individual officers involved. To do so would be contrary to the very guidance found in *Graham v. Connor* and its progeny. However, we are questioning the initial operational and tactical decisions to deploy SWAT—setting up a deadly force encounter where one need not have occurred.

Law enforcement is a dangerous occupation. Nearly a quarter of all line-of-duty law enforcement deaths occur at traffic stops. This statistic is reflective of the fact that (1) cops most often interact with citizens pulled over for traffic violations, and (2) vehicles are often the instrumentality of criminals. But, every car stop shouldn't be performed like a felony car stop, with officers aiming drawn pistols and taking up a tactical position behind their vehicles. It is important that officers are trained on recognizing preassaultive behaviors and, hopefully, will stay ahead of the bad guy's decision cycle. This is good, common sense, and police should be alert and vigilant at every traffic stop. However, everything cannot revolve around officer safety, no more than the conduct of military operations must be guided only by minimizing casualties. For if it did, every police-citizen interaction would involve a SWAT unit, hostage negotiator, and barricades just to check for a valid driver's license.

So, the question becomes, when is it tactically reasonable to use SWAT? As we shall see, using SWAT has unintended consequences that should be balanced against legitimate concerns. It is clear that SWAT brings a critical asset to law enforcement that needs to be maintained with the training and resources necessary. It is also clear that if it is overused, society runs the risk of living in a police state whereby the government knows everything and can coercively impose its will—even to the point of deadly force—on society. That world would be the antithesis of what our founding fathers envisioned when they created our great and free constitutional republic.* It is for this reason alone that police policy makers should carefully develop rules or decision matrices on SWAT utilization.

---

* Contrary to what our public educational system has brainwashed many kids to believe, we do not live in a democracy. A democracy quickly becomes a tyranny of the majority. Our Constitution was designed to protect us all from that horror. Governments have killed millions more than any criminal element.

FAIRFAX COUNTY, VIRGINIA: USE OF SWAT TO KILL AN OPTOMETRIST FOR GAMBLING

The authors could have recited the facts from news accounts or told the story in their own words, but author Radley Balko did such a fine job it bears repeating:

> Sal Culosi is dead because he bet on a football game—but it wasn't a bookie or a loan shark who killed him. His local government killed him, ostensibly to protect him from his gambling habit.
>
> Several months earlier at a local bar, Fairfax County, Virginia, detective David Baucum overheard the thirty-eight-year-old optometrist and some friends wagering on a college football game. "To Sal, betting a few bills on the Redskins was a stress reliever, done among friends," a friend of Culosi's told me shortly after his death. "None of us single, successful professionals ever thought that betting fifty bucks or so on the Virginia–Virginia Tech football game was a crime worthy of investigation." Baucum apparently did. After overhearing the men wagering, Baucum befriended Culosi as a cover to begin investigating him. During the next several months, he talked Culosi into raising the stakes of what Culosi thought were just more fun wagers between friends to make watching sports more interesting. Eventually Culosi and Baucum bet more than $2,000 in a single day. Under Virginia law, that was enough for police to charge Culosi with running a gambling operation. And that's when they brought in the SWAT team.
>
> On the night of January 24, 2006, Baucum called Culosi and arranged a time to drop by to collect his winnings. When Culosi, barefoot and clad in a T-shirt and jeans, stepped out of his house to meet the man he thought was a friend, the SWAT team began to move in. Seconds later, Det. Deval Bullock, who had been on duty since 4:00 AM and hadn't slept in seventeen hours, fired a bullet that pierced Culosi's heart.
>
> Sal Culosi's last words were to Baucum, the cop he thought was a friend: "Dude, what are you doing?"
>
> In March 2006, just two months after its ridiculous gambling investigation resulted in the death of an unarmed man, the Fairfax County Police Department issued a press release warning residents not to participate in office betting pools tied to the NCAA men's basketball tournament. The title: "Illegal Gambling Not Worth the Risk." Given the proximity to Culosi's death, residents could be forgiven for thinking the police department believed wagering on sports was a crime punishable by execution.

In January 2011, the Culosi family accepted a $2 million settlement offer from Fairfax County. That same year, Virginia's government spent $20 million promoting the state lottery.*

The use of SWAT in this case decreased the peace and law-abiding character of this community. There is no reasonable argument why this arrest needed to be made by a specialized police element using military tactics in the hours of darkness. A simple knock on the door or, if they had probable cause already, the issuance of a criminal summons would have been much more appropriate. Often, police will attempt to justify the use of SWAT by claiming they had reliable information that "there was a gun in the house." Again, the authors caution that having a gun in the house is a constitutionally protected right, and that the mere presence of a potentially dangerous instrumentality does not give rise to an armed incursion more relevant to a combat zone than a peaceable society. Such unnecessary instances of SWAT utilization also stress the police–populace relationship.

ALBUQUERQUE POLICE SWAT ARREST A HOMELESS MAN IN A SUBURBAN PARK

In March 2014, a homeless man was camping out in one of the region's public parklands. This man, later identified as James Boyd, was shot to death one Sunday during a confrontation with Albuquerque police SWAT officers.

Officers were initially called to the 800 block of Piedra Vista after neighbors spotted a suspicious man camping in the foothills. *Note*: Such camping is prohibited by local ordinance and therefore illegal. It was also reasonable to expect the neighbors to ask that he be removed. However, illegally camping in a suburban area is not what most citizens would expect to require SWAT. Such ordinances are known as *mala prohibita* crimes, not *mala in se* crimes. Legal scholars have used the terms *mala prohibita* and *mala in se* to draw the distinction between legally proscribed and morally proscribed offenses. The former are those offenses that are wrong simply because there exist formal, codified rules prohibiting them, like

---

* Balko, Radley, *Rise of the Warrior Cop: The Militarization of America's Police Forces* (New York: Perseus Books Group, 2013).

"no parking," "no gambling," "no speeding," or "use of brake retarders prohibited." The latter are intrinsically evil crimes, such as murder, rape, and robbery. Just as in the Virginia gambling case, James Boyd was engaged in a *mala prohibita* activity, hardly one requiring the force and firepower of a SWAT team.

After the shooting, Albuquerque Police Department chief Gorden Eden said James Boyd continued to threaten to kill police officers despite attempts by officers to calm him down. (We question how surrounding a mentally ill person with a SWAT detachment and K-9 dogs, and then employing beanbag guns and flash bang grenades, would be considered calming to a paranoid individual, but we digress.) The officers also noticed the suspect had several knives on him, as well as several layers of clothing. A resident said he heard the person screaming and yelling angrily. The resident said the tone was hateful and that they had never heard anger of that intensity.

The fat, agitated suspect, James Boyd, was armed with two camping penknives, was on uneven ground, and there were large boulders between himself and the suspects. The suspect's ability to close the distance between himself and the officers was hampered because of these facts. As discussed in Chapter 6, there is a commonly accepted 30-foot rule that police are trained on, as that distance represents the distance, on even ground, that an individual armed with an edged weapon can close within the time it takes an officer to successfully shoot the threat. It is dangerous to second-guess the officers, but the facts seem to indicate that the officers were not in imminent danger from the suspect.

As the situation progressed, the police began moving in against the suspect, who was actually shot multiple times in the back as he turned from the police. While this might reasonably be explained by the fact that it takes an average of approximately one-third of a second to stop shooting in response to the absence of a visual stimulus, the question is not "When did the officers stop shooting?" but rather "Why did they start shooting in the first place?" Boyd was shot with M4-style rifles, not pistols. These rounds were clearly fired by a member of the SWAT team, and they create more grievous wound channels than pistols. But, if deadly force was authorized, the police officers' weapons of choice are irrelevant.

This March 16, 2014, shooting of James Boyd, a mentally ill homeless man illegally camping in the foothills to the east of the city—and who seemed to be posing no imminent threat to the officers—was captured on a helmet cam worn by one of the shooting officers. The video quickly went viral and sparked protests by hundreds of people in the city, which were dispersed with tear gas by riot police. Obviously, this incident did not increase the safety and security of the city, and it increased the gulf between law enforcement and those they serve. The YouTube video is very disturbing for a number of reasons: (1) The police officers continued to treat the subject as a military objective to be conquered, as in "We have to take that hill from him!" raising the question, "Why?" (2) There did not appear to be any physical threat to anyone (until a threatening situation was created by poor police tactics). (3) Why was SWAT called in and used to enforce a simple *mala prohibita* crime?

Police routinely handle hundreds of cases of mentally disturbed individuals (10-86 was the radio call sign for mental cases in some jurisdictions, and 10-86 became the nickname for "crazies"). If at all possible, we approach them slowly, gently, and calmly in an honest effort to get them treatment and shelter.

It is always possible to escalate force, but it is very hard to de-escalate once you have raised the level of aggression. Approaching a paranoid schizophrenic dressed like blitzkrieg *soldaten* will not have a calming effect on the situation, nor will it increase the safety and security of a community. One can always ratchet up the force if things go crossways, but it is really difficult to put the violent toothpaste back in the tube after a suspect gets a taste of that first.

This leads to an important discussion that is not happening with enough frequency in America: SWAT is a highly specialized skill that takes recurrent (and expensive) training to maintain. Simply kitting-out police officers in high-CDI-factor* equipment is not enough. Moreover, assuming a department invests the time and money to properly train its SWAT/ERT members, it still needs to ensure that there is adult leadership involved in decisions to employ such teams. Mere cowardice on the part of patrol officers is not enough in our view. Policing is an inherently risky business. We do not mean to demean the value of the life of any officer, but oftentimes the job requires one to make that car stop, knock on that door to investigate a possible crime, or serve that warrant. Every possible encounter with a criminal need not involve SWAT.

---

* *Chicks dig it* (CDI) is now commonplace terminology among operators and wannabe operators. In other words, "If I dress up like a member of SEAL Team 6, I must be a stud." Obviously, it isn't that easy, but it sure sells a ton of unnecessary tactical equipment.

10

Being Poor Is Not a Crime

This is a short chapter, but a very important one. Growing up in the suburbs or rural areas of America, many police are not intimately familiar with dire urban poverty. Coming from an environment of relative affluence and raised by a two-parent family, it is almost unimaginable to take cognizance of the despair, violence, mistrust, and chaos in which some are raised. When an officer from the suburbs is suddenly thrust into an environment where the walls move with roaches, tenants urinate in the hallways, and a walk to the corner store can be a perilous journey, that officer quickly succumbs to an "us-versus-them" mindset. But, as many wise men and prophets throughout history have pointed out, being poor is not a crime.

In fact, the vast majority of poor Americans stuck in bad neighborhoods are just trying to survive. Policing in such neighborhoods takes an extra degree of patience, understanding, and a cultural shift that many young officers are never taught. It is easy as a young cop to fantasize about making that big bust or winning a shoot-out with the bad guys. This is all well and good, but normally, as so eloquently stated by Josemaria Escriva,

> Heroism is in the little skirmishes of each day. When you put up a continuous fight, with love, in apparently insignificant things, the Lord is always present at your side, as a loving shepherd: "I myself pasture my sheep, I myself will show them where to rest—it is the Lord Yahweh who speaks. I shall look for the lost one, bring back the stray, bandage the wounded, and make the weak strong.... They will feel safe in their own pastures. And men will learn that I am Yahweh when I break their yoke straps and release them from their captivity."*

---

* Escriva, Josemaria, *Christ Is Passing By* (New York: Scepter Publishers, 2002), p. 191.

At first glance, this passage seems to be written for priests or other persons of the cloth. In reality, Josemaria Escriva wrote it for everyday workers—people doing God's work, *Opus Dei*, in their everyday work. Saint Josemaria lived, preached, and worked in civil war Spain in the 1930s—a society where the very fabric of civilization was grossly breached. Churches were burned down, priests and parishioners were murdered for saying Mass, and people were killed for a loaf of bread. It desperately needed community policing, but instead ended up in a spiral of mistrust and civil war. The enduring truths of what Josemaria wrote were beautifully captured in the movie *There Be Dragons*, about the torment of men's souls in this perilous time. Again, we do not want America to tumble down the road to such civil unrest. Preventative community policy can prevent that from happening.

Faced with both a real and a perceived growing disparity between the poor and the better off, the United States could fall into a chaotic postapocalyptic type of world if its police continue down the road of being either glorified prison guards or a thin blue line. We must not throw our hands in the air and believe that our most impoverished of societies—the Detroits and West Baltimores of the country—are simply corrals in which we keep untouchables penned. For instance, in Maryland, 23 of its 24 counties are essentially taxed in order to keep one jurisdiction, Baltimore, fiscally afloat and segregated.

Baltimore's criminal justice system is so overwhelmed that the prosecutors often keep criminal defendants in pretrial confinement for so long that the defendants simply plea out to time served and no fact-finding trial is ever held. All well and good if they were, in fact, guilty. Often, however, as we illustrated in Chapter 6, they are simply victims of lazy or incompetent police officers and an overwhelmed system. This is a feverish cycle leading to further mistrust between police and populace. Real community policing can slowly turn this around. As discussed in Chapter 18, New Haven, Connecticut, is one example of the proper use of comparative statistics (COMSTAT) and how all the elements of community resources can turn a bad situation around. But, this takes patience, resources, and a virtuous police force.

Departments need to teach their recruits that they serve all citizens: the poor, the sometimes ungrateful, and persons of all faiths, denominations, and standings in life. Supervisors need to get out of their offices and patrol cars to observe how their subordinates are treating the citizenry, especially the poor. It is easy to be polite to the banker or shop owner, but how a nation treats its poor is a true reflection of its character and virtue.

11

Peace Officers Versus Professional Law Enforcement Officers

Our friend Gary's father and grandfather were both police officers in a small New Jersey town just across the river from New York City. In the 1920s and 1930s, at least a few times a year, Gary's grandfather would bring home an intoxicated man and put him to bed on the family couch. In the morning, Gary's father—then a young lad—would stare at George until he woke up. The big man would shake open his eyes, see the young man, and bellow, "Good morning, young man, what's for breakfast?" Gary's grandmother would then make George a big breakfast of a dozen eggs, bacon, pots of coffee, and orange juice. Then, Gary's granddad would drive George home across the river. George would always leave a hundred-dollar bill (real big money in those days) folded under the family Bible in the hallway. You see, "George" was George Herman "Babe" Ruth. Gary's family never told a soul about this, and George's photo didn't end up on the front pages of *The New York Times*.

Gary's grandfather was a peace officer, not a professional law enforcement officer driven by arrest statistics and self-aggrandizement. Similarly, when one of the authors was a patrolman in Baltimore, he would occasionally roll up on a carload of young teenagers sharing a joint of marijuana in Southeast Baltimore. Instead of arresting them, he would tell the youths, "I am going to turn my back, count to 15, then search your car, and I better not find anything on you or in the car!" As he turned his back, he could hear the kids scurrying to dump their nickel bags of pot and roach clips down the storm drains. He would then sit the kids on the curb and explain how a narcotics-related arrest could ruin their futures. He was a peace officer, acting as part of the community instead of acting in an "us-versus-them" world. He also extended the same courtesy to a car full of Naval Academy midshipmen who, while a bit inebriated by alcohol, had just wrapped a then-new Nissan 280Z around a streetlamp post. To him, it would make no sense to ruin the four-year investment our nation just expended on these young men.

Unfortunately, even back in the 1980s, there was a growing breed of patrolmen who would have used that opportunity to get five narcotics-related arrests for the evening. One in particular was quite adept at padding his drug busts. Not too surprisingly, he went on to become a Drug Enforcement Administration (DEA) agent. People do what they are rewarded for doing. Gary's father was not working in a system that rewarded patrolmen based on how many arrests they made. Keeping track of what a patrolman or even a department is accomplishing is essential, but how we go about keeping track of that will have an effect on the individual patrolman and on the department. The outcome of this type of record keeping can be both positive and negative at the same time. With the increased use of statistical tools and computers, it becomes much easier to measure the arrest performance of a department. Unfortunately, it has become much more difficult to measure the performance of a department in its community relations and the tremendous good that officers do by using their discretion.

In the two examples above, there would have been little good to society or to the individuals involved had they been arrested and given criminal records. If patrolmen are rewarded for how many arrests they make, then they will tend to make more arrests and use less discretion. Without a doubt, this increases the police–populace gulf in our society. Police officers are changed from peace officers into professional law enforcement officers. We do not believe this is necessarily a good thing.

Instead, we believe that police leadership—from the squad corporal on up—must reward officers for exercising their individual moral courage and discretion when it helps the community. And, leaders must recognize not only the value, but also the limitations, of monthly comparative statistics (COMSTAT) meetings or quarterly training briefs. As discussed in other chapters, COMSTAT can be an effective tool to allocate both the whole of government and private community resources in a high-crime area. It is a terrible tool in the hands of a tyrant, and it is a poor substitute for thoughtful leadership and mentorship.

Police leadership, from the very top on down, must train and trust their young officers to specifically consider *discretion* a positive tool in their tool belts. Young officers must be given the authority to use discretion: Everything should not be about the arrest or stats. If leaders can't trust their subordinates to use wise discretion, then perhaps more work needs to be done on assessment, selection, and training of their officers. Young officers need to be rewarded when they appropriately use discretion in their daily work, and then need to be trusted to do so in the future. Young officers will make mistakes. So long as the mistakes are made without malice or ill intent, the officers should not be punished for making them (unless it becomes a pattern of misconduct).

Keeping the peace and trust of the community is far more effective than just locking up everyone for every on-view infraction. Leaders also need to understand that young officers are going to make mistakes. Again, so long as those mistakes are honest ones and done without malice, officers should be mentored and taught better ways to do things, rather than disciplined or fired. Learning self-control takes time. One doesn't find wise old heads on young bodies. It takes time and patience to teach and train a peace officer. Most people learn best by testing their boundaries and sometimes making minor mistakes. If they are lucky, they sometimes learn by watching others' mistakes. It takes nothing to train a professional law enforcement officer as an automaton, as a robot or drone could be similarly trained. As we will discuss later, one enduring purpose of a police department is to not only assist in the identification of bad actions and bad actors, but also reward positive actions and actors, and encourage the latter while discouraging the former. "Robocops" can't do this very well, but human beings, when properly trained and encouraged, are exceptional at it!

A palpable fear of lawsuits or political correctness alleging racial profiling also tempts police administrators to veer away from allowing discretion. This is not a new concept or problem:

> You have to have confidence in your commanders and must give them authority. If they make a mistake out of malice you punish them and if they make a mistake out of ignorance, you actually reward them because you want people to continue to have flexibility and creativity. Desire risk taking in commanders who are not afraid of opportunities.[*]

While the authors seem to disparage Machiavelli in Chapter 2 as a model for strategic leader in a constitutional republican form of governance, we acknowledge and agree with his observations concerning tactics and leadership skills. A newer potential impediment to Machiavelli's sage

---

[*] Machiavelli, *The Discourses on Livy.*

leadership advice is the advent of real-time technology. The ability for leaders to observe the actions of their subordinates as they occur often tempts seniors to intervene with the proverbial "10,000-mile screwdriver":

The U.S. Army War College and other senior service schools recognize the ill effects of technology-driven time compression on leadership. Formerly, commanders and individuals at the unit level had immense authority and discretion to lead. Being on scene and in a position best suited to assess threats, combined with the authority to act at the lowest tactical level, best allows our forces to get inside adversaries' decision cycles. But, this requires senior leaders to trust their subordinates. Technology can interfere with this trust. If not handled deftly, the hue and cry for all police officers to be equipped with digital body cameras can create a similar dilemma for police departments:

> President Obama, grappling with how to respond to the racial unrest in Ferguson, Mo., and a wave of anger at law enforcement officials across the country, said Monday that he would tighten standards on the provision of military-style equipment to local police departments and provide funds for police officers to wear cameras.[*]

This creates many unintended consequences. For instance, 200 years ago Navy ship captains had absolute authority and discretion. At the strategic and operational levels of war, Army commanders have never had that level of discretion, as their bosses were always close enough by to be consulted before major campaigns were unleashed. But, police officers are generally operating at the tactical level. As technology such as that advocated by Obama makes communications easier and easier, discretion becomes less and less easy to achieve.

Therefore, it takes a morally courageous and trusting senior leader to delegate to the lowest level of leadership as possible: often the cop on the scene. The individual on the scene always has a clearer picture of the tenor and tone of the society in which he is operating. A bird's-eye view from an unmanned aerial vehicle, drone, or police command post is often deceiving in its seeming clarity. Camera lenses cannot process sounds, emotions, and other sensory information that a human on the scene can. With the ubiquity of security cameras, facial recognition software, and predictive

---

[*] Landler, Mark, "Obama Offers New Standards on Police Gear in Wake of Ferguson Protests," *New York Times*, December 1, 2014.

analysis, the need for real human leadership on the scene is more important than ever.

Additionally, just like comprehensive use-of-force guidelines, such
camera footage can improperly be used offensively against an officer if
judged by the unknowing or corrupt. A perfect example of this was when
the U.S. Federal Air Marshals (FAMs) were first writing their use-of-force
policies and the issue came up of how to write rules for striking weapons
(like ASP batons). A colleague of ours, Doc, who is an experienced SWAT
trainer, supervisor, and team member, wisely advised the FAMs not to
specify what type of striking instruments their agent may use. Instead,
the policy allows for the use of improvised weapons that may be readily
available: a passenger's cane, a jug of water, or a suitcase. For, if the FAM
manual specified or implied that the agents had to use an ASP baton, then
callous members of the plaintiffs' bar, ignorant members of the media,
or even their own leadership would use that rule offensively against the
FAM agents if they bonked a suspect with anything other than an ASP.
Welcome to the world of lawsuit-happy America!

Leaders should be and usually are held responsible for their subordinates'
actions. This drives a natural tendency for leaders to know and control
what their subordinates are doing. In high-risk situations, this perceived
need for control is only exacerbated. Within the military especially, as
technology has improved, this has led to more and more attempts to
control an individual's actions on the battlefield.

One can easily point to the changes in warfare that landline telephones
had in World War I, through the changes in wireless communications in
World War II, to the ability today for the commander in chief to watch
in real time an actual raid halfway around the world. It becomes extremely
seductive for a leader to direct and control the actions of his subordinates
under these conditions, especially when the outcome of the actions is of
national importance. So, too, police and political leaders now have the
ability to analyze incidents before, during, and after a critical encounter
of a policeman with the public. The leadership challenge, as always, is to
know the difference between doing what you *can* do and doing what you
should do. Leaders that have a properly trained force are more likely to
trust that force in times of peace and duress.

The benefit of having a police or peace officer among us instead of a law
enforcement officer should be obvious from a social perspective as well.
The police officer has the community's families' interest at heart, rather

than the supervisor's or systemic need to feed the statistical machine. While more difficult to quantify—ask warriors of the Vietnam era how well Secretary of Defense Robert McNamara's statistical machine worked to forge leaders—the leadership of human dynamics and trust works much better over the long run. Locking up every 1 out of 420 Americans has not gone so well in the short term—at least since Nixon's "war on drugs" took root in the early 1970s. As we lose more and more of our privacy due to the invasiveness of technologies, virtuous policing, restraint, and concern for humanity become all the more important for the police and populace.

One of the author's cousins, Michaela, and her boyfriend, Bob, were traveling along the Virginia–North Carolina border on vacation from their tough, yet rewarding work running a horse farm in Rhode Island. Both are mature, nice people who are the epitome of law-abiding, tax-paying middle-class citizenry. While driving along a rural highway going toward the Outer Banks of Carolina, they saw a policeman on the shoulder of the road with his emergency lights activated. There were no other cars in front of the officer's car, and the officer was safely ensconced in his vehicle. Bob, out of courtesy, attempted to move to the left lane. Unfortunately, another car was blocking his ability to change lanes. To Michaela and Bob's surprise, the officer pulled them over and issued Bob an expensive moving citation for "failure to change lanes for a stopped emergency vehicle." Bob, a commercial driver's license (CDL) holder, tried to explain that he was precluded from shifting lanes by the other vehicle and was unaware of a new law Virginia had passed in this regard. The officer was polite to the point of obsequiousness, saying, "You can always come down and fight it in court," knowing full well that an average American cannot afford to take two days off from work to drive or fly down from Rhode Island to challenge a $125 ticket. Moreover, even if he did so, there would be no guarantee that the local judge would still not find him guilty and then tack on extra court costs (a not-so-cute euphemism for another extralegal tax) to boot.

When, after the ticket was issued, Michaela told the officer, "You are not being nice at all," the officer responded, "I always spoke politely to you throughout this stop." Michaela rightly pointed out, "Being polite is not the same as being nice." The point Michaela was making was soon proved to be true, as she and Bob then staked out the officer for the next two hours and watched him as he would pull the same "fake car stop" and then only ticket out-of-state cars less likely to fight this random tax in court.

This behavior, while we are sure was rewarded within his department, further widens the gulf between police and populace. While the underlying law—requiring drivers, when safe to do so, to move a lane away from an emergency vehicle during a car stop situation—was written to try and prevent officers from being injured by vehicles striking them while they are in that dangerous position between the stopped vehicle and the active lane of traffic immediately adjacent to the car stop, its application here was nothing short of state-sponsored extortion. To set up a fake car stop just to hand out tickets defeats the spirit of the law and increases citizenry's righteous indignation and anger against the police. It also shows law enforcement in the light of a tax collector instead of a public safety officer.

It should be obvious that when the police are used to collect taxes, as opposed to protecting and serving the public, the bond between them and the public they serve is severely damaged. This outcome of the breakdown between the public and police is predictable and with precedent. When the federal government instituted a 55-mile-per-hour speed limit, the results on that bond were not positive. Up until that time, traffic engineers, who used a method that addressed both safety and human dynamics, generally set speed limits. When the speed limit was changed in a manner that most drivers perceived as unreasonable, they simply drove faster than the posted limit, but at a speed that most drivers (and safety engineers) would consider safe.

The reaction of the federal government was to threaten the states (who enforce speed limits) with a loss of money if they could not demonstrate a lowering of the actual driven speed. This led to actions such as the state police driving 55 miles per hour in all lanes of traffic on a highway that was designed for speeds in excess of 70 miles per hour, causing enormous congestion and a significant increase in the likelihood of an accident. It was clear to anyone watching such an event that the state police were increasing the risk of an accident on the highway and angering most citizens. The citizenry reacted in a way anyone could have predicted. The state police, whom many perceived as increasing the danger to them, became an enemy to be avoided. This was in spite of the fact that likely very few state policemen personally supported this tactic. They were simply following the orders of their superiors. Thankfully, this artificial limit has changed, but it is unknown what long-term effects this aberration may have had on the relationship between police and drivers.

Similarly, when a local police force targeted a four-lane highway in one of the authors' rural towns, a similar reaction was noted. The highway is a divided four-lane road with a speed limit of 45 miles per hour. There is a stretch of that road of about 3 miles without any lights or significant intersections. Traffic routinely drives at about 50 to 55 miles per hour on that section, and it is not known for accidents. The local police force gathered support from the surrounding counties and set up a speed trap on this road, and by using radar ticketed a large number of drivers over a several-hour period one afternoon. The tickets were almost all reduced to "driving with improper equipment," a term of art stating that the driver's speedometer was inaccurate. This is obviously false, or in English, a lie. Few, if any, of the drivers had points added to their driving record, and their insurance did not go up. A number of attorneys in the area were paid to fix the tickets. Again, there was no pretense that any of the automobiles actually had faulty speedometers.

The attorneys and the drivers functionally lied to the court in order to reduce the penalty, while allowing the county to collect its tax. The court certainly understood this, but also saw this as a way to get a conviction without much trouble or expense. Money from the fines went into the local coffers. Within two days of the traps ending, the average speed on this road returned to the safe, but higher than posted, limit. Who in the community was served by this action? More importantly, how will those drivers who were ticketed inappropriately think about their police department in the future? Perhaps it will not matter, but it is another slight tear in the bond between the community and its police.

Red-light or stoplight cameras are often another chimera: tax collectors posing as safety devices. At certain well-defined and -researched traffic intersections, where accident rates are demonstrably high due to red-light violators, such devices may be an effective and fair tool to enhance public safety. But, as the Internet has quickly educated citizens, the private companies that sell them not only promise revenue increases to municipal and state governments, but also take a cut of the fines as payment in kind. This is nothing more than a shakedown, and citizens know it.

Moreover, some studies indicate that accident rates *increase* at some intersections where these devices are used due to drivers suddenly, unexpectedly, and unnecessarily slamming on their brakes to avoid getting "flashed" by cameras timed to a short yellow signal. Research has demonstrated that the best predictor of red-light violations is the length of the yellow signal. Unfortunately, lengthening this where cameras are established would reduce the number of violations, and thereby the income from these violations. Such commonsense alterations of the length of the yellow lights are often not allowed by the contract that places the cameras in the first place. Money trumps common sense and decency.

What happens as police become more and more slaves of technology and tools of these law enforcement taxation schemes instead of peace officers? The population will begin to lose respect for the rule of law and begin to fight back, and the reputation of the profession will suffer. It is miraculous that more so-called speed cameras do not fall victim to sawzalls or thermite bombs. If the gulf between police and populace is not healed, then such targeting—along with playing "sporting clays" with government drones and worse—will become ubiquitous. There is a catchphrase from *Unintended Consequences*, John Ross's 1996 underground bestseller, that alludes to this very real possibility: "It is time to feed the hogs." We pray and hope that America never becomes a hog feeding ground.

It is critically important, then, for police leaders to teach and encourage virtuous behavior among their force, concentrating on magnanimity and goodness instead of small-minded behavior that glorifies and feeds upon itself. A force that seeks only statistics can quickly become a self-licking ice cream cone: There is more crime, so we need more officers, who in turn make more arrests, which shows we have more crime and generates more "income" through asset forfeiture schemes and federal grants for more equipment. A law enforcement agency's mission should *never* be for it to grow itself. The mission should be dictated by true community needs and requirements, and with a view toward keeping the peace, not enforcing every law dreamed up by a bored and "do something, even if it's stupid" legislature.

12

When Society Embraces the Bad Guys: The Sad Song of Sergeant Johnnie Riley

In 2003, in an affront to the safety and fair peace of the community of Prince George's County, Maryland, a young resident named Kalvin Kyle decided to go for the big time by carjacking another citizen's car. Unfortunately for Kalvin, yet good for the citizens, the victim he chose was an off-duty police officer. The officer shot and arrested Kyle. Sentenced to a lengthy jail term for that carjacking, Kyle was supposed to spend many years in prison.

In the meantime, the good guy of our story was in full stride of living the American dream with his wife and family. Sergeant Johnnie Riley, married to the same woman for two decades, a proud and involved father of a small family, and a weekly churchgoer, was a policeman and a soldier too. He first served in the vaunted 101st Airborne Division and later in the Maryland Army National Guard; he served in Iraq as an infantryman, where he earned both the Combat Infantryman's Badge and the Bronze Star Medal for his service to our republic. As a police office in District Heights in Prince George's County, Maryland, he was recognized as officer of the year on four separate occasions.

Now, sometime after serving only a part of his original sentence for the 2003 carjacking, Kalvin Kyle was released from prison on parole. Did he learn from his mistakes and become a model citizen? No. He was back on the streets of Prince George's County acting out his hoodlum ways. And, on an early September evening of 2012, he ran into our story's good guy, resulting in an absolute tragic and unjust sequence of events that is summarized as follows.

The relevant facts occurred in District Heights, Maryland. District Heights is a Maryland suburb of Washington, DC.* On September 6, 2012, District Heights police sergeant John Riley, an 8-year police veteran and 20-plus-year military veteran, was working a uniformed patrol post in an unmarked Ford Crown Victoria equipped with emergency lights and siren. At approximately 5:15 p.m., near Marlboro Pike and Foster Street, Sergeant Riley attempted to conduct a traffic stop of a young Black male operator of a Honda CBR600RR motorcycle for a traffic violation. In the vicinity of the motorcyclist just prior, during, and after the traffic stop was an SUV (possibly a Chevrolet Tahoe) occupied by two individuals who seemed to be acting in concert with the motorcyclist. In an apparent attempt to elude the officer, the operator of the motorcycle—later identified as Kalvin Kyle—entered the wrong way on Foster Street, which is a one-way street halfway between Marlboro Pike and County Road. Due to high vehicular traffic volume at the intersections of Foster Street and County Road, the motorcyclist was unable to escape and stopped the motorcycle right at that intersection.

After getting out of his police vehicle, Sergeant Riley approached the operator of the motorcycle, had a brief discussion with the motorcyclist, and told him he was under arrest for fleeing and eluding and possession of a stolen motor vehicle. It is not exactly clear at what point Sergeant Riley became aware that the motorcycle was stolen, but it clearly had an ignition that was tampered with and a "kill switch" installed in its place. At the time of arrest, Kalvin Kyle was sporting a dreadlock haircut, which later becomes relevant to the decision by Sergeant Riley to use force. Initially, Kalvin Kyle resisted arrest and physically tussled with Sergeant Riley, resulting in Johnnie Riley having to forcibly take Kyle to the ground, where he was eventually handcuffed. Citizens in the area witnessed much of this. A second officer—Prince George's County police officer McMillan—responded to the incident and assisted Sergeant Riley in securing Kyle by seat belt in the front seat of Sergeant Riley's police cruiser. Kalvin Kyle initially gave his name as Kalvin Patterson or Kalvin Paterson. His misspelling, or not knowing how to spell his own last name,

---

* According to the 2010 census, there were 5,837 people, 2,050 households, and 1,505 families residing in the incorporated city of District Heights. The population density was 6,276.3 inhabitants per square mile. The racial makeup of the city was 6.0% White, 90.1% African American, 0.2% Native American, 0.6% Asian, 1.1% from other races, and 1.9% from two or more races. Hispanic or Latino of any race made up 3.7% of the population.

gave the officers at the scene the correct impression that he was hiding his true identity: a typical tactic of felons wishing to hide a criminal history.[*] Also briefly appearing at the initial scene was District Heights deputy chief of police, Wendell Brantley. Unfortunately, both Officer McMillan and Deputy Chief Brantley, believing the scene to be secure, left the scene after only a few minutes.

During the traffic stop and arrest of Kalvin Kyle, Sergeant Riley again noticed the SUV with 22-inch custom wheels, operated by unknown persons—but described by other witnesses as being operated by a Black male with "dreads" (slang for dreadlocks)—circling the area of the motorcycle stop.[†] This particular area of District Heights, just off of a main thoroughfare, was a higher-crime area compared to Maryland as a whole.[‡] However, this particular block of Foster Street contained a mix of residential and commercial properties, including a day care facility. After arresting Kalvin Kyle and handcuffing and securing him by seat belt in the front[§] of the patrol vehicle, Sergeant Riley requested a subject check through police communications and began to photograph the stolen motorcycle. He was again distracted by the activities of the occupants of the suspicious SUV, which had circled the block and appeared to be "eyeballing" the arrest scene. The term *eyeballing* is used in police parlance to indicate deliberate, nefarious observation by a third party.

Just as Sergeant Riley began to process and photograph the stolen motorcycle, he again noticed the suspicious SUV. This time, it was traveling slowly on County Road and its driver was partially hanging out of the vehicle's window, motioning with his arm, giving a "come along"

---

[*] At some point after the arrest, Sergeant Riley either became aware or suspected that Kalvin Paterson was actually Kalvin Kyle, a subject with a violent criminal past, which included a conviction of robbery with a dangerous weapon and transporting a handgun. During that incident in 2003, Kalvin Kyle tried to take the car of an off-duty police officer. Amazingly, the police shot Kyle during that incident, too.

[†] See, *inter alia*, witness statements and grand jury testimony of Deputy Chief Brantley at page 25, where he specifically and timely reports Sergeant Riley's statement to him immediately after the shooting describing this vehicle. Another witness—a citizen—also saw this SUV.

[‡] Annually, District Heights suffers 167 crimes per square mile compared to an average of 65 crimes per square mile for the state and 39.3 crimes per square mile for the nation. Sources: Neighborhoodscout.com and Maryland state government.

[§] Most police jurisdictions secure and transport prisoners in the backseat of their patrol vehicles, areas that are segregated from the front seat by a metal cage. Sergeant Riley's patrol car did not have a caged area, so officers in his situation often transport criminal suspects in the front seat of a police vehicle. This is done not only in Prince George's County, but also by other major jurisdictions, such as the Pennsylvania State Police, when transporting suspects with a lone police escort.

sign to Kyle. At this very moment, Sergeant Riley caught movement in his peripheral vision and noticed that Kalvin Kyle[*] had extricated himself from the patrol vehicle and was now running away, possibly toward his colleagues in the SUV, who were believed to be circling the block in the direction of Kyle's escape route. Either way, a felony suspect who had already demonstrated his dangerousness to the police and the community was escaping lawful custody.

After unsuccessfully attempting to stop Kyle by futilely throwing his baton at the fleeing subject, Sergeant Riley fired three .40-caliber S&W rounds from his Glock Model 22 duty pistol at Kalvin Kyle, striking the subject once in the lower back. The first two rounds missed Kyle and lodged in an unoccupied vehicle parked nearby.[†] At the time he first noticed Kyle escaping, Sergeant Riley's vision was impaired by the police cruiser, which was between him and the suspect. Numerous other psychophysiological factors, such as tunnel vision, inattentional blindness, and sequential thinking, negatively impacted his ability to precisely assess the threat. Human eyes are not cameras: We process information with our brain, using trained schemas to interpret our environment. Police officers' schemas, based on their training, knowledge, and experience, are very different from the average juror's, who often assesses the reasonableness of a policeman's actions based on what Hollywood and TV shows teach them.

The occupants of the suspicious SUV quickly sped away before any more information could be obtained about their identities or motives. However, Kyle later admitted that he was acting in concert with the occupants of the SUV. Sergeant Riley notified emergency services and an ambulance

---

[*] It would be incorrect to infer that Sergeant Riley, at the time he fired his weapon, knew or believed that Kalvin Kyle was still handcuffed from behind. It is common police knowledge that felons often practice not only getting out of handcuffs, but also wriggling the cuffed hands from behind, under their legs, so that the cuffs are in front. Moreover, the officer's ability to quickly analyze the situation is negatively impacted by the stress of the moment. Deputy Chief Wendell Brantley, in his grand jury testimony at page 50, articulately explains this phenomenon as it happened to him on one occasion: "As a Prince George's County police officer I have had someone escape from a car when I was assisting another officer. We gave foot pursuit. The one officer I was assisting fell. I continued pursing that person. He was moving so fast to this day I cannot tell you if he was still handcuffed or not. *The only logical assumption I could make is he somehow had got out of the cuff* because he was able to scale a ten-foot wooden fence in Kentland. He was running so fast that I could not see if he was still handcuffed or not" (emphasis added). This testimony is from an extraordinarily well-trained supervisory officer with at least 18 years of experience.

[†] According to Department of Justice (DOJ) statistics, police officers miss their intended targets approximately 80% of the time when firing in real-life use-of-force scenarios.

was dispatched to the scene. He also immediately provided trauma care to Kyle—hardly indicia of intent to kill or unlawfully injure. In addition, he immediately reported to his supervisor, Deputy Chief Brantley, his concerns about the suspicious SUV. In fact, an LOF (look out for) radio dispatch was announced over police channels describing the SUV.

Once in the backseat of Chief Brantley's police vehicle and after Sergeant Riley gave a quick situational report of what had happened, Chief Brantley reminded Sergeant Riley of his rights under the Law Enforcement Officer's Bill of Rights not to make a formal statement. Instead of focusing their investigation on why a reasonable officer might, indeed, use deadly force under these circumstances, the subsequent state's investigation ignored the criminal culpability and decisions of Kalvin Kyle and his possible co-conspirators in the SUV. Because of the wide gulf that has existed between police and the populace in Prince George's County for decades, they went after Sergeant Johnnie Riley!

Within weeks—despite clear evidence of a complete lack of criminal intent on Sergeant Riley's part, and the fact that the relevant constitutional law specifically allows for split-second errors when such incidents unfold—the politically appointed state's attorney for Prince George's County sought and obtained a grand jury indictment of Johnnie Riley, charging him with first-degree attempted murder, second-degree attempted murder, first-degree assault, and use of a handgun in the commission of a felony! This also despite the fact that the state's own use-of-force experts—two experienced police officer trainers and patrolmen—opined that, at worst, Johnnie Riley made an error in judgment. Moreover, both of the prosecuting attorneys assigned to the case did so because they were ordered to do so by their superior—the politician.

Sadly, after improper jury instructions were given—instructions that said that the jury could infer criminal intent to kill based on the officer's pointing and firing a weapon in the line of duty at a criminal suspect—and three days of contentious deliberation, a Prince George's County jury convicted Sergeant Johnnie Riley of first-degree assault, felony handgun use, and criminal misuse of office. Kalvin Kyle—the miscreant behind this tragedy—was never charged* and was unjustly awarded with hundreds of thousands of dollars from the public coffers. Sergeant Johnnie Riley, because Maryland has a mandatory minimum sentencing guideline, was sentenced to five years in prison.

---

* Charges were dropped in exchange for his testimony against Sergeant Riley.

DISCUSSION

The old common-law fleeing felon rule that allowed peace officers to shoot fleeing felons such as Kalvin Kyle was written not only to physically stop them, but also to induce them to "surrender peaceably" if they dared commit inherently dangerous felonies, rather than allow them to "escape trial for their crimes." In 1984, the U.S. Supreme Court, in *Tennessee v. Garner*,[*] revised that rule to a new standard: whether an "officer has probable cause to believe that the suspect poses a significant threat of death or serious physical injury to the officer or others."

When officers have probable cause to believe a suspect committed a crime "involving the infliction or threatened infliction of serious physical injury," it is reasonable under the Constitution to use deadly force, if necessary, to prevent escape of such a person. If not, "this suspect will remain free in the community for the time being, and law enforcement officers will be consumed in an effort to find him. When they do, perhaps he will surrender quietly, or perhaps he will violently resist. While he is at large, perhaps he will not commit another crime, or threaten to inflict serious injury. The point is that the *burden of risk is on the dangerous suspect rather than on the community.*"[†]

MISUNDERSTANDING THE TACTICAL DYNAMICS OF AN ENCOUNTER

> The race is not to the swift or the battle to the strong ... but time and chance happen to them all.
>
> **—Ecclesiastes 9:11**

Much of the confusion facing those investigating and assessing deadly force encounters flows from their ignorance of the tactical dynamics of a deadly force encounter. There are many ways to break down the tactical dynamics of a deadly force encounter, but the opinions and concepts of most experts can be set forth into the following three categories: action

---

[*] 471 U.S. 1 (1984).

[†] Patrick, Urey W., and Hall, John, *In Defense of Self and Others—Issues, Facts, & Fallacies: The Realities of Law Enforcement's Use of Deadly Force* (Durham, NC: Carolina Academic Press, 2010), p. 285.

versus reaction, fight-or-flight syndrome (emotional intensity), and wound ballistics. Not only does the relevant case law recognize these factors when assessing the efficacy or lawfulness of a shooting, but also those professing to be tactical instructors must be intimately familiar with them before attempting to write and teach in this arena. Unfortunately, there are too many so-called firearms or tactical experts who have never grasped the fundamentals of these dynamics. Most attorneys, judges, and jurors are woefully, and sometimes willfully, ignorant of these facts.

Action Versus Reaction

Bad guys—be they insurgents in Iraq or criminals on the streets of New Orleans or Ferguson—only have one decision: when to initiate an attack. They are nearly always at a tactical advantage over a police officer. This is true whether it is time to press the "clacker" on an improvised explosive devise, fire the first shot in an ambush, or punch a police officer in the face during a routine car stop or field interview. Good guys (and society must start from the premise that the police officers are the good guys) have at least three decision points to assess before initiating any defensive actions.

    First decision point. One has to first recognize the threat. Far too often, due to a combination of poor threat recognition training, bad luck, poor situational awareness, and perhaps a skilled opponent, the good guys get shot or punched in the face before even recognizing a threat exists. The multiple instances of law enforcement officers being killed with their own weapon[*] prove the maxim that "good guys can never afford to be unlucky, and bad guys need only be lucky once." This is one message tactical operators always need to remember. John C. Hall, perhaps our nation's preeminent expert on the constitutional law concerning use of force, is fond of reminding students that we must not forget the role chance plays in every encounter. He routinely cites Ecclesiastes 9:11 when lecturing to emphasize that role.

    Second decision point. After recognizing a threat, goods guys have to determine an appropriate level of response, because not all threats require a deadly force response. This is why it is extremely important not to burden officers with a checklist of conditions that must

---

[*] In an average year, approximately 17% of officers killed in the line of duty are shot with their own weapon after their "unarmed" assailants gain access to it during an initial altercation.

be met before deadly force is authorized. "Last resort" language in particular is foolhardy because deadly force may, in fact, be the first resort in such an encounter. Another factor that negatively impacts this second decision point is a factor known as Hick's law. A psychologist[*] wrote a 123-page article describing what should be obvious: The more factors a brain has to filter, the longer it takes to reach a decision. Unfortunately, too many police, security, and military leaders who are in charge of drafting deadly force policies ignore this fact. Confusing and tactically impractical guidance builds in delay and creates deadly hesitancy.

Third decision point. Assuming one recognizes the threat and then determines that deadly force is an appropriate level of response, our brain then has to tell our bodies to react. This step, all by itself, can take an average of 1.5 seconds under ideal circumstances. By way of reference, a law enforcement study presented experienced cops with a range of scenarios whereby the first two decision points were already solved: The threat is a steel target at 15 meters distance, and the appropriate level of response is deadly force. On command (the sounding of an air horn), the officers were to draw and fire on the steel targets. The average response time was over 1.5 seconds—an eternity in a firefight. Even if a weapon is drawn, the average response time from a visual stimulus to the first shot being fired is over a half second. An opponent of average skills can fire two shots at the officer in that half second.

For these reasons, we must divorce ourselves from Hollywood's notions of a gunfight. Officers must never wait until an opponent points or fires a weapon before applying deadly force. Movies and television shows are littered with situations where good guys either wait until being shot at before returning fire or attempt to talk the bad guys into surrendering.

---

[*] Hick, W. E., "On the Rate of Gain of Information," *Quarterly Journal of Experimental Psychology*, 4, 11–26, 1952; R. Hyman, "Stimulus Information as a Determinant of Reaction Time, *Journal of Experimental Psychology*, 45, 188–196, 1953. Hick's law, or the Hick-Hyman law, is a human–computer interaction model that describes the time it takes for a user to make a decision as a function of the possible choices he or she has. Given n equally probable choices, the average reaction time T required to choose among them is approximately $T = b \log 2(n + 1)$, where b is a constant that can be determined empirically by fitting a line to measured data. *See also* Stuart K. Card, Thomas P. Moran, and Allen Newell, *The Psychology of Human–Computer Interaction* (CRC Press, 1983). According to Card et al. (1983), the +1 is "because there is uncertainty about whether to respond or not, as well as about which response to make."

This is Hollywood at its finest, but deadly if used as a model for any real use-of-force situation.

The police officers firing in the range study above were firing in a controlled setting, at static targets, and were expecting it. Real-world decision making is further negatively impacted because shooting incidents are most often characterized by the following:

- Sudden, unexpected occurrences. This is nearly always true, because if an incident is expected, presumably an officer would bring something larger than a handgun or rifle.
- Rapid and unpredictable movement by the target(s) and, hopefully, the police.
- Limited target opportunities.
- Frequently under low light or from partially obstructed vantage points.
- Life-or-death stress of sudden, close, personal violence, which leads us to the second dynamic of a tactical encounter, the emotional intensity or fight-or-flight response.

Fight-or-Flight Response (Emotional Intensity)

We are fearfully and wonderfully made.

Psalm 139:14

Fight or flight, better described as emotional intensity, is how one's body most likely reacts when engaged in mortal combat due to certain autonomic functions that occur when one recognizes a life-threatening situation. This effect is induced via a psychological function. In other words, one must *perceive* the threat as serious. Nevertheless, once perceived, the following physiological effects follow:

1. Norepinephrine, cortisol and epinephrine are dumped into the bloodstream.
2. Both heart rate and contractility of the heart increase, leading to increased blood flow.
3. Vasoconstriction—the body's involuntarily action of drawing blood from one's extremities and routing it to the central cortex in order to provide maximum oxygenation of vital organs and the brain

housing group—occurs in the major organs of the body, excluding the brain, and vasodilation occurs in the major muscle groups. The need for digestion is minimal, but you need as much strength in your arms and legs as possible. The brain is never short on blood supply, even in the cold, although it is reduced in areas affecting vision.

4. Body temperature increases, blood pressure increases, and pupils dilate. This often results in a small loss of close focus.
5. Perspiration increases.
6. Blood sugar increases, allowing more energy transfer to the major muscles.

Most are familiar with examples of enhanced strength and heart rate increases associated with the adrenaline dump—a woman who lift a car's wheel off of her trapped child and other examples of incredible weights being lifted—but many are unfamiliar with the often negative effects of vasoconstriction and the other physiological and psychological effects of adrenaline. In 2004, author and retired Army ranger Dave Grossman published his book *On Combat*, detailing these effects on warriors and police officers under high-stress situations. Grossman's book, as well as John Hall's and Urey Patrick's *In Defense of Self and Others*, should be required reading for anyone involved in analyzing the reasonableness of a use-of-force encounter. Lieutenant Colonel Grossman, Dr. Bill Lewinski and his team of dedicated experts at the Force Science Institute,* and others have identified certain physiological and psychological phenomena that occur under situations of close personal violence:

- **Loss of fine motor skills.** Evolutionarily, it was very important to have a sudden surge in gross motor skills, increase in speed, and insensitivity to pain. Fighting off saber-toothed tigers or fellow men armed with clubs was extremely important. This enhanced a person's ability for basic fighting skills: hand-to-hand and blunt weapons. But such physiological occurrences can be terrible for modern weapons, which require trigger sensitivity, precision shooting, and fine cognitive processing. This "clubbiness" of fingers further degrades one's ability to draw, reload, and manipulate weapon systems.
- **Cognitive processing deteriorates.** Under high-stress events, a person's sympathetic nervous system (SNS) begins to take over

---

* See http://www.forcescience.org.

control of the situation. This is a basic primal response, an automatic reaction to a perceived survival threat. When this happens, there will be errors in judgment, errors in performance, and a negative impact on memory and motor skills. Because the midbrain begins to take over, the cognitive or thinking portion of the brain often loses control. Many police officers die screaming for help into their radio microphones or repeatedly ordering armed subjects to "drop the weapon" when, instead, they should be engaging the bad guy with overwhelming deadly force.

- **Decision errors and performance errors.** The average junior high school ball player practices around 400 hours a year developing complex motor skills and, hopefully, increased mental processing ability under the "stress" of the game. Yet, his performance is typically mediocre. No one, except his parents and girlfriend, wants to watch him play. The average law enforcement officer, due primarily to budgetary constraints (ammunition and time cost money), practices less than 40 hours a year in all forms of defensive tactics. Moreover, officers typically do not practice on moving targets under high-stress conditions. They "qualify" on static targets with the only stress extant is that the event is timed. In the case of Prince George's County, officers are required to fire their weapons only two hours per year. But, society expects Olympic-class performance at "game time."

  Again, Hollywood is much to blame for these expectations. If the 100-pound female officer on TV can use judo to defeat the 240-pound drunken steel worker, how come the officers in real life had to shoot the guy?

- **Inattentional blindness—humans filter out noncritical stimuli.** A good sports example might be the often viewed video of Toronto Blue Jays second baseman Jay Bell throwing a baseball directly into an umpire's face. Even though the fans and audience clearly saw the umpire, Jay Bell did not. So practiced in the art of pivoting and throwing to first base, he was focused on the first baseman's glove to the exclusion of what was clearly visible to the television audience and the crowd; he simply did not see the umpire. In part, this is because the human eye is not a video camera. Humans see with their brains, not their eyes. Jay Bell filtered out all extraneous information—to include what is a blinding flash of the obvious to uninvolved witnesses. This is one very real and probable reason why Sergeant Johnnie Riley never even saw the handcuffs on Kalvin Kyle.

He defaulted to his trained schema: A fleeing felony suspect with a bent elbow equaled a threat. And Johnnie Riley acted in response to that threat. Moreover, this is why requiring police to wear lapel video cameras will not solve the problem. In fact, what those cameras record will often later be used offensively by the uneducated against the officer because the camera sees things differently than a live officer does under stress.

We look, but we do not see. We listen, but we do not hear.

Sherlock Holmes* and St. Paul†

- Selective attention. Also, once a person intently focuses on any specific thing, it is very difficult to focus on other things. See, for example, "The Invisible Gorilla" video at Dr. Dan Simons's website‡ for a visual demonstration of this fact. It is an amazing video in its own right, but when viewed in context of an officer making decisions under the stress of close, personal violence, it takes on a far graver meaning. Yet, most jurists and investigators never take this into account when accessing an officer's actions after the fact.
- Hyperventilation due to fear-induced stressors causes a significant reduction in blood flow to the visual cortex portion of the brain. The result is missed cues, misidentified objects, and near blindness. What might be obvious to a nonparticipant witness might be totally missed by a participant in a life-or-death struggle.
- Auditory exclusion. Many police officers and soldiers never hear their own weapons discharge during a firefight. Sir Winston Churchill noted this phenomenon in one of his many memoirs. Recalling his participation in the last horse cavalry charge of the British Empire at the Battle of Omdurman in the Sudan (September 2, 1898), Churchill wrote that despite the rattle of musketry, the crash of artillery, the thundering of horse hoof beats, and all of the sounds attendant to a modern battlefield, it was "like watching a silent movie." He also commented on the role of chance, stating, "Chance is unceasingly at work in our lives, but we cannot always see its workings sharply

---

* Doyle, Arthur Conan, "Sherlock Holmes, a Scandal in Bohemia," *The Strand Magazine*, London, 1891: "You see, but you do not observe. The distinction is clear."

† Jowett, Benjamin, *The Epistle of St. Paul to the Thessalonians, Galatians, Romans: With Critical Notes and Dissertations*, "St. Paul's Epistle to the Romans 11:8" (London: John Murray, 1855).

‡ See http://www.theinvisiblegorilla.com/videos.html.

and clearly defined."* Officers, and those later judging them, need to understand that they may not hear their partners' warnings or threat activities or vocalizations. This can be very disconcerting if they are not prepared for it.

- Time–space distortion. Anyone who has been in an automobile accident and saw the accident unfolding before impact—such as when losing control on a long patch of black ice or when looking into the rearview mirror and seeing the idiot behind you standing on his brakes as his car screeches toward impact with your vehicle—has probably experienced time–space distortion. What takes mere seconds may appear to take minutes as our brain goes into the "oh no!" mode. This often happens to police officers and other combatants, who have variously reported seeing their empty brass cartridges discharging in slow motion (sometimes appearing "as large as trash cans") or actually seeing their bullets impact into their target. Experienced warriors and athletes can sometimes tune their bodies to use this phenomenon to their advantage, such as Ted Williams's claimed ability to slow a 93 miles per hour fastball down to the point where he could see the seams on the ball. Not many folks realize that Ted Williams was also an ace Marine fighter pilot in WWII and Korea. His uncanny ability to control time–space distortion, as well as his superior hand–eye coordination, most likely made him a great fighter pilot too. But, such skills are either genetically endowed or require tremendous amounts of practice.

  Again, if not prepared for this, it can be very disconcerting and further negatively impact both the shooters' decisions to use force in a timely and appropriate manner and their aim. Shooting on a qualification range is rarely an indicator of how well an individual will shoot under the stress of a deadly force encounter.

- The myth of multitasking. Brains think sequentially, focusing very quickly on one thing, then the next—not at the same time. For those that have attempted to text while driving, in that one second you are focused on your cell phone, your vehicle could travel 88 feet (at 60 miles per hour). It is also irrelevant whether the distraction is auditory rather than visual. Simply focusing on the conversation rather than the roadway will have the same disastrous effect on one's

---

* Churchill, Winston S., *A Roving Commission: My Early Life* (New York: Charles Scribner's Sons, 1930), p. 66.

driving. The reason why texting and handheld devices are outlawed in most states is an enforcement issue: It is easy to spot a hand to the ear or hands in one's lap instead of the steering wheel. It is nearly impossible to detect hands-free devices. But, even using hands-free devices causes driving impairment akin to a 0.08 to 0.015 blood alcohol content (BAC) percentage. It is very clear, in terms of both common sense and scientific documentation, that once something arises that captures your attention, your external focus immediately narrows down to just that one area. Yes, you can walk and talk at the same time, one of the most simplistic forms of multitasking. But once you trip, you can no longer carry on the conversation because your full attention is concerned with dealing with your tripping. Imagine how this phenomenon impacts an officer under stress.

- Loss of peripheral vision (tunnel vision). Field of vision during high-stress encounters narrows to 1° to 3° of the focal plane. Hold a thumb out at arm's length—what the thumb obscures at 15 feet approximates a 3° field of vision. Things outside this field are necessarily excluded from the decision-making process. Based on this factor alone, it is entirely possible that Sergeant Riley never saw that Kalvin Kyle was still handcuffed.

- Memory gaps. Often, persons involved in high-stress events forget much of what they and others did during the event. Sometimes, after a period of at least 24 hours of decompression, their memory is restored somewhat. That is why it is critical that commanders do not allow criminal investigators to interview participants in a line-of-duty shooting until after this period has lapsed. Moreover, the fact that the recollections of the shooter and other participants, and the physical evidence—for example, the number of rounds fired and their direction—might be wildly divergent should not suggest or imply untruthfulness on anyone's behalf. They report what they believe they saw.

- Intrusive thoughts. A participant's mind, under the high stress of a gunfight, may think of things entirely unrelated to the critical events at hand. Police officers, as well as warriors in combat, often report this phenomenon.

Wound Ballistics

Again, Hollywood has done much to distort and craft our perceptions and beliefs concerning how bullets work and their effect on the human body.

Years of portraying suspects getting blown through plate-glass windows by Clint Eastwood's .44 Magnum or vehicles exploding or rolling over after being hit by small arms fire has created deeply imbedded myths that must be exposed.

The truth is that many police officers—as well as the bad guys—do not even know that they are shot until after the gunfight is over. Unless a person receives a devastating head shot or the cervical spine is severed—causing immediate disruption of the brain housing group and brain-nerve function—the body, physically, can keep on fighting until volumic blood loss (around 40%) deprives the brain-nerve function of enough oxygen to work. That is why officers are trained to apply force until the threat is over. They are never taught to shoot to kill.

Based on all of his training, knowledge, and experience, Sergeant Johnnie Riley, just as any reasonably trained officer who uses force in defense of self and others, was clearly attempting to stop the threat, not kill Kalvin Kyle. Absent some specific evidence of malice aforethought—for example, a prior personal evil animus of Johnnie Riley toward Kyle or involvement as a co-conspirator in a drug gang (neither of which exists)—an officer's decision to use force under the high stress of a deadly force encounter is with the intent to stop the threat. Both of the state's experts testified to this fact at trial.

But, before one can understand why this is so, gaining an understanding of how bullets work is critically important. Bullets work both psychologically and physically.

HOW BULLETS WORK PSYCHOLOGICALLY

Many have preconditioned their minds into believing how bullets work. Again, Hollywood is responsible for most of this folly. The FBI, in its exhaustive studies of law enforcement-related shootings, has found many examples of experienced police officers winning the initial phase of a gunfight by accurately engaging suspects, and then ultimately losing by not finishing the mission. Sometimes cops who, in the middle of a firefight, stop and actually look at their weapons because they aren't "working like they are supposed to work" experience this to their peril. In other words, the cops had preconditioned their expectations as to how a suspect they had just shot was supposed to react. And when the suspects did not immediately fall to the ground (or get blown backwards or through the plate-glass window), it caused a moment of hesitation on the cop's part, sometimes with fatal consequences.

More importantly, instead of immediately falling to the ground, suspects sometimes continued to aggressively assault or return fire on the officers. In the opening seconds of the famous and tragic FBI shootout of April 1986 in Miami, Florida, FBI special agent Jerry Dove fired a Winchester Silvertip 9-mm hollow-nosed round into one of the suspects, Michael Platt. This round severed Platt's right brachial artery before it entered his upper thoracic cavity, where it collapsed his right lung and caused further arterial bleeding. That one round fired by Jerry Dove caused a fatal injury to Platt. That means, by expert medical opinion provided postincident, it was believed that even had Platt received immediate trauma care, he still would have expired.

But, Michael Platt didn't perish for an additional 4 minutes, until he either exsanguinated (bled out) or succumbed to a head shot adminis-tered by FBI agent Ed Mireles during the closing moments of the firefight. But, in this additional 4 minutes, Platt killed two FBI agents, including Jerry Dove, and grievously wounded five others. While the mechanics or physical aspects of wound ballistics—how and why it took so long for the suspects to bleed out—played a role in their ability to continue the fight, it was the suspects' psychological determination that proved so deadly to the FBI. Yet, despite the damage received by the FBI, they also managed some payback of their own that day:

All five of the FBI Agents who were wounded continued to function and fight back despite their wounds. The best example for this discussion is FBI Special Agent Ed Mireles. SA Mireles had lost the use of his left arm due to a gunshot wound suffered in the opening stages of the fight that destroyed flesh and bone in his arm. He was on the ground and fading in and out of consciousness due to the cumulative effects of shock and blood loss, but continued to fight back for the duration of the shoot-out. SA Mireles fired five shotgun rounds from a pump-action shotgun he had to operate with one hand, inflicting buckshot wounds on both assailants. Then he regained his feet and approached Platt and Matix as they sat in Grogan and Dove's Bureau car and ended the gunfight by shooting both in the head with his handgun. By his own account, SA Mireles was not aware of his injury until he tried to use his arm to push himself up off the ground and could not, which caused him to look at his arm and see the wound and exposed bones. By the end of the gunfight, he was functioning on sheer will and rage.[*]

There is good news and bad news when dealing with the psychological aspects of how bullets work. Because we are fearfully and wonderfully made, the human body can withstand huge trauma and still fight and still survive, so long as we receive decent trauma care within the "golden hour." As good guys, we must always remember that and train to fight through our adversaries' and our own injuries. The bad news is that the bad guys are also fearfully and wonderfully made, and in addition to their own bodies' inherent strengths, they may also bring a powerful will to the fight (as did the two subjects the FBI faced in Miami). In the United States, drug use is pandemic.

In fact, earlier in his shift, Sergeant Riley arrested another suspect: a PCP user. This officer—four times officer of the year—was obviously not one to sit out his shifts at a local Dunkin' Donuts or 7-Eleven store. He was constantly vigilant for the criminal elements within society. Kalvin Kyle was one of those criminal elements.

HOW BULLETS WORK PHYSICALLY

Despite all the fantasy out of Hollywood and misinformation in many gun magazines, small arms rounds[†] do not possess knockdown or stopping power. Small arms projectiles physically incapacitate an individual by crushing, tearing, or destroying flesh and bone—hopefully with enough depth of penetration and permanence to either directly disrupt the body's brain-nerve function or cause enough blood volume loss to keep oxygen from adequately feeding that brain-nerve function. The goal is stopping the bad guy from performing his ill deeds. Police officers, as most soldiers, really do not shoot to kill: They shoot until the threat is over. It is entirely

---

[*] Patrick, U. W., and Hall, J. C., *In Defense of Self and Others* (Durham, NC: Carolina Academic Press, 2005), pp. 66–67.

[†] The authors are referring to handgun rounds and rifle/carbine rounds up to 7.62 NATO. It is certainly true that .50-caliber Browning machine gun (BMG) rounds or 12-gauge rifled slugs do possess superior stopping power compared to the aforementioned rounds, but the reality is that even these larger rounds are still governed by the general principles of wound ballistics. Once the principles of wound ballistics are grasped, it can be readily understood that projectiles that create larger and deeper holes increase the probability of timely results. However, in each case, we are still only talking about increasing probabilities.

irrelevant to the outcome of the shooting incident whether the bad guy dies. In the FBI shootout, Michael Platt died, but not soon enough. This is part of the reason why, on average, police officers fire three rounds in a line-of-duty shooting.

The preeminent scholar in the field of wounds ballistics, retired Army surgeon Colonel Marty Fackler, had this to say about the shock or knock-down power of a small arms projectile: "The shock from being hit by a bullet is actually much like the shock from being called an idiot; it is an expression of surprise and has nothing to do with physical effects or psychological trauma."[*] The ground truth is that the amount of physical energy inflicted on the body by a small arms round is equivalent to being hit by a Major League fastball.[†]

It is impossible to accurately predict with any degree of certainty the effects of wounds created by small arms projectiles. That is why it is absurd to draft into rules of engagement (ROE) guidance or a use-of-deadly-force policy such language as "use only the rounds necessary," "shoot to wound," or "shoot and assess." If a subject presents an imminent threat of death or serious bodily injury, then he must be shot until he ceases to present such a threat. Shooters and policy drafters alike must understand this concept of how bullets work, or they will continue to be subject to the other's folly.

When a bullet enters the human body, it creates a temporary wound channel and a permanent wound channel. Of the two, one can only reliably count on the permanent wound channel to destroy, crush, or tear flesh or bone. Even so, there is no accurate way to predict the course and effect of a small arms projectile on the human body.

A *temporary wound channel* is the larger temporary displacement of flesh or tissue caused by the transfer of energy within the body. The body has an amazing elastic quality that will absorb energy by temporarily stretching. Unless the bullet impacts close to a hard organ such as the liver or spleen, this temporary stretching will cause little or no diminution of the body's ability to function. The tissue will simply expand, and then collapse back unto itself. For those familiar with the blocks of gelatin portrayed in many gun magazines that purport to show the knockdown power of a particular round, the large, opaque area represents the temporary wound channel.

---

[*] Fackler, M. I., "Questions and Comments," *Wound Ballistics Review, Journal of the International Wounds Ballistics Association*, 4(1), 5, 1999.

[†] Patrick, U. W., and Hall, J. C., *In Defense of Self and Others*, p. 69, quoting Douglas Lindsey, MD.

Such depictions, while visually impressive, are nearly meaningless in assessing the efficacy of a particular round.

A *permanent wound channel* is the permanent path of destruction through the body caused by the passage of the projectile through flesh and bone. It is the permanent hole caused by the size, depth of penetration, and course of the bullet as it traverses though the body. Many variables effect the permanent wound channel, to include, but not limited to, the velocity of the round, round fragmentation, deflection (either before or after entering the body), and size of the projectile.

Unless the permanent wound channel directly disrupts the brain-nerve function, one cannot ever assume or anticipate immediate incapacitation. The human heart can be eviscerated by a direct hit from a 7.62 × 51 mm NATO round (the standard sniper round within most police and military inventories), and still there will be enough oxygen in the brain for the assailant to continue to function for an additional 10 to 15 seconds: a seeming eternity in a firefight.

IN DEFENSE OF SELF OR OTHERS

Did Sergeant Riley have reasonable belief that Kalvin Kyle presented an imminent threat of grievous bodily injury to Riley or innocent others at the time he used deadly force? The old common-law standard clearly recognized that officers did not have to be *right* in their actions, only *reasonable*. This is still the standard. Moreover, *imminent* does not mean *immediate*. As Associate Justice Oliver Wendell Holmes so eloquently noted in *United States v. Brown*, "Detached reflection is not demanded in the presence of an uplifted knife."[*]

After the United States partially lifted the veil of sovereign immunity by diverse Federal Torts Claims Act statutes in the 1970s, the Supreme Court gradually began to take cognizance of use-of-force cases against federal, state, and local law enforcement officers: cases claiming some sort of violation of the individuals' constitutional rights based on the officers' use of force. The landmark cases from the 1980s—applying the Fourth Amendment standard of reasonableness—are *Tennessee v. Garner* and *Graham v. Connor*.

---

[*] 256 U.S. 335, 343 (1921).

The Constitution simply does not require police to gamble with their lives in the face of a serious threat of harm.[*]

We must avoid substituting our personal notions of proper police procedure for the instantaneous decision of the officer at the scene. We must never allow the theoretical, sanitized world of our imagination to replace the dangerous and complex world that policemen face every day. What constitutes "reasonable" action may seem quite different to someone facing a possible assailant than to someone analyzing the question at leisure.[†]

This standard was slightly modified by the 2001 case of *Saucier v. Katz*. In essence, the court set forth the standard that "no reasonable officer would have acted in a similar manner."

In December 2004, the Court decided *Brosseau v. Haugen*. In *Brosseau*, the Court further examined how to evaluate law enforcement uses of force to determine whether such actions were excessive. This decision refines the current trilogy of U.S. Supreme Court decisions that define when law enforcement officers are civilly liable for uses of force. *Tennessee v. Garner*, *Graham v. Connor*, and *Saucier v. Katz* comprise those cases. *Garner* and *Graham* set out the general approach to defining constitutional constraints on the use of force by law enforcement, stating that force used by officers constitutes a seizure under the Fourth Amendment and is objectively evaluated for reasonableness. The *Katz* decision profoundly impacted the way courts analyze civil rights lawsuits brought pursuant to Title 42, Section 1983 of the U.S. Code (and its federal counterpart *Bivens v. Six Unknown Agents*). In *Katz*, the Court established a two-step approach to these lawsuits. It held that courts first view the alleged facts and establish whether a constitutional violation could exist pursuant to the principles enunciated in *Garner* and *Graham*. If no possible constitutional violation occurred, then the court would summarily dismiss the lawsuit. However, if the court found a constitutional violation, then it would determine if the officer involved should be entitled to qualified immunity. The evaluation of whether the officer can receive qualified immunity constitutes a separate and distinct analysis from the initial determination of whether the force used was constitutional.

In *Katz*, the Court specifically held that law enforcement officers may apply force that eventually is determined to be unconstitutional yet remain protected by qualified immunity. In the words of the Court, "[q]ualified immunity operates to protect officers from the sometimes hazy border

---

[*] *Elliot v. Leavitt*, 99 F.3d 640, 641 (4th Cir. 1996).
[†] *Smith v. Freland*, 954 F.2d 343, 347 (6th Cir. 1992).

between excessive and acceptable force." The Court plainly stated that while uses of force by police occur that are clearly excessive or clearly appropriate, a gray area remains in between. The Court went on to say that when an officer's use of force falls within this gray area, *deference must be paid to the officer and qualified immunity granted.** (emphasis added)

The authors—in the clear vision of 20/20 hindsight—are not saying that Johnnie Riley was right in his decision to use deadly force; rather, we believe he is due the deference that the Supreme Court offers in *Katz*. After the *Katz* decision, there were numerous cases evaluating whether police uses of force fell in the "hazy border" between the clearly excessive and the clearly constitutional, as defined in that decision. *Brosseau* was the U.S. Supreme Court's first vehicle to address this issue. FBI supervisory special agent Tom Petrowski explains this in a *Law Enforcement Bulletin* article:

Like virtually all case law related to law enforcement use of force, *Brosseau* was a civil rights lawsuit brought by Kenneth Haugen against Officer Rochelle Brosseau of the Puyallup, Washington, Police Department. A former crime partner had complained that Haugen had stolen tools from his shop. Brosseau later learned that a felony no-bail warrant existed for Haugen's arrest on drug and other nonviolent offenses. The day after receiving the associate's complaint and verifying the arrest warrant for Haugen, Brosseau responded to a report that Haugen and others were fighting in the yard of his mother's home. When Brosseau arrived, Haugen ran out of his mother's yard and hid in the neighborhood. Brosseau requested assistance, and, shortly thereafter, two officers and a canine arrived to assist in locating and arresting Haugen. The two associates, with whom Haugen had been fighting, as well as Haugen's girlfriend and her 3-year-old daughter were at the scene. Haugen's SUV was parked in the driveway facing his girlfriend's car (occupied by her and her child) with about 4 feet between the two vehicles. The two associates were in a pickup truck parked on the street in front of the driveway about 20 to 30 feet away.

After being spotted by a neighbor who alerted the officers, Haugen appeared and ran into the driveway. With Brosseau in pursuit, he jumped into the driver's seat of his SUV and closed and locked the door. When she caught up, Brosseau pointed her gun at Haugen and ordered him to get out of the vehicle. Haugen ignored her command and attempted to find his keys to start the SUV and escape. Brosseau repeated her commands and struck the driver's side window several times with her handgun. This had

* Petrowski, Thomas D., "When Is Force Excessive?" *FBI Law Enforcement Bulletin*, September 2005, p. 27.

no effect on Haugen. On the third or fourth strike, the window shattered. Brosseau then tried to take the keys away from Haugen and struck him on the head with her gun. Haugen, still undeterred, started the SUV. After it started but before it moved, Brosseau jumped back and fired one shot through the rear driver's side window at a forward angle, hitting Haugen in the back. She later testified that she shot Haugen because she was "fearful for the other officers on foot who [she] believed were in the immediate area, [and] for the occupied vehicles in [Haugen's] path and for any other citizens who might be in the area." In justifying her use of force, Officer Brosseau also cited the fact that Haugen had a no-bail drug warrant and that she had probable cause to believe that he had committed a burglary. She also stated that she originally thought he was attempting to access a weapon when he ran to his vehicle.

Even though he was wounded, Haugen accelerated aggressively and drove through the small, tight space between the other vehicles. He swerved across a neighbor's lawn and proceeded down the street. After going about one-half blocks, Haugen realized that he had been shot and stopped. In deciding this case, the Supreme Court assumed for the purposes of its decision that Officer Brosseau's conduct was unconstitutional and presented this case as illustration that officers *still* may be entitled to qualified immunity even though they used force in an unconstitutional manner.[*]

Such may be the case in Sergeant Riley's instance. In the clear vision of 20/20 hindsight, other less intrusive means might have been available to him. But, nothing in the case suggests that Johnnie Riley acted so outside the bounds of reasonableness as to deny him qualified immunity under the *Brosseau* standard. It is then axiomatic that he should have been immune from criminal liability, absent some showing of specific *unlawful* intent to murder Kalvin Kyle. Nothing in the evidence suggested the presence of such ill will or unlawful intent. Johnnie Riley was convicted and sent to prison absent evidence that he did anything wrong except make an error in judgment under the high-stress moments of a felony arrest.

Brosseau provides one example of a use of force by a police officer that, while constitutionally questionable, was certainly in the "sometimes hazy border between excessive and acceptable force," and therefore the officer was entitled to qualified immunity. It is our sincere belief and professional opinion that such is the case concerning the facts confronting Sergeant Riley in September 2012. In a broader sense, the U.S. Supreme Court in *Brosseau* reminds society that it must pay great deference to law

---

[*] Petrowski, Thomas D., "When Is Force Excessive?" *FBI Law Enforcement Bulletin*, September 2005, p. 28.

enforcement officers in use-of-force situations, and that the law clearly reflects this deference.* The Prince George's County state's attorney and the jury never gave Sergeant Riley such deference.

In 2007, in *Scott v. Harris*, the Supreme Court had the opportunity to directly reexamine the standard set forth in *Tennessee v. Garner*, concerning the reasonableness of the force used to stop a fleeing and potentially dangerous suspect. It is relevant here for a number of reasons, as it not only reaffirms *Graham*, but also examines the conduct of both the police and the subject who gets shot by the police. *The court properly places an onus on citizens not to act in a manner that endangers human life.* Escaping from lawful arrest and fleeing down a crowded street clearly endangers human life—at a minimum, it would be reasonably foreseeable that police would give chase and either they or innocent others could get hurt in the ensuing melee.

The court held that because Harris started the high-speed car chase, creating a dangerous situation that threatened the lives of innocent bystanders, it was reasonable for Scott to try to stop it even when it put Harris in danger of serious injury. To reach that conclusion, the court first had to decide the factual issue of whether Harris's behavior endangered human life.

Harris argued that his driving was controlled and nonthreatening, and that his path was clear of other traffic and pedestrians. His arguments were successful in the court of appeals, but after viewing the police videotape of the chase, all but one of the Supreme Court justices disagreed with the appellate court. The Supreme Court concluded that Harris's driving did pose an immediate threat to the lives of others.

On the question of whether the force used was reasonable, Harris argued that to be reasonable, Scott's attempt to stop the chase using force must meet standards set forth in *Tennessee v. Garner*. There, a police officer shot an unimposing, unarmed burglary suspect in the back of the head as the suspect fled. The *Garner* court held that the officer's use of deadly force was not reasonable because (1) the suspect did not pose an immediate danger to others, (2) the deadly force was not necessary to prevent the suspect's escape, and (3) the officer gave no warning. The *Scott* majority rejected Harris's *Garner* arguments. They held (1) that *Garner* did not establish any across-the-board test for determining the reasonableness of

---

* Ibid., pp. 27–31. The preceding lengthy section in this report discussing Brosseau quotes the Petrowski article almost in its entirety and nearly verbatim. The authors are indebted to Supervisory Special Agent Petrowski not only for his scholarship in this arena, but also for his professional instruction on diverse occasions in the past.

Fourth Amendment seizures, and (2) that it was distinguishable on the facts. In both *Garner* and the case before it, the court applied the standard Fourth Amendment reasonableness test to the circumstances of that case. Was it objectively reasonable for Scott to do what he did?

Looking to the circumstances of the car chase, the court held that it was reasonable for Scott to take the actions he did. Moreover, the majority noted, if the court were to rule otherwise—in effect, requiring police to let speeding suspects get away—it would give criminals an incentive to drive recklessly just so the police would have to break off pursuit.

The same rationale would apply in Johnnie Riley's case. Do felony suspects, with violent criminal histories, who are lawfully arrested, have a right to escape from lawful custody and flee toward a position of tactical advantage or freedom? Holding Sergeant Riley *pecuniarily* liable would fly in the face of the Supreme Court decision in *Scott*. To allege that he should be *criminally* responsible is simply legally unjustifiable in light of the relevant case law and societal needs. It is unconscionable, unlawful, and immoral that the state of Maryland would charge this matter as a criminal concern.

It is doubly fantastic that a jury would find evidence beyond a reasonable doubt and convict this man. But, because this occurred in Prince George's County, Maryland, a jurisdiction with a huge gulf between police and the populace, the good guy gets convicted and jailed, while the bad guy not only gets off scot-free criminally, but is also enriched from the public coffers as the result of a civil suit that should have never been settled.

MISTAKEN BELIEF

An analysis of Sergeant Riley's reasonableness does require him to be right in the clear vision of 20/20 hindsight. In fact, a federal appellate court rightly notes the following:

> It is not necessary that the danger which gave rise to the belief actually existed; it is sufficient that the person resorting to self-defense at the time involved *reasonably believed* in the existence of such a danger, and such reasonable belief is sufficient even where it is mistaken.* (emphasis added)

---

* *Davis v. Freels*, 583 F.2d 337, 341 (7th Cir. 1978).

So, whether Kalvin Kyle *actually* presented an imminent threat to Sergeant Riley or innocent others is not required under the law, but only that Riley's belief that he did so was objectively reasonable under the circumstances. Reasonable does not mean correct or right.

Additionally, in *Klein v. Ryan*, the Seventh Circuit held that a reasonable officer in the position of Sergeant Riley could have believed that the use of deadly force was justified. In *Klein*, the officers had been investigating the burglary of a Laundromat. Using surveillance photos, the officers identified a suspect, Klein. One night, while surveying the area around the Laundromat, they spotted Klein in a car a few feet away from the Laundromat. Klein entered the Laundromat and proceeded to open the machines and remove the money. After obtaining backup, several officers took strategic positions outside the Laundromat, and as Klein exited, one of the officers commanded him to halt. Klein did not heed the warning and ran for his vehicle. After he got to his car, Klein started the engine and began backing up. An officer then jumped out of the way and, after regaining his position, fired two shots at Klein as he fled the scene. Klein was later arrested after checking into the hospital to be treated for gunshot wounds. The court determined that the actions taken by the law enforcement officers in attempting to stop the fleeing suspect were reasonable *as a matter of law*. In its analysis, the Seventh Circuit explained:

> Police officers tell a person, who they reasonably suspect of having committed a forcible felony, to halt. They reasonably believe that the suspect heard them, but the suspect continues to flee. The suspect gets in the car and begins to drive away, with no resistance from any other officer. In this situation, a police officer could reasonably believe that deadly force was necessary to prevent the arrest from being defeated by resistance or escape.[*]

DUE PROCESS VIOLATIONS

Additionally, the Supreme Court has also analyzed law enforcement use-of-force cases pursuant to a due process review under the 14th Amendment. Usually, all that is required for a 14th Amendment violation to occur would be deliberate indifference on the part of the police. However, in situations such as vehicle chases and other tactical situations that are tense,

---

[*] *Klein v. Ryan*, 847 F.2d 368, 373 (7th Cir. 1988).

uncertain, and rapidly evolving, the standard is lower. As so eloquently explained by Urey Patrick and John Hall in their seminal book *In Defense of Self and Others*:

> Conceding that "deliberate indifference" would be the appropriate standard in some circumstances, the Court observed that such could only be true when *actual deliberation* is practicable. For example, The Court explained that claims of inadequate medical care for pre-trial detainees must be viewed differently from claims that officers used excessive force in response to a violent disturbance. In the former case, there is time and opportunity for "deliberation" whereas, in the latter instance, police *"are supposed to act decisively and show restraint at the same moment, and their decisions have to be made in haste, under pressure, and frequently without the luxury of a second chance."* In such circumstances, *"... only a purpose to cause harm (emphasis added) unrelated to the legitimate object of arrest will satisfy the element of arbitrary conduct shocking to the conscience, necessary for a Due Process violation."* Applying this standard to the facts, the Court concluded that even if the officers' decision to engage in and continue the high-speed pursuit "offended the reasonableness upheld by tort law or the balance struck in law enforcement's own code of sound practice ..." it did not violate Due Process.[*]

So, as applied to Sergeant Riley's circumstances, absent showing some specific criminal intent unrelated to his intent to stop Kyle or effect an arrest, this case would not even meet a 14th Amendment due process violation. There is nothing in the case file to remotely demonstrate any criminal animus or intent on the part of Sergeant Riley. Even viewed in the worst light possible, his actions would, at most, amount to simple negligence. This is not sufficient to sustain a conviction for any crime, especially when one considers it was an act committed by a police officer in the line of duty. Again, *In Defense of Self and Others* eloquently states this point of law and order:

> I decline utterly to be impartial as between the fire brigade and the fire.
>
> *Sir Winston Churchill (1926)*

There are some topics about which decent folk cannot afford to be impartial. Sir Winston's statement provides a good example. There is an obvious parallel between the fireman and the policeman. Just as the fireman's helmet

---

[*] Patrick, U. W., and Hall, J. C., *In Defense of Self and Others*, pp. 58–59, citing and quoting *County of Sacramento v. Lewis*, 118 S.Ct. 1708 (1998).

represents our determination as a community to protect ourselves from the dangers posed by fire, the law enforcement officer's badge and gun represent our determination as a community to protect ourselves from the dangers posed by individuals whose actions threaten our safety. *The folly of taking a neutral stance between that which is dangerous and that which we create to protect us from that danger should be self-evident.*[*] (emphasis added)

Also relevant to this case is the Prince George's County Police Department's own *Use of Force Training Guide and Continuum* (2010), which specifically cites the *Graham v. Connor* standard, stating *inter alia*:

- It is the policy of this Department that each incident involving the application of any degree of force upon the person of another, must be evaluated upon the facts known to the officer at the time of a particular incident. The totality of the circumstances, at the time of the incident, will be considered when reviewing use of force incidents. An officer's use of force will be measured against the standards found in the 4th, 5th, 8th and 14th Amendments to the U.S. Constitution. There are three distinct standards that may apply to an officer's use of force upon a person. The first is the 8th amendment and the "cruel and unusual punishment" standard. The second is the 5th and 14th amendments and the "shock the conscience" standard. The third is the 4th amendment, and the "objective reasonableness" standard.
- The Department recognizes that officers are expected to make critical decisions in circumstances that are tense, uncertain and rapidly evolving. It also understands that the amount of time available to evaluate and respond to a situation, or lack thereof, may impact the officer's decision.

If the above-stated policy is true, why then did the office of the state's attorney rush to prosecute Sergeant Riley based on facts all clearly discerned in the clear vision of 20/20 hindsight? The answer to that is complex too, but mostly it is because of political expediency and moral cowardice.

Because of the great power and sway a prosecutor's office holds over the public, it is important that they impartially and with great self-control apply the law to the facts. The prosecutor in Ferguson, Missouri, possessed such courage. Unfortunately, for Johnnie Riley and his family, the one in Prince George's County did not. It is also readily apparent that the populace there is inferring that their sons and daughters have a right to steal motorcycles, violate parole, and scuffle with police officers.

---

[*] Id., p. xv.

Was it possible that Sergeant Riley could have used less intrusive means? Of course. He could have used a Taser device (assuming he had one and was within that weapon's effective range), sent a K-9 dog after Kyle (although, as noted by a federal appellate court, one would then expect a different type of lawsuit to ensue), chased the subject with his patrol vehicle, or chased and tackled the subject. The latter option, however, would have placed the officer in extreme danger not only from Kalvin Kyle, but also the group of unknown subjects in the SUV.

Neither the law nor reason requires a law enforcement officer to use the least intrusive means available to stop a threat or effect an arrest, only an objectively reasonable means. Johnnie Riley's actions, while questionable in the clear vision of 20/20 hindsight, were still objectively reasonable as set forth by the U.S. Supreme Court. Accordingly, he should be shielded from not only personal liability, but also criminal liability, which required a much stronger degree of culpability and burden of proof.

A jury, likely dumbed down by television and already possessing a strong animus against the police, is not the vehicle to assess the reasonableness of an officer-involved shooting. The prosecutor's office should have been the impartial arbiter in this case. Their own exert witnesses told them, "I think, at worst, Sergeant Riley made an error in judgment, but I do not think what he did was criminal." One of the authors—an expert witness in this case— was warned not to refer to Kalvin Kyle and his criminal cohorts as thugs or hoodlums because many in the jury would see Kyle as their son, grandson, or brother! A society that is incapable of self-governance and that has lost the ability to discern between good and evil is doomed to failure. It appears that Prince George's County, Maryland, falls squarely in that defined category.

Sergeant Riley—despite being named police officer of the year four times and possessing a distinguished military record, to include being awarded the Bronze Star Medal and Combat Infantry Badge—was not given the benefit of the doubt by the society he so valiantly served. There simply was no evidence that Sergeant Riley possessed criminal motive or criminal negligence in his shooting of the subject on the evening of September 6, 2012. He made a decision in seconds, and his actions are now being judged in the clear vision of 20/20 hindsight. If Kalvin Kyle had been allowed to escape or reach his comrades, another officer, Sergeant Riley, or other innocents could have been killed. Kalvin Kyle was clearly the author of his own misfortune.

Tragically, on June 10, 2014, a jury in the circuit court for Prince George's County convicted Sergeant Johnnie Riley of first-degree assault, use of a handgun in a felony, and misuse of office. This conviction is legally unsupportable in light of the corpus of extant Supreme Court law sur-rounding law enforcement's use of force. This jury was instructed with pattern jury instruction written and applicable to civilian criminal defen-dants, not police officers serving in the line of duty.

In Maryland, police officers possess qualified immunity from civil liability, which is decided at a much lower preponderance of the evidence standard. It seems axiomatic to all but the either woefully or willfully ignorant jurists that if an officer's actions, viewed from the perspective of an officer on the scene rather than in the clear vision of 20/20 hindsight, could not even hold him liable for monetary damages, then he could never be found guilty of criminal misconduct based solely on his decisions made under the mere seconds of a highly stressful encounter with a felon.

The Georgia qualified immunity statute—see *State v. Bunn* as an explana-tory example—provides immunity from criminal as well as civil pros-ecution for these types of police shootings. It seems that the Maryland General Assembly, by not specifically stating the obvious—that if an officer is immune from *civil* liability, then no sane prosecutor would ever expose him to *criminal* liability—placed far too much trust and confidence in the prosecutorial discretion of the offices of the state's attorney in these matters.
   Also,

> when criminal indictments and charges are instituted against a law enforce-ment officer for using deadly force, the impetus is predominantly political. The shooting incident was controversial in the public eye, inflamed seg-ments of the community, and the filing of criminal charges is a political response to allay the emotional outrage of the affected activists. It is a politically driven act, not a public interest one—*a refutation of the existence of a civil system of law designed and intended to deal with precisely such issues in which harm was done but without criminal elements.*[*]

Officers should not have to survive based on chance, luck, and the belief that their adversaries will be poor shooters. Moreover, they should not have to worry that a court and team of prosecutors—woefully ignorant of the dynamics of such encounters—will judge them from the cool, calm perspective of 20/20 hindsight. Society should be physically and emotion-ally ill that Johnnie Riley has been convicted of a crime that he did not commit. Had he shot Kalvin Kyle in Texas—or Cecil County, Maryland, for that matter—at worst, Johnnie Riley would have lost his job.

---

[*] Id., p. 277.

Moreover, peer-reviewed scientific studies have demonstrated that law enforcement officers will make decisional errors 13% of the time. In plain words, in 9% of instances, officers will see a gun where there is none present, and in 4% of cases, officers will miss a gun when they should have spotted it. Additionally, because, in part, they understand the role chance plays in their lives, officers filter their world based on their training and make recognition-primed decisions that are sometimes wrong. But, there is no criminal intent or motive in these actions. Absent some superseding, intervening motive, police officers—the good guys—ought to be given the benefit of the law and doubt.

Instead, the citizens of Prince George's County seem to have accepted that many of their sons have turned out to be criminals, embracing the false idols of "street cred" and the faddish violence of the modern music world. And, Johnnie Riley is an African American: a fact that the NAACP found extraordinarily inconvenient after racing down from New York to investigate this matter in 2013. Meanwhile, Johnnie Riley—the tragic hero of this story—remains in jail as of now. We hope and pray that the appellate courts in Maryland reverse this tragic outcome.

How does this happen? Well, the state's attorney who forced this prosecution to trial was incompetent, lacked moral courage and self-control, and in the end, was not after justice—he was only seeking to placate an ignorant populace stirred by an equally ignorant media. All they cared about was the 10-second sound bite: "Officer shoots unarmed, handcuffed man in the back."

The problem remains, just as in Ferguson, Missouri, or New York City (where the 1999 Amadou Diallo shooting occurred), that these cases are complex and not easily translated into a 10-second sound bite. They require review by a competent Serious Incident Review Team (SIRT) that understands the dynamics of such encounters. Too many uninitiated and uneducated persons in positions of power make their decisions based on ill-founded notions they viewed on television shows such *CSI* or the über-liberal *Law & Order* series.

The truth of the matter is that shell case patterns, number of rounds fired, and shot timing and placement are mostly irrelevancies in discerning the reasonableness of an officer's decision to use deadly force. Before any person begins to judge an officer-involved shooting, he or she would do well to read Hall and Patrick's *In Defense of Self and Others* and attend a gold-standard program like Force Science Institute's certification course.

Two other sad and disturbing notes to this case include the following:

1. Sergeant Johnnie Riley sat in jail for seven months before his trial even began. He was confined in part because the prosecution argued—and an ignorant judge agreed—that Johnnie Riley represented a danger to society, in part because he was an Iraq War veteran with a Bronze Star Medal and other combat awards.* It is nothing short of disgraceful to argue that a combat veteran, someone who risked his life to protect and defend our republic, is somehow a threat to society because of that service. Unfortunately, as the populace has shifted from one where Hollywood actors (Jimmy Stewart, Clark Gable, Tyrone Power, etc.), sports stars (Ted Williams, Bob Feller, Ton Landry, etc.), and even preppies (George H. W. Bush) volunteered to serve in combat, a very small percentage of Americans have served in our volunteer Armed Forces. One of the consequences is a mistaken belief, again fueled by Hollywood and television, that combat somehow transforms people into raging homicidal sociopaths.

2. At his sentencing hearing, while the prosecutor was making closing arguments against Riley's good character and nature, Johnnie Riley finally snapped emotionally. He lunged at the prosecutor in a fit of rage and was tripped by his own counsel and tackled by sheriff's deputies in the courtroom before any physical harm was done. Not to excuse such an outburst, but is it any wonder that Johnnie Riley might alas feel a bit betrayed by the very system he fought for and defended both in Iraq and on the streets of Prince George's County? The two experienced trial prosecutors in this case are both very good attorneys and very good people. This chapter is not directed at them or the state's experts. The fact that their politically appointed master forced them to take this case to trial on charges that simply did not fit the alleged facts† is simply another tragic note here.

---

* By the state's reasoning, all three authors are a threat to society, as we have at least a dozen combat deployments among us, with the requisite awards and decorations that must indicate our clear and present danger to society.

† The state should have charged Johnnie Riley with the more appropriate Maryland Criminal Code 3-204: Reckless Endangerment, a misdemeanor charge with the following elements: A person may not recklessly engage in conduct that creates a substantial risk of death or serious physical injury to another. Had the state done this, the case could have quietly been handled with a pretrial agreement. Instead, the state sought to destroy Johnnie Riley. To that end, it has succeeded—so far. We pray that Maryland's appellate courts will right this wrong.

13

Redefining the Role of State: Back to a True Liberalism

Today, most Americans need a basic civics lesson on how truly unique the political experiment known as the United States of America has been in the course of human history. With the examples of ancient democratic Athens and the Roman republic foremost in their minds, the founders of our country established an exceptional form of government. For much, if not all, of recorded history prior to the American Revolution, the compact between the individual and the government was always one whereby the individual was subordinate to the government: to the Crown in England, the state in Prussia, or the emperor in China. Even the subsequent French Revolution placed the individual subordinate to the rule and tyranny of the mob (democracy in its pure, unfettered form—to the surprise of many Americans, including most newscasters, the United States is *not* a democracy, but rather a constitutional republic).

The individuals who painstakingly crafted our Constitution understood the risks of being human. As stated by Robert Kaplan in his book *Warrior Politics*,[*] before the first president was sworn into office, our Constitution established a method to remove him from office. The checks and balances built into our government are well known by every schoolchild, but the implications may not be so easily understood. In order to control the universally corrupting effects of power, controls on human behavior must be established. These checks must be not only on individual leaders and those we place in positions of power, but also on groups of people. We established checks not only on individual branches of government, but also on ourselves. The Bill of Rights established limits not only on the federal

---

[*] Kaplan, Robert, *Warrior Politics: Why Leadership Demands a Pagan Ethos* (Toronto: Random House, 2002).

government, but also on the power of the majority to enforce their will on a minority. The founders understood that all people, to include our elected leaders, are human. There is no utopia in this life. Our country grants no human being absolute power. But it is a natural process for human beings to strive for more power. We all need checks and balances. It is natural for both political parties to try to increase their power and influence. To believe otherwise is delusional. That is one reason why the difference between Republicans and Democrats is merely the flavor, not the size, of the ever-growing and resultantly tax-hungry state. This has led to a terrible trend whereby citizens spend ever more of their time and money serving the state. One predictable result is how they view and treat law enforcement and vice versa. Witness this scandalous news report out of Chicago:

Drivers in Chicago have gotten wise to speed cameras, budget figures show, and now the city needs to come up with $50 million in revenue. Chicagoans are costing the city tens of millions of dollars—through good behavior. Mayor Rahm Emanuel underestimated the intelligence of Chicago drivers, and the city paid for it big time. On a smooth, wide, well travelled stretch of Irving Park Road, running between two cemeteries—no homes, no stores, no parking—the city of Chicago is trying to balance its budget. Each flash means a photo; each photo, a violation. Each violation: a hundred bucks, from red light and speed cameras. CBS 2 has learned the speed cameras caught far fewer speeders than expected. According to the Mayor's 2015 Budget Overview, there have been "lower than expected violation rates." How much lower? Fifty million dollars lower. Emanuel's administration had figured on $90 million in fines to help balance this year's budget, but they can only count on $40 million. That's a $50 million shortfall, putting pressure on the next spending plan. "It was a combination of the camera company's salesmanship and the city's greed," says camera critic Barnet Fagel. The city was expecting a nearly $100 million windfall by flooding the city with the speed cameras, using proximity to schools and parks as justification. The speed camera on Irving Park is listed as close to Challenger Park, which actually looks more like a parking lot—and is, during Cubs games. Critics have said red light cameras don't enhance safety and are more of a cash grab for the city government. A report by Inspector General Joe Ferguson maintained, "The City cannot prove red light camera locations are based on safety considerations." And a University of Illinois at Chicago study concluded "red light cameras are not effective in improving safety."*

* CBS-Chicago, "City's Speed Traps Backfire," 2014, https://screen.yahoo.com/videos-for-you/obey-law-bankrupt-city-041400714.html.

The story, while amusing on one level—a mayor counting on electronic speed traps to fund his bloated budget—is extremely disturbing on another. Any honest politician faced with a budget shortfall should simply do the obvious: limit the size, scope, and intrusiveness of government so that it does not, in turn, need to resort to such chicanery to fleece its citizens of their hard-earned money. Otherwise, he should be run out of town on a rail. Unfortunately, if there is not an appropriate check on the behavior of the politician, we are foolish to believe he will be honest. Instead, he will act in his self-interest, which usually involves having more funds to disperse in a way that will help him. The impact on the public's trust and respect for such a government is difficult to measure, but when people suspect that law enforcement is more interested in meeting a budget shortfall than it is in protecting and serving the public, only bad things can follow.

Red-light cameras and speed cameras are just the tip of the iceberg of the ways and means by which governments rob their citizenry. It is entirely reasonable and expected that law enforcement officers should ticket or arrest reckless drivers, drunken drivers, or those committing dangerous acts in violation of the public peace and order. That is a critical portion of the social contract that police have with their citizenry. Instead, in more and more jurisdictions, they have become the tools of unscrupulous politicians to take by force dollars from the average workingman in order to feed the ever-expanding government. And below is another example, this time out of the District of Columbia:

> Since 2009, D.C. officers have made more than 12,000 seizures under city and federal laws, according to records and data obtained from the city by *The Washington Post* through the District's open records law. Half of the more than $5.5 million in cash seizures were for $141 or less, with more than a thousand for less than $20. D.C. police have seized more than 1,000 cars, some for minor offenses allegedly committed by the children or friends of the vehicle owners, documents show.*

These are robberies in the sense that they are the taking of the property of another by force or threat of force. The only debatable point is whether it is an *unlawful* taking. But, when legislatures and executive branches pass laws and edicts by fiat, laws and regulations hidden from most in their making by the slick use of legislative riders and executive orders, they are indeed contrary to the natural law and dignity envisioned by the

---

* O'Harrow Jr., Robert, and Rich, Steven, "D.C. Police Plan for Future Seizure Proceeds Years in Advance in City Budget Documents, *Washington Post*, November 16, 2014.

founders of the republic. When this happens, the feedback system that allows checks on their behavior is quashed.

This sounds like semantics, but it is not. We have shifted from a people that understood and agreed to a very limited system of government that served the natural rights of man to a people that now believe that they possess only those civil rights that the government allows. Thomas Jefferson articulated the inherent right to life, liberty, and property ownership in the Declaration of Independence. He viewed these as essential to the establishment of a government of free people. While these freedoms are certainly not absolute, it is simple math: The greater a government infringes on them, the less freedom we have.

More importantly, greater infringement damages the social contract between the citizens and our government. Few would argue that if an individual commits a crime of violence against a peaceable neighbor, we should not lock that person away from the rest of us, infringing on that criminal's liberty. Some would argue that the wholesale locking up of a generation of poor young men for drug crimes pushes this in the wrong direction. But our established form of government is life, liberty, and unmolested property ownership. Exceptions must occur, but they should be exceptions to the freedom of the individual, not the other way around. These fundamental rules for human behavior were critical to the writing of our Constitution, and became the law by which we live.

Unfortunately, many now loathe the notion that citizens possess God-given or natural rights. For instance, the rights of the modern state, like the Civil Rights Act of 1964, are purely the creation of legislation and can be changed at any time. In contrast, the natural rights of man, which were articulated in the Declaration of Independence, and later formed the theoretical basis for our Constitution, are the *inherent* right to life, liberty, and property ownership. One of the greatest examples of the limitations of the human condition, and why it is critical to establish and maintain checks on the behavior of us all, is with the primary writer of the Declaration. Most educated people know that the same man who wrote the words establishing the fundamental concepts of our political freedom also held slaves and viewed these human beings as his property. No one is immune from being human. All of us have the potential for both good and evil. We all need checks on our behavior. But, Thomas Jefferson's ownership of slaves does not negate the sound principles he wrote of concerning the relationship between the state and the individual.

Because of their inherent nature, these rights formally codified in our Constitution were meant to be permanent. Our Constitution was written to protect this sacred relationship in which the individual was never subordinate to the state. But, through the creeping incrementalism of the last 100 years of our history, Americans have ceded most of their wealth, freedoms, and now seemingly every right to privacy to the government. "The package of civil rights proffered by progressives in place of natural rights is long but mainly serves to shield the individual from the hurt feelings that can result from people exercising the natural right of free association while offering no protection against the most dangerous threat to any individual: the violence of the state."[*]

The common man's definition of insanity is when an individual sticks his face into a chainsaw, says "ouch," and then does it time and again. America's war on drugs may be the social equivalent. As further explained by author and political analyst James Ostrowski in his book *Progressivism: A Primer on the Idea Destroying America*,

> when drugs were treated as private property, as they were throughout most of American history (through 1914), they were not a serious social problem even though you could buy "hard drugs" cheap over the counter or by mail order. From the onset of drug prohibition in 1914, they have been a major social problem. The progressives' disruption of the natural order in this regard has been a catastrophic failure. The state cannot effectively shut down the flow of illegal drugs in the black market. Drugs are available even in maximum-security prisons. The prohibition of drugs tends to make drugs more dangerous as quality control is reduced. The ban on hypodermic needles helped spread the AIDS virus. Drugs become more potent as more potent drugs are more easily smuggled. The market for mild coca leaf tea, which Pope John Paul II drank on occasion, no longer exists in the United States. Prohibition stimulates gang violence over turf wars and, by greatly increasing the price of drugs, encourages the kind of petty theft ("car popping," shoplifting, etc.) that is common throughout the country. Illegal drugs draw in many young people with otherwise limited job prospects because of the poor education in the progressive government school and the structural unemployment caused by various progressive policies such as the minimum wage. Most end up with criminal records that render them even more unemployable. Some end up dead or maimed in drive-by shootings. There is a massive amount of data and research condemning the drug war and not a single study that shows that its benefits outweigh its costs.[†]

---

[*] Ostrowski, James, *Progressivism: A Primer on the Idea Destroying America*, Kindle ed. (New York: Cazenovia Books, 2014), Kindle locations 2063–2064.
[†] Id., Kindle locations 1543–1555.

Or, this gem from Afghanistan:

> Cultivation of the illegal poppy plant in Afghanistan has reached an "all time high" following a $7.6 billion counternarcotics campaign paid for by the United States, according to government oversight investigators.
>
> Despite the spending to combat growth of the poppy plant, which is used to make drugs such as opium and heroin, cultivation has reached an "all time high," especially in places once declared "poppy free," according to new report by the Special Inspector General for Afghanistan Reconstruction (SIGAR).*

And lastly, this spot-on observation of William F. Buckley Jr.:

> More people die every year as a result of the war against drugs than die from what we call, generically, overdosing. These fatalities include, perhaps most prominently, drug merchants who compete for commercial territory, but include also people who are robbed and killed by those desperate for money to buy the drug to which they have become addicted.†

It would only surprise a bureaucrat that spending $7.6 billion of taxpayers' hard-earned money to artificially create a black market for illicit drugs would actually *increase* the supply and demand for that very commodity. The failure of the war on drugs is a first cousin to the failure of LBJ's Great Society. A belief that a government can, by force or threat of force, fairly redistribute wealth from free men to the betterment of others defies rational thought, logic, and all notions of true liberty. Ten generations of fatherless families, single mothers being paid to have more generations of victims, and then further ridiculous schemes to fix these problems that were of the government's making in the first place must stop. Does America need more cities like Detroit or suburbs like Ferguson?

The authors are very hesitant to criticize America's war on drugs, as we have all been intimately and personally involved on the front lines of that war. We have worked with and have the greatest respect for many of the individuals involved in that fight. We respect their integrity, motives, and individual courage. Too many of our friends have died in this fight for us to cavalierly dismiss the war as a failure. We believe, however, that the nation needs to take a knee, access where it is going, and perhaps vector the war

---

* Kredo, Adam, "Afghan Poppy Cultivation at 'All-Time High,'" *The Washington Free Beacon*, October 21, 2014.
† Buckley Jr., William F., "The War on Drugs Is Lost," *National Review*, February 12, 1996.

away from locking up millions of persons for simple possession and focus instead on the power nodes and true financiers in this world. Moreover, it should *never* be a fight about feeding the enforcement machine with asset forfeiture funds.

Additionally, much more attention should be spent on demand reduction: stopping America's seeming insatiable thirst for illicit narcotics. It is very difficult to convince Juan Valdez to grow coffee rather than coca leaves for cocaine production or poppies for heroin when weak-willed Americans are intent on polluting their bodies and souls with these foul drugs.

The salvation of cities like Detroit will not come from more government intervention. It will only come when America removes the shackles of progressivism and returns to the freedoms our ancestors proposed and articulated: the belief and reality that by hard work and ingenuity, one could start and build a prosperous business. And, with a belief in divine providence, society could live peaceably and successfully. The unparalleled success of this country has come from such beliefs and from the resultant following of natural law. Most politicians recoil at this notion, because for them the state is their god. If this trend is not reversed, America's people of faith and those that believe in the natural rights of man will be in direct, violent conflict with the apparatchiks of the secular, progressive state.

Having all served in war-torn parts of the world, we do not want that to happen in our country. But diverse voices of right reason—Alan Dershowitz, Ben Carson, Andrew Napolitano, Walter Williams, and Patrick Buchanan—have all recently expressed concern over the mounting police state in America. We should all be concerned. None, however, should be surprised at America's continued slouching toward Gomorrah.[*]

The U.S. prison population is now hovering near 2.5 million: a number that has quadrupled since Ronald Reagan's first presidential election. One out of every 100 American adult males is behind bars. Prison is an environment ripe for the preaching and recruitment of radical Islamists—again, another unintended consequence of putting people in prison.

This disproportionally high prison population is not an accident or random spike. Progressivism, or big government, as we now know it, is a mindset that favors the use of aggressive governmental force to solve all social problems. Such force, combined with people's reliance on government, from kindergarten to old age, is a blight on our dignity as a

---

[*] From Robert H. Bork's prophetic book *Slouching Towards Gomorrah: Modern Liberalism and American Decline* (New York: Harper Collins Publishers, 1996).

race of supposedly free people. Prison is one of government's main tools of coercion. It is the not-so-subtle threat behind every governmental edict, from Environmental Protection Agency (EPA) rules that bankrupt small farmers to incomprehensible Internal Revenue Service (IRS) tax regulations.

If you don't go to prison by violating the more commonly known criminal statutes—ones like robbery, rape, or murder that are logically predicated on the natural and common laws of man—you can nevertheless now find yourself in the hoosegow by failing to abide by some obscure federal regulation. And companies, once the province of geniuses like Thomas Edison and John Moses Browning, are now crushed by onerous regulations and invasive government actions. A dear friend of ours works fairly high up within DuPont. His horror stories of the tens of thousands of man-hours and hundreds of millions of dollars wasted just maneuvering through all of the administrative and legal mazes imposed by federal and state governments are discouraging.

Also, look at the direct threats made by the Department of Justice against Internet providers and wireless cell phone carriers to turn over all telephonic metadata of every single phone call made in our country—no probable cause requirement, just the voracious appetite of the beast. Or, the armed SWAT-style raid on the iconic Gibson Guitar factory in Tennessee. Gibson's alleged crime? Being the end importer of some supposedly endangered species of wood! In the end, we see that big government, in its thirst to rake in fines and covet the goods of private citizens, really does not care about people. This must stop before we all end up in the gulag or government re-education camps: "Got my mind right now, Boss!"

Why can't a person—not a criminal suspect—buy an airline ticket and fly without showing an ID card? Does anyone truly believe that a terrorist would have any problem obtaining such an ID? Infinitely more important is that the "papers please" mindset is so shockingly reminiscent of Nazi Germany. Nonetheless, many states have passed legislation that citizens must present ID to police officers on demand, without any probable cause that a crime is afoot. We are creeping closer and closer to an all-knowing state. Think of all the individual liberties we have surrendered in the last generation in the name of state security against terror, the war on drugs, or whatever bogeyman is proffered in support of such actions.

Not happy with stealing by force or threat of force nearly half our earned income, the government is now seriously into the previously illegal business of selling lottery tickets. Americans spent over $65 billion on lottery tickets in 2012. Lottery tickets are heavily advertised, and their odds are heavily in the government's favor. Furthermore, instead of relieving tax burdens, the proceeds simply create golden handcuffs for a government now addicted to this illusory windfall. To add salt to this wound, the lottery programs always start out promising to fund some seemingly altruist goal, such as improving schools. The desire to increase revenue drives these lotteries, while at the same time, in many locations, there are now state-funded programs to help gambling addicts. The insanity of this type of behavior can only be called that: insane. Progressivism and modern man's overreliance on government are truly forms of insanity.

The notion that the government is the solution to man's problems is a lie unto itself. Any notion that more police presence or intrusions into our private lives will make us safer is illusory at best and dangerous as hell to our principled, free lifestyles.

For instance, suppose I work hard and save $5,000 over the course of a year to buy a motorcycle. Happily, on my way to purchase my new bike one Saturday morning, I get pulled over by some eager-beaver young police officer for a simple traffic violation. Now, suppose my pile of cash is lawfully sitting in my center console. No big deal, right? Wrong! Nowadays, that police officer will likely seize my hard-earned cash as evidence of some nebulous wrongdoing, give me a receipt (if I'm lucky), and then say, "Prove you didn't come by this money by illegal means!"

This is happening across America all the time. In fact, many departments specifically train officers on how to pull over people on a technicality, just as a ruse or pretext to gain access to Fourth Amendment-protected areas of a person's car. This notion of asset forfeiture is a mortal affront to our dignity and security as free citizens, yet most Americans either turn a blind eye to it or are totally ignorant that such activities could possibly be happening in our republic. Yes, drug dealers, gangs, and more typical bad guys often do carry large sums of cash. But, we should *never* place the legal cart before the horse, making citizens prove that an otherwise lawful commodity in their possession is rightly and justly theirs.

This is not to say that officers, responding to a bank holdup call, should not seize fresh stacks of $100 bills from a suspect matching the description of the bank robber. Nor are we saying that police shouldn't seize money contemporaneously to illegal narcotics sales. But, to take money from people just because it is in plain view and then place the onus on that citizen to prove it is his or hers in the first place is directly contrary to the inherent, God-given rights of humanity. It makes otherwise honest citizens nervous when a police cruiser pulls behind them. The second-order effect of this distrust of our police destroys the critical relationship between the citizenry and the police who serve them. This cannot stand. Supervisors that reward their officers for such asset forfeiture seizures are only fueling the fires of tyranny. Asset forfeiture money is very much akin to crack cocaine or methamphetamine: easy to access and extraordinarily addictive.

Since 9/11, this willingness to be scanned, probed, frisked, and molested by strangers to make us feel safe is proof-positive that the terrorists won. George W. Bush, a Republican, was responsible for the creation of a gigantic, invasive, costly, monolithic agency in search of a mission: the Department of Homeland Security. Perhaps that agency's most visible and annoying spawn is the Transportation Security Administration (TSA). First, any honest security professional will admit that the TSA is merely eyewash to the public. It is sickening to hear otherwise intelligent Americans say, while waiting in horrendously long lines to be probed, "Well, so long as it makes us safe!" The truth be told, once terror groups used the tactics of 9/11—namely, to seize an airliner with box cutters—that tactic ceased to be viable. The tactic of using knives to take over a plane was no longer effective by the end of the day on September 11.

The brave men and women of United Airlines Flight 93 proved that we would no longer be victims in such a situation. All that TSA does now is to ensure that good Americans are stripped of both their dignity and any defensive weapons, to include nail clippers, while traveling. Even more outrageous, and done like a thief in the night, is when one gets to the final destination, opens his checked baggage, and finds that his neatly packed private possessions have been pawed over by a faceless, nameless, and unaccountable minion—all without probable cause. Almost as if a demonstration of how silly some of this is, recently several individuals were arrested for routinely smuggling firearms into New York by carrying the weapons in their carry-on luggage. How is this possible? The perpetrators were airline employees, and therefore not screened.

What was once a joy and privilege[*]—airline travel—is now miserable. The Department of Homeland Security, like most federal agencies, was

---

[*] For those post–baby boomers reading this, some perspective is in order. When flying, men used to wear coats and ties and ladies wore dresses (think Cary Grant and Ingrid Bergman in *Notorious*). There was nothing diminutive in calling a stewardess a stewardess, people generally acted civilly, and one could meet family members at the gate. Now, one is lucky if the person sitting next to you has even bathed that same morning. Passengers routinely wear pajamas, tracksuits, or tank tops, and surly "flight attendants" have replaced the polite stewardesses of yesteryear. This is not progress.

created to fix a problem that did not exist. It is time for Americans to reclaim their basic individual inherent rights as set forth by history's true liberals: Thomas Jefferson and most of our founding fathers. We have ceded too many of our rights and responsibilities to the government. If we do not, the friction points between a coercive government and its citizens will only become more stark and violent.

The relevance of this discussion to law enforcement and virtuous policing is long-term. The problems of today were not created overnight. They have been festering and brewing since at least FDR's New Deal, but certainly since the abject failure of LBJ's Great Society programs of the 1960s. As a starting point to fix these entrenched problems, it is important that we as a society reexamine our inherent social contract between government and ourselves. We should (1) recognize that we, the people, do not serve government, but that it serves us, and (2) shrink rather than expand the size, scope, and function of government. Doing so will fundamentally help professional law enforcement officers return to being peace officers more concerned with working as members of society than being its gatekeepers or a "thin blue line." Every action by a police officer should be grounded on service to the citizens he or she protects. When this foundation is lost, regardless of the cause, only very bad results will occur.

Agencies and individual officers interact with the public they serve on a minute-by-minute basis. They must know and practice their craft in accordance with the rules of the road for a virtuous and free society. Here is an example showing a stark demarcation between the actions of a constitutionally focused and virtuously led agency (Nashville Police Department) and an abusive, authoritarian office of another (the U.S. Secret Service):

> It's rare to receive a 911 call from the Secret Service, but that's exactly what happened in January 2013 in Nashville, Tennessee, according to a new letter to the House Oversight Committee. The Secret Service agents had gone to a Nashville resident's home to investigate Facebook comments the Tennessean had made against the President. Unsurprisingly, the Obama critic—who hadn't violated any laws—wasn't willing to come out of his home and be investigated by the federal government.
>
> "He shoved the door in our face and went around the corner," the Secret Service agent told the 911 operator, "Possibly, he had a gun in his hands."
>
> Of course, slamming a door in someone's face isn't against the law, and neither is having a weapon. The man, who's a law-abiding gun owner, made no threats. He only demanded to see their warrant. They didn't bother to get one, but that inconvenient fact didn't stop them. One of the agents

asked the Nashville police sergeant to "wave a piece of paper" in order to fool the resident into believing they actually had obtained a warrant.

So, let's recount this, shall we? The Tennessean criticized the President in a non-threatening way ... as is his First Amendment Constitutional right. The Tennessean had a gun to defend his home ... as is his Second Amendment Constitutional right. The Tennessean asked to see a warrant ... as is his Fourth Amendment Constitutional right. None of these rights were respected by the Secret Service agents.

But you gotta love the Nashville Police. Chief Steve Anderson wrote a letter to the former Nashville Secret Service Director Julia Pierson and Assistant Director A.T. Smith detailing these abuses. "I think you can see that had the MNPD officers complied with the directive from the Secret Service agents," he wrote, "there was likelihood for this event to have escalated into a serious and/or embarrassing situation for both of our agencies."

He never heard back from Pierson, but Smith responded with a "condescending and dismissive" tone. When Anderson went to their office to discuss whether they thought it was right to wave around a piece of paper to pretend they had a warrant, the Secret Service agent allegedly answered, "I don't know. I'm not a lawyer."

It's good to see local authorities standing up to a corrupt, bloated federal government hell-bent on taking away our individual rights. Rep. Jim Cooper (D-Tennessee), one of the committee members who received the letter, thinks this is an outrage. "There's already a lot of fodder to attack the Secret Service with, and this will be more," he said, before saying that the Secret Service's tactics were grievous Constitutional violations.

Here's the best part of the story. Chief Anderson says that his officers are no longer allowed to work with the Secret Service unless they get a directive from the top. Why? He wants to make sure his officers aren't asked to engage in questionable and possibly unconstitutional activities.

Kudos to the Nashville police for standing up to a bloated, corrupt federal government and saying, simply, "no more."[*]

Such a story is troubling, too, in that it involves an agency, the U.S. Secret Service (USSS), that should be in the top echelon of law enforcement in terms of recruiting standards, training, and professional behavior. Its own Office of Professional Responsibility and the Department of Justice's Civil Rights Division should be actively investigating this matter. More importantly, if found to be true, the agency should be demonstrating

---

[*] Meckler, Mark, "Nashville Police Refuse Secret Service Illegal Search of Obama Critic," *The American Spectator*, October 16, 2014.

sincere remorse and a commitment to training to ensure such abuses do not occur in the future. Criticism of a president, no matter how harsh, is not a crime in our republic. Only activities that might be reasonably construed as in furtherance of a crime or threat against the life of a president are potentially criminal in nature. If the USSS investigates and places persons merely critical of a president, Barack Obama or George Bush, in the category of criminals or persons of interest, then half the country or more would be so titled! This should never happen lest the agency wants to be known by the last two letters of its acronym.

Again, some of out dearest friends are and were special agents of the U.S. Secret Service. Their dismay over how their agency has been ill led in the past decade is palpable. This probably will not be fixed until a change in administrations. But, it only takes a few years to ruin decades of goodwill and work. We pray that their agency will survive this era intact.

Agencies and those individuals whose duty it is to protect and serve their populace should remember that degree of humility necessary to prevent treating fellow citizens as the enemy. To prevent war crimes or other nonchivalrous acts, virtuous military leaders look for signs among their subordinates of depersonalization of others: persistently calling civilian noncombatants "Gooks" or "Slopeheads" in Vietnam or "Ragheads" or "Hajis" in more recent conflicts. The culture that led to the My Lai massacre in Vietnam did not happen overnight.

The same devolution can happen in law enforcement, especially in high-crime areas where the police–populace gulf is already wide. This is why it is so important for police officers to maintain allegiance to the objective natural law rights of all mankind, rather than the pettiness one acquires by treating others as objects, statistics, or animals. Saint Augustine, who had a bitter experience when he sought happiness outside the natural law of God, said: "You have made us for yourself, O Lord, and our hearts are restless till they rest in you!"*

Again, seemingly little steps and little things matter. Devolution into constant use of foul language in the ordinary course of business is also an indicator of a problem within a police force. Locker room language may be fine in the locker room, or even a squad room on occasion, but never in public. Barking profanities at a citizen is never appropriate. If, for no other reason than protecting oneself from future liability (as an officer never knows when his actions are being recorded, and it plays badly in front

---

* From Saint Augustine of Hippo, *Confessions*, Book 1, chap. 1.

of a jury when an officer uses profanity), police leaders should insist on courteous and professional language. Leading by example in this regard is very important.

Law enforcement agencies are full of many good virtuous men and women who want to do the right thing. However, it is incumbent upon their leadership and society as a whole to hold them to the highest standards of respect for individual liberty and private property rights. Absent such guidelines provided by the natural law, even good men and women can devolve into mindless drones of the state. Nazi SS troops were not born that way. Everything they did was lawful under the statutes of the Third Reich, and all that was required for them to gain the untenable power and strength they had by 1939 was for good and righteous men to remain silent and acquiesce in 1933. We ought not be fooled into believing we are somehow a better or different species.

14

Police in Our School Systems

A generation ago, schoolchildren caught fighting in the corridors, sassing a teacher or skipping class might have ended up in detention. Today, there's a good chance they will end up in police custody.[*]

—Wall Street Journal

America's public school system's plunge into mediocrity was jump-started by Madeline Murray O'Hare's 1963 atheist victory in the Supreme Court.[†] Denied the right to freely exercise their religious beliefs, students and schools embarked upon a rudderless journey, in search of the false ethereal nirvana promised by the hippies of the 1960s.

> Imagine there's no heaven
> It's easy if you try
> No hell below us
> Above us only sky
> Imagine all the people living for today

Very easy advice from a millionaire and former Beatle, but John Lennon's lyrics offer horrific guidance for the rest of society. The problem is that someone eventually has to pay the piper for "living for today."

The resultant chaos that passes for education, especially in our urban areas, should be of surprise to no one. The public school teachers' unions, most visibly the National Education Association (NEA), continue to

---

[*] Fields, Gary, and Emshwiller, John R., "For More Teens, Arrests by Police Replace School Discipline," *Wall Street Journal*, October 21, 2014.

[†] See *Murray v. Curlett*, which was consolidated on appeal to the Supreme Court in the case of *Abington School District v. Schempp*, 374 U.S. 203 (1963). In that landmark case, school-sponsored Bible reading in public schools in the United States was declared to be unconstitutional.

browbeat and hoodwink politicians and society alike into believing that we should simply throw good money after bad. "If only we had more money," they bemoan. How, then, does one explain the fact that the District of Columbia public school system spent $29,349 per pupil in the 2010–2011 school year, yet fully 83% of the eighth graders in these schools were not proficient in reading and 81% were not proficient in math?*

Parents, not the government, should be the moral barometer and decision makers for where, how, and by whom their children are educated. Believing otherwise has turned our nation's public schools into institutions that resemble penitentiaries instead of more wholesome places of learning. Replacing reading, writing, history, science, and arithmetic with a mushy amalgamation of "social studies" could be the subject of an entire other book. But, it is important to recognize this serious flaw in our society as we address virtuous policing, for without a fundamental understanding of the rights and responsibilities that are supposed to underpin a constitutional republic, students will not become good citizens. They will not learn resiliency and peaceable forms of conflict resolution. Nor will they recognize and know how to exercise self-defense when another—be it a politician or hoodlum—is trying to deprive them of one of their rights.

The nanny state now constantly intervenes when boys are simply being boys. Even a fair playground fight or martial discipline—harken back to Spencer Tracy in *Boys Town* or *Captains Courageous*—previously held forth as honorable, good, and necessary for young men to experience, is now relegated to the dustbin of history. Now, schools discipline kids for biting their Pop-Tarts into the shape of a pistol. In their *Wall Street Journal* article, Gary Fields and John Emshwiller report on the following incidents: a seventh-grader in Mississippi charged with disturbing the peace as a result of a minor hallway altercation, a teenager in Wisconsin charged with theft for sharing a classmate's chicken nuggets, a Florida child charged with a felony weapons rap as the result of a science experiment gone awry, and, lastly, a student in Texas who was given a misdemeanor ticket for wearing too much perfume!

In the fall semester of 2014, in Chester County, Pennsylvania, thousands of school-aged children were subjected to breathalyzer tests when

* Jeffrey, Terrence P., "DC Schools: $29,349 per Pupil, 83% Not Proficient in Reading," May 14, 2014, CNSNews.com.

coming to attend high school football games. One parent says she was "troubled" watching 11-year-old middle school students line up to be tested. As well she should be! If there were some indication of probable cause, then perhaps it would not be so outrageous to test those individual suspects. The notion that somehow because everyone gets searched there is no Fourth Amendment violation is ludicrous. But, here is the underlying and truly frightening part of this: Some parents voiced opinions such as the following:

> "If they didn't have that breathalyzer, you never know what could happen."
> "I think it's an invasion of privacy, but in today's world, it might be a good idea!"

To the first statement, one could posit that snapping one's fingers and counting to three keeps pink elephants from landing on one's head. In other words, there is no defined condition predicate to warrant mass searches: only a fear of the unknown. And, there is no evidence that causally links giving breathalyzer tests (like snapping one's fingers) prevents alcohol-related incidents (the pink elephants from falling). But, so long as they "feel safe" is enough for some to surrender others' fundamental liberties. And to the second statement, we ask, "So, in today's society, the Constitution goes out the window and we all line up like good little subjects because of some bureaucrat's bright idea?" Truly, as Ben Franklin observed, "Those that sacrifice liberty for security deserve neither."

Here is another chilling sidebar to this story. One parent called the school to complain and was advised with that huffy tone that only an entrenched bureaucrat can muster, "The breathalyzer policy is in the student handbook." Oh, so if anal and vaginal cavity searches were "in the student handbook," they too would be OK?

Mindless, spineless zero-tolerance policies have taken the place of wise discretion and critical-thinking skills. We are witnessing the emasculation of our young male society on one hand, and then depriving them of any moral compass to guide their natural passions and predilections on the other. So, teachers are now stuck with a group of children without a moral compass or resiliency, and are left only with the coercive power of the state to intervene when violence erupts in the classroom. That, or they resort to huge dosages of Ritalin, Xanax, or other pharmaceuticals that are now routinely prescribed to school-aged children.

While it is not reasonable to expect trips to the principal's officer, suspensions, and other administrative threats will stop 18-year-old, 6-foot-4-inch inner city Detroit public school "students" from assaulting teachers and innocent others, teachers ought to be able to resolve classroom disciplinary problems at the elementary and middle school grade levels without calling law enforcement officers. After speaking with many dedicated and hard-working public school teachers, we know that calling the police is not their first choice.

Part of the problem is with a complete lack of parental guidance at home, as well as parents who take the side of their "Little Johnny" in the face of overwhelming evidence that their child has been a juvenile delinquent, but cops should not be involved in these scholastic matters unless life or limb is at risk. It leads to what has become to be called the "schoolhouse-to-jailhouse track." The train on this track must be derailed.

The presence of law enforcement in and around schools should be limited to "safety days" and other special circumstances where students can learn in a positive environment about the role of police in a secure society. If principals and teachers feel compelled to call law enforcement to instill discipline in their schools, perhaps they are in the wrong line of work. And, perhaps police departments should stop sending officers to such ridiculous calls for service. Any competent police shift lieutenant should tell these principals to stop wasting officers' time and to do their own jobs. Why would anyone that is supposed to be in the business of educating young people want to see their young wards branded with a criminal arrest for such minor disciplinary infractions?

In these days of intrusive electronic surveillance, the powers of computers using link analysis, and nearly unlimited digital memory capacity, any record of involvement with law enforcement can tarnish a kid for the rest of his or her life. Accordingly, those instances in which children are fingerprinted, photographed, and entered into the National Crime Information Center (NCIC)* system ought to be infrequent and limited to very serious crimes. Calling someone names, texting "I want to kill you," and all the stupid things children have always done when young and

---

* NCIC is a computerized index of criminal justice information (i.e., criminal record history information, fugitives, stolen properties, and missing persons). Run by the Department of Justice, its information is available to federal, state, and local law enforcement and other criminal justice agencies. It is operational 24 hours a day, 365 days a year. See http://www.fbi.gov/about-us/cjis/ncic.

impulsive should not now be handled by our criminal justice system. It is busy enough handling real criminal investigations. At least it should be. But, school systems will become lazy if they are not forced to resolve their internal problems. If it is easier to just dial 911 than expend the time and energy disciplining kids and separating the wheat from the chaff, schools will do the former. And, so long as law enforcement goes down that road it does not need to go down, finds the manhole, and jumps in with both feet, then we end up where the *Wall Street Journal* has warned we are headed.

The second order of effect of resorting to police intervention in schools is that it desensitizes children to the shame and fear that they once had about being arrested or detained by the police. When one of the authors was a youngster growing up in Baltimore, he and a group of friends sneaked out of their homes one evening to play tag and get into mischief ("Nothing good ever happens after midnight" rings as true now as it did then). The group of three friends was caught trespassing atop a gas station's roof by an alert police officer. Two got away (including the author), but the third, "Tommy," was nabbed by the cop and driven home to his parents. The two friends who got away hid in the bushes outside Tommy's house and watched through the window as Tommy's dad spanked Tommy right in front of the police officer. It put the fear of God in all of us, and we thought twice about sneaking out again. And, Tommy did not end up with an NCIC record to stain his future.

Today, assuming they took Tommy home instead of processing him at the police station and calling social services to take him into the system, the police would probably arrest Tommy's dad for spanking him. Our society is turned on its head, and it needs to right itself before succumbing to the self-inflicted, mortal wounds that a statist, socialist government always inflicts on its citizens. If one has any doubt about this, and can't see the dangers staring him or her in the face here in America, then he or she need only look to the insane regulations unleashed by the European Union on the peoples of its member states.

Again, courageous police leaders can help prevent this by refusing to stray into lanes that should be occupied by parents and teachers. To do otherwise creates a self-licking ice cream cone for the demand for a coercive, intrusive government force by a school system unwilling to govern itself. Every one of man's foibles, and especially a child's, need not be subject to state action or response. Again, the goal of this book is to counter the forces and trends that create the police–populace gulf we find in many of America's ghettos. If we want Main Street to look and act like old Baltimore's public housing projects, so accurately portrayed in *The Wire*, then we need only to begin to treat all of our children as potential criminal suspects—if you give a mouse a cookie....

While the authors recognize that the criminal problems of such blighted places as East and West Baltimore are the result of complex social, economic, and societal failures, it is simply an observation that those populations' opinion of the police begins at an early age. If children are exposed, processed, and integrated into a criminal justice system at an early age, it is very likely they will remain tarred and feathered by that very system for the remainder of their lives. Moreover, if their experience with the police is a negative one, the basic trust required for a peaceful, symbiotic relationship will be lost.

Witness the public's knee-jerk reaction to the police shooting incident in Ferguson, Missouri. Despite clear and convincing evidence that the suspect, Michael Brown, (1) was a neighborhood bully, thief, and street criminal (2) who just committed a strong-arm robbery at a convenience store and (3) then initiated a violent assault on a uniformed police officer, the citizens of Ferguson were predisposed to seeing this event solely as a racial issue. And, despite more and more forensic evidence to the contrary, the same citizenry continued to view the situation through the myopic straw of their racially charged antipolice bias.

While the seeming disparate demographics between the police population (overwhelmingly Caucasian) and the citizenry (almost 65% Black) in that community may also have been a condition predicate to this mistrust, there must be much more behind such angst and anger. Race disparity alone would not account for the problem, as even more disparate demographics exist in medical treatment facilities, yet such levels of mistrust are not present in those surroundings. The relationship scars present in Ferguson were created by repetitive negative interactions. A healthy relationship between police and the community would be further degraded if police officers were used to enforce minor disciplinary infractions in schools.

Such bias starts at an early age and is extraordinarily unhealthy for society. The police should be able to rely on good and decent folk to support them and children to wave to them on the street, and generally be happy when they see a patrol car in their vicinity. Accordingly, the relationship must be a two-way street. Both the police and the community they serve have a responsibility in better forging this trust. It seems almost intuitive that if the police-student relationship at the elementary school level becomes one of enforcer and suspect, then the foundation of a healthy relationship in later life becomes cracked and brittle. If kids start correlating police with only negative life events (arrests of self or parents) and are never exposed to police in healthy, normal circumstances, the likelihood is low of their trusting police when it really counts.

So, what types of positive interactions can police have with America's youth? At an individual level, simply getting out of a patrol car and talking with school kids at a street corner can do amazing things to make things personal in a positive manner. It is very easy to be mean or uncaring to someone you don't know—hence the ease by which email communications can quickly get nasty. Bringing a K-9 dog to a school so that kids can pet it sounds easy: Allowing an officer to carve time out of a busy patrol schedule takes a visionary police shift commander who can see beyond the next comparative statistics (COMSTAT) thrashing.

Organizationally, police leaders that take the time to forge a more positive relationship with the schools within their jurisdictions will be rewarded in the long run. That kid, whom otherwise might ignore doing the right thing, may turn out to be a key witness in a homicide or robbery. More lastingly, however, it just might help the students onto a path of becoming good, responsible citizens. We know this all may sound too much like Joe Friday of television's *Dragnet* fame, but Jack Webb, as a character and citizen, was mostly right.

The cynical cop, cut from the pattern of the characters of Joseph Wambaugh's novels (and every big department has them), will pooh-pooh this idea and simply despair of the situation. But, we have a moral, ethical, and legal (natural law) responsibility not to succumb to such despair. We must never simply think of society's children as future felons. Again, most police officers begin their careers with altruistic motives. Those that do not are hopefully weeded out in the psychological screening process.[*] Departments should do everything they can to ensure their officers do not become jaded. The violence and scourge of television and video games, where eight-year-old kids murder rival drug gang members, shall not be the end state of our great republic. But it will be so if we simply expect or allow it.

Studies from as early as 1970 from the University of California–Los Angeles (UCLA) have noted the correlation between families that do not have a father (or positive masculine role model) and lower income and crime. The out-of-wedlock births among all races have skyrocketed

---

[*] Amazingly, some departments do not perform basic psychological screenings of their applicants. They mostly all give polygraphs, but a sociopathic personality can pass a polygraph all day long!

over the past four decades. That reality is readily apparent in most urban environments, but the trend is also occurring in suburban areas. This is not to assert that being poor is a crime or that being poor makes one a criminal. But, it is undeniable that criminal behavior more easily takes root in impoverished areas. That is why positive role models, as set forth below, can have such great effect in diverting youth away from the criminal track. There are some tremendous private-sector initiatives in this arena as well, such as that at the Ignatius Academy in Baltimore, whereby children from the projects are given a real opportunity to achieve and excel in school and the workplace. Over 90% of that institution's students go on to successfully matriculate in undergraduate programs. Law enforcement can't do it all by itself and needs to team with such private enterprises and charitable initiatives to chip away at the roots of criminal behavior.

POLICE ATHLETIC LEAGUE

Police Athletic League (PAL) programs have been in existence for decades. Often, law enforcement officers volunteer their time to help organize community sports leagues and other positive outlets for youths' energies and interests. Some famous Americans who are alumni of PAL programs are General Colin Powell, singer Billy Joel, and NBA legend Oscar Robertson.[*] PAL's member chapters work to prevent juvenile crime and violence by building the bond between cops and kids. For PAL to be successful, it is very important that departments, private charitable institutions, churches, and local politicians actively and synergistically support these programs. The NFL and NHL, among other organizations, actively sponsor PAL programs. Interestingly, St. Louis has a PAL chapter, but it is unclear as to whether or not Ferguson falls under its jurisdiction.

Encouragingly, Prince George's County, a jurisdiction previously plagued by a history of poor police–community relations, and the one involved in the tragic story of Sergeant Johnnie Riley in Chapter 12, is taking many steps to improve that relationship. It has an Explorer post (see below) at each of its districts and a PAL league operational in the summer. It also partners with the Maryland Park Police for a summer youth initiative that provides summer internships for youth. One of Prince George's

---

[*] See http://www.nationalpal.org/content/alumni.

County's senior trainers recognizes the importance of strengthening the relationship between the community and the department. This affirmation from an officer in a position of authority is very important for such programs to succeed. Even for adults, they offer a citizen police academy. Citizens are also empowered via a citizen advisory council and a citizen complaint oversight panel. Prince George's County should be commended for taking these measures to include the community in what is going on within their police department.

POLICE EXPLORERS

A more narrowly focused program than PAL is the Police Explorers. Typically, they are organized for young men and women in ninth grade and above, between 14 and 20 years of age, who have an interest in law enforcement. These programs can serve as a stepping-stone or entry portal for a career in policing or the criminal justice system. By way of example, the Delaware State Police, one of the nation's most respected and professional departments, has an Explorer program that introduces its members to the principles of fingerprinting, evidence collection, radar operation, criminal investigations, and patrol procedures. The Delaware program specifically mentors its students for a career in law enforcement. It also strives to instill leadership, responsibility, commitment, and professionalism—essentially, the cardinal virtues!

One limiting factor of most Police Explorer programs is that they typically require a minimum grade point average and no criminal arrest history. If police start arresting and processing students for minor school disciplinary concerns, then programs like this one become out of reach of otherwise capable and eligible students.

The Explorers also actively support community service and charitable events like state fairs, Special Olympics, and polar bear plunges* in support of charity. Like the Boy Scouts, Trail Life USA, and other civic-minded youth groups, Police Explorer programs help shape and form tomorrow's leaders. Not enough departments have or support Police Explorer

---

* The annual Plungapalooza event, sponsored by the Maryland State Police, is the largest polar bear plunge in the United States. Held at Sandy Point State Park near the Chesapeake Bay Bridge, it raises funds for the Special Olympics.

programs, as they require a commitment of time and resources that are in competition with other departmental requirements. But, their long-term benefits may help heal old community wounds. The problems society is now facing were not created overnight, but with perseverance, faith, and virtue, we can make a much safer, better, and freer tomorrow.

Police departments can't fix all of the social and cultural problems in American schools. Community policing will not magically transform listeners of violent, misogynist rap music into aficionados of Ralph Vaughan Williams. But, they can takes strides toward humanizing themselves and those they serve. When each group, respectively, begins to see each other as fellow human beings rather than statistics to be arrested or authority figures to be feared, then the gulf will shrink in size and scope. Keeping our children out of the adult criminal justice system, and a coercive police presence out of our schools, will help better achieve that goal.

A nihilistic, violent postapocalypse society where zombies abound may make entertaining video games and movies, and spark survival equipment and firearms sales, but it is hardly the vision for a healthy American future. The short-term cures for many problems in our schools should not spawn longer-term divisions and hatreds in our population. Arresting children, exposing them to violent prison populations, scarring them with indelible criminal records, and setting up an even greater "us-versus-them" world between the state and its commoners is not a good recipe for success. Schools should be creating self-sufficient, freedom-loving citizens. Prayerfully, America will true her moral compass, and this issue will not remain the one it has become of late.

15

On Notice and the Presumption of Innocence

Two of the fundamental underpinnings of the common law, that body of law from which most of American jurisprudence is derived, are the concepts of notice and presumption of innocence. Driven by the need for ever-more dollars to fuel their explosive growth in the past two decades, and now hooked on the fiscal crack known as asset forfeiture, modern governments have resorted to taking citizens' property without either.

Notice is that requirement that governments take steps to make persons aware of *mala prohibita* (man-made) crimes. *Mala prohibita* crimes, like "no texting" or seat belt laws, generally require some sort of notice to be given to the public before police can start arresting or charging persons for violations. Hence, when one drives from Maryland into Virginia, there are big roadside signs that warn people—especially out-of-staters—that radar detectors are illegal in the Commonwealth of Virginia. *Mala in se* crimes (wrongs in themselves), by contrast, are reasonably known to be wrong: Rape, murder, robbery, and burglary are all *mala in se* crimes. Because *mala in se* crimes are violations of the natural law, there is almost no requirement that the state give notice of the criminality of these intrinsically evil acts.

Presumption of innocence should need no further explanation. A person shall be presumed innocent until the state proves otherwise, beyond a reasonable doubt. But, based on the actions of diverse local, state, and federal law enforcement and intelligence agencies of late, perhaps the concept needs some reinforcement either by judicial enforcement or otherwise. For instance,

an Iowa woman named Carole Hinders saw her bank balance go from $33,000 to zero thanks to IRS confiscation. Hinders, who owns a small, cash-only Mexican restaurant, has not been charged with any crime and is not suspected of tax fraud. The IRS says they took her money solely because she deposited too little of it at a time, and the agency claims she did so to avoid the required reporting of any bank transaction over $10,000. She says she just thought it was helpful to save the bank paperwork.

Though the $10,000 rule is ostensibly designed to help catch terrorists and drug dealers, it is far more often used on regular citizens who are unlikely to ever see their money returned. "I don't think [the IRS is] really interested in anything," said a lawyer representing another seizure case. "They just want the money."

To keep her restaurant afloat following the confiscation of her savings, Hinders has had to take out a second mortgage and max out her credit cards. "How can this happen?" she asks. "Who takes your money before they prove that you've done anything wrong with it?"*

So, a government agency, without probable cause, seizes the business assets of a citizen of the United States because she followed the rules? Moreover, it then shifts the burden of proof onto that citizen to, in essence, prove a negative: that they didn't obtain the money by unlawful means! If people lose faith in the integrity of those enforcing the law, then Katy bar the door! For "stripping motivated people of their dignity and rubbing their noses in it is a very bad idea!"†

Recently, FBI special agents impersonated repair technicians at the Caesars Palace resort in Las Vegas in order to surreptitiously collect evidence. What was the alleged crime that underscored this warrantless search? Not an imminent terrorist attack or some other exigent circumstance that *might* excuse a warrantless entry, but online sports betting during the 2014 World Cup!

In accordance with the Fourth Amendment of the Constitution and scores of Supreme Court cases, a person should be secure from warrantless search and seizure by government agents unless the person knowingly waives such protections or the law enforcement agents obtain a warrant. Allegedly, not only did the agents involved violate this sacrosanct right, but they also ignored clear advice from the U.S. Attorney's Office not to

---

* Kristian, Bonnie, "IRS Seizes Woman's Entire Savings Because She Deposits Less Than $10,000 at a Time," *The Week*, October 27, 2014, theweek.com.

† Ross, John, *Unintended Consequences* (New Brighton, MN: Accurate Press, 1996), from author's note, p. 10, describing the unintended consequences governmental actions may have on a populace.

proceed with such tactics.* The FBI is supposed to be the paradigm of virtue among law enforcement agencies. Incidents such as this tarnish its reputation among the profession and public alike. The Constitution is not a document to be cleverly circumvented.

The dirty and corrupt cops described in books and movies like *Serpico* and *Prince of the City* unlawfully seize citizens' cash and property for private gain. Their corruption was felt to varying degrees throughout the country, but it was a major contributing factor in the lack of trust between police and populace in 20th-century urban America. Now, in certain circumstances, law enforcement officers are trained and used to seize the private property of others without adequate probable cause or due process of law.

Now, though, they do it not for personal gain, but to enrich the coffers of the state. While this might be done under the letter of the law, the end result is the same, if not worse: The population loses respect for the law. Eventually, the people will begin to ignore it or take violent, physical actions against it. Progressives and conservatives alike will clamor for more and far more restrictive laws. The end of that road is a totalitarian, all-knowing state that will annihilate the freedoms upon which our republic is founded. One of the main reasons for us writing this book is to hopefully avert this tragic consequence.

In addition to the IRS's notorious abuses, as exemplified by the case set forth above, the following examples of law enforcement's putting the cart (presumption of guilt) before the horse (the rights of the public to remain free from unlawful searches and seizures) are the mere tip of the iceberg.

The Bureau of Alcohol, Tobacco and Firearms (ATF) spent hundreds of thousands of taxpayer dollars investigating a former soldier over his alleged sale of an old, used shotgun with an 18-inch barrel to one of the ATF's informants. The shotgun in question had a barrel that was considered lawful by federal regulation. But, unknown to the suspect (and to most Americans), the overall length of the weapon was allegedly only 25.5 inches—a half-inch shorter than what is required under the National Firearms Act of 1934.† It is unclear whether the informant, the suspect, or the ATF had sawed off a half-inch of the weapon's wooden butt stock,

---

* Associated Press and MailOnline Reporter, "FBI Agents Under Fire for Posing as Repairmen at a Las Vegas Hotel and Entering Rooms Without a Warrant to Bust Illegal World Cup Gambling Ring," *The Daily Mail*, October 29, 2014.
† There was some evidence that the informant himself sawed off a half inch of the wooden stock in order to make it illegal.

thereby making possession of it a *mala prohibita* felony under federal law. Most American firearms owners, including the former soldier in this case, know of the silly proscription against possessing a sawed-off shotgun, but most incorrectly assume it applies only to the barrel's length. Nonetheless, with this federal crime at hand, the agency descended upon the person and property of Randy Weaver of Ruby Ridge, Idaho, in order to arrest him for what is, in essence, a tax stamp violation—for the National Firearms Act of 1934 was and is a tax measure that gave the out-of-work "revenuers" something to regulate after Prohibition was repealed a year earlier.

In the end, Weaver's wife, Vicki, son, Sammy, and U.S. Marshal William Francis Degan were all unnecessarily killed as the result of this lack of virtue of certain agents of the ATF. When the Weaver case was passed from the ATF to the U.S. Marshals Service, no one in the ATF informed the marshals of the fact that the ATF had attempted to solicit Weaver as an informant. The ATF also related false information concerning Weaver's actions, threats, background, and temperament. In short, the ATF agents involved lacked competency, moral courage, a sense of justice, and certainly, self-control in initiating an investigation of a man who simply wanted to be left alone. Randy Weaver and his family moved to the forests of northern Idaho to freely associate with those whom they wanted. Wanting to associate with one's own racial tribe and cultural group is not a crime in America, and Weaver is certainly not alone in that desire. Simply observe the seating arrangements in most high school and collegiate cafeterias to confirm this phenomenon. Interestingly, on August 24, 1992, on the fourth day of the siege at Ruby Ridge, Deputy Assistant Director Danny Coulson of the FBI wrote the following in a memo:

Something to Consider

1. Charge against Weaver is Bull Shit
2. No one saw Weaver do any shooting
3. Vicki has no charges against her
4. Weaver's defense: He ran down the hill to see what his dog was barking at. Some guys in camys (camouflage) shot his dog. Started shooting at him. Killed his son. Harris did the shooting [of Deputy US Marshal Degan]. He [Weaver] is in pretty strong legal position.

No kidding! Congress initiated a lengthy hearing on the Ruby Ridge incident, primarily focusing on FBI special agent Lon Horiuchi's actions as a member of his agency's elite Hostage Rescue Team (HRT) and their rules of engagement.* Unfortunately, Congress missed the incident's jugular: the Keystone Cops antics of the ATF that led to the involvement of the U.S. Marshals and FBI in the first place. Congress just assumed that there was sufficient probable cause underpinning the federal arrest warrants for the alleged National Firearms Act (NFA), violation. They made the same mistake in investigating Waco three years later: another fiasco initiated by ATF incompetency, lies, and general lack of virtue.

Again, this is not an indictment or criticism of individual special agents of the ATF, many of whom are friends and colleagues of the authors. But, when citizens begin to feel helpless or at the mercy of an unbridled bureaucracy, whether or not such feelings are totally justified, the resultant breakdown of a decent, orderly, and free society will occur. Either the citizens will become mindless working drones who sacrifice freedom for a false sense of security, or they will rebel in violent and unpredictable ways. Playing silly administrative games and regulations just because one can is not a path to success as a person or agency. The ATF should not be looking for ways to make felons of average Americans based on what they might possess in their homes or gun lockers. We find it offensive when politicians and policy makers point toward the European Union (EU) as a model for us to follow, especially in the matters of gun control. Rifles kill less than 1/20th the number of persons that motorcycles do, yet no one is militating for banning motorcycles (nor should they). And, motorcycles are not specifically protected by the Bill of Rights.

Most Americans enjoy their freedoms and do not want to become another member of the EU. We fought a violent revolution to become unshackled from that world. The freedoms that were earned for us by our forefathers are easily perishable, though. In one generation, we are halfway back to that nanny state mentality where people look to the government to solve every little problem or dispute. The methods and ways by which we agree to be policed are an important part of this equation. If we idly

---

* *Rules of engagement* is a military term that really should have no relevance to domestic law enforcement policy. The FBI operates under a Department of Justice-approved use of deadly force policy, which is derived from relevant federal constitutional case law such as *Graham v. Connor, Tennessee v. Garner,* and their progeny. Law enforcement's trend toward using military terms like the *objective* and *ambush* and *overwatch* needs to be reversed. It is important to note that Horiuchi was found to have acted objectively reasonable based on what he knew at the time. The authors' quarrel here is not with Lon Horiuchi or the FBI. Rather, it is with the ATF's actions here and on numerous other occasions where they have infringed on American citizens' fundamental rights of self-defense and to be secure from unreasonable search and seizure (as recognized by the Second and Fourth Amendments).

sit by, keep our mouths shut, and take it as we are prodded, probed, and groped at airports, or mailed hundred-dollar speeding tickets for alleged camera violations, or if we allow departments to conduct BS warrantless searches of vehicles based on supposed drug-sniffing dogs "alerting" on our vehicles, then we deserve what we get.

But, we deserve better treatment than all of this. Actively engage with your representatives, let them know that we, the people, are angry and are not going to take it any more. Vote! It is disgusting that even in important contested political races, less than 50% of those eligible actually vote. Take the time to talk with police in your communities. They should not be faceless report writers who you see only when you are robbed, involved in an accident, or your home is burglarized. Police are living, breathing human beings. They have good days and bad days. Having a citizen say hello or buy them a cup of coffee can be refreshing for them and you.

Members of police departments and law enforcement agencies must possess the virtues in order to abide by their oaths to protect, uphold, and defend the Constitution of the United States. This must not be mere lip service, but a daily, active calling. For the notions contained within it are under constant assault by those within government who want to cast fellow citizens as the enemy merely for their political or religious beliefs or, shockingly, for their support of the Constitution.

This is not hyperbole or scare tactics. Two Department of Homeland Security (DHS) documents from 2009 actually characterized the following groups as extremists:

- American citizens who voice their beliefs in the U.S. Constitution
- Those who support a third-party candidate
- Christians who believe in the second coming of Jesus Christ (a core tenet of most major Christian faiths, including Roman Catholics)
- Those who oppose state-sponsored abortion
- War veterans from Iraq and Afghanistan

According to this official DHS guidance provided to local, state, and federal law enforcement agencies, these people—our brothers and sisters in our great republic—are now to be considered "potential terrorists," "radicalized" citizens, and "extremists." This is not just reminiscent of Nazi Germany via artistic license: It is exactly what the Gestapo and SS did within the German population in the 1930s. Painting citizens as criminals for their political thoughts or religious beliefs is the only extremist activity here, and the fact that it was done by a federal law enforcement agency should send shivers down the spine of every American.

It is activity—not thought—that forms the basis for articulable reasonable suspicion and probable cause. For instance, if a person who opposes state-sponsored abortions starts bombing abortion clinics, then that activity on his part is illegal—not his belief that human life begins at conception! Moreover, there are millions of citizens who oppose state-sponsored abortion. They peacefully protest and voice their political opinions, but would never dream of committing a violent act. If an Iraq War veteran suffers from extreme posttraumatic stress disorder (PTSD) and goes on a killing rampage (this has not happened), then that individual's actions are criminal. But, mere combat service in Iraq or Afghanistan does not make a person an extremist or even a suspected extremist. Again, all three authors—individually and collectively—have multiple combat tours in Iraq and Afghanistan. It is personally and professionally offensive as hell that a branch of the very government we served is now labeling us as extremist threats to our fellow citizens because of our service and belief in the Constitution.

This categorizing of large segments of the American population with suspicion (at least a million people on the Transportation Security Administration's [TSA] "no fly" list) runs so contrary to the Constitution's letter and spirit that it is difficult to use polite language to describe it. Not only is it indicative of an anticonstitutional spirit, but also it is clearly lacking in virtue. Doing so is intellectually lazy (lack of competency), patently unjust, and demonstrates a complete lack of self-control, and those that "go along to get along" are moral cowards. These are times that require virtuous leadership.

It is possible, and even prudent, for law enforcement to understand and be able to assess patterns of crime, similar to an epidemiologist discerning the spread of blood-borne pathogens.* For instance, if one is a young African American gang member in Chicago, you stand a 13% chance of being shot—about the same odds as playing Russian roulette with a six-shot revolver!† So, used properly, link analysis of social trends can

---

* See, for example, the works of Andrew Papachristos, a Yale University sociologist, on the topic of gun violence. A fascinating video, in which Papachristos explains portions of his findings, can be viewed at http://gunculture2point0.wordpress.com/2014/10/10/tragic-but-not-random-andrew-papachristos-on-gun-violence/. He also correctly points out that focused enforcement actions, instead of sweeping enforcement ones (such as rampant stop and frisks or traffic check points), work better to address these societal problems.

† Id., at approximately the 28:00 minute mark.

appropriately aid law enforcement in discerning and preventing criminal activity. But, placed in the hands of ignorant or malicious law enforcement officers, such grasps for information can be devastating to the health of our society.

It is very important to note two aspects of the Chicago study referenced: (1) The race of the suspect is not important, but the cultural shortcomings of his associated gang members are, and (2) a very large number of people living in the affected high-crime areas are not criminals. Therefore, these types of analyses and reports must be accurate, limited in scope, and done with extreme care so as not to trample everyone's freedoms in the cure of a very specific illness. The 2009 DHS document mentioned above is an example of an ignorant abuse of statistical analyses. Conversely, intelligent and focused enforcement based on comparative statistics (COMSTAT) or link analysis trends, such as that being practiced by the New Haven Police Department, can positively impact criminal behavior while still protecting all of our constitutional freedoms.

If police begin to see and utilize the powerful analytic tools at their disposal in a manner inconsistent with our free and open society, either we will slip into a coercive police state or good and otherwise honest people will rebel. Many individuals in our society are wise to the ways of the former and will resort to the latter if pushed too far. Why, then, would departments want to force this issue? If they lack the cardinal virtue of self-control and humility, they might simply do it because they can: the classic "bully cop" syndrome exemplified by a 2013 article in *Esquire* magazine.* Here are two snippets from that article:

> My entire adult life has been dedicated to the deliberate management of violence. There are no two ways around that fact. My job, at the end of the day, is about killing. I orchestrate violence.
>
> We will pry your gun from your cold, dead, fingers. That is because I am willing to wait until you die, hopefully of natural causes. Guns, except for the three approved categories, cannot be inherited. When you die your weapons must be turned into the local police department, which will then destroy them.

That article, written by Robert Bateman, purportedly an active-duty Army officer and police officer, grossly misinterprets the law of the land and is replete with factual errors and highly selective statistics. More

---

* Robert Bateman, "It's Time We Talk About Guns," *Esquire*, December 3, 2013.

disturbingly, the author openly threatens the coercive use of governmental force—to include deadly force—to seize *lawfully* owned firearms from his fellow citizens. Such rhetoric dangerously threatens the natural rights of man and is a prime example of why many otherwise law-abiding and good citizens mistrust and hate law enforcement. It is a trend that must be reversed if we are to survive as a constitutional republic that recognizes and defends the liberties of her citizens.

It is disconcerting that a person who took an oath to uphold and defend the Constitution not only would write words so derisive of it, but also knows so little about the document that he swore to defend. Moreover, it is appalling that an active duty military officer would incite and encourage others to kill or arrest persons exercising their individual and constitutionally protected rights.

SECOND AMENDMENT

Justice Antonin Scalia and the majority in the seminal Supreme Court case of *Heller v. District of Columbia*, 554 U.S. 570 (2008), articulated both the current and age-old traditional interpretation of the Second Amendment to the U.S. Constitution. The current interpretation of the Second Amendment is the same as the traditional interpretation. The process of judicially interpreting the Constitution and the law of the land is the foundation of our system of government.

The five-justice majority opinion in *Heller* stated, "the Second Amendment protects an individual right to possess a firearm unconnected with service in a militia." This is clearly consistent with the writings of the founding fathers as elucidated in *The Federalist Papers*, as well as other writings of the authors of the Constitution. As Alexander Hamilton stated so clearly in Federalist Paper 29, "Concerning the Militia," "The best we can hope for concerning the people at large is that they be properly armed."

We encourage readers to study Justice Scalia's controlling opinion in its entirety. It is the law of the land, and serving military officers are bound to uphold it. In fact, many argue that the decision did not go far enough in detailing the historical fact that the founding fathers and framers of the Constitution were talking about an inherent individual right to possess arms—in their own words:

Patrick Henry: "The great objective is that every man be armed....
Everyone who is able may have a gun."

George Mason: "To disarm the people [is] the best and most effectual
way to enslave them."

Samuel Adams: "The Constitution shall never be construed ... to prevent the people of the United States who are peaceable citizens from
keeping their own arms."

Moreover, in the eyes of the authors of the Constitution, the Second
Amendment does not merely *confer* a right granted to us by government;
rather, it *acknowledges* a God-given natural right that belongs to all human
beings by virtue of our birth. It is, literally, a birthright. If it were repealed
tomorrow, one would still have an inherent right to own arms and use
them to protect oneself.

We can only hope that the author was using hyperbole in his writing,
and that his stated actions were not his intent, although such inflammatory use of language is indeed disturbing coming from one serving in a
position of responsibility in our government. We expect and demand a
more measured, reasoned, and mature approach from a senior officer in
our military. We also note that the term *well regulated* did not mean what
he thinks it meant at the time of the founding of our country. A better
explanation of the phrase in today's usage would be *well functioning*.
As the Supreme Court understood, the *preparatory* phrase does not in this
case limit the *declarative* statement.

CRIME AND WEAPONS

Statistically, as clearly demonstrated by Professor John R. Lott Jr. and
others, crime is reduced in states that acknowledge the right of their
citizens to carry concealed weapons for protection. It is very interesting
to compare the crime statistics from New York (where concealed carry
laws are only for law enforcement and society's elite—Senator Chuck
Schumer, an ardent gun control advocate, has an unrestricted concealed
carry (CCW) permit in New York, to include New York City) and Vermont
(where citizens have an unrestricted right to carry). Invariably, the violent
crime rates in the adjacent New York counties are higher.

In the United States, crime is inversely proportional to civilian firearm ownership. In states and municipalities that have strict gun control, crime flourishes. Examples include Detroit, Chicago, Baltimore, and other large urban areas where law-abiding citizens are disarmed, leaving only criminals with firearms. Strict gun control is directly proportional to crime. Moreover, the average time for police to respond to a serious incident is approximately 14 minutes. Hence, law enforcement rarely stop crime and are mostly involved in report taking and follow-up criminal investigation after the fact. In other words, they clean up the mess but rarely arrive in time to protect people. In fact, courts have explicitly stated that it is not the duty of the police to protect citizens. See *Warren v. District of Columbia*, 44 A.2d. 1 (D.C.Ct. of Ap. 1981) and *Castle Rock v. Gonzales*, 545 U.S. 748 (2005).

The most effective way to stop a violent intrusion, armed robbery, or other violent criminal act while it is happening is by force of arms in the hands of the victim or other citizens. If a law-abiding person knowingly decides to go about unarmed in a violent crime-plagued area, that should be the individual's rather than the state's choice. Such ignorance should not be projected upon others who make the choice to be responsibly armed in order to protect themselves and innocent others.

In summary, the Constitution is clear. There is an individual right to own firearms for self-defense. The statistics are also clear: Gun control is strongly related to increased crime. Believing otherwise in the face of the data today is simply fantasy, perhaps driven by an unreasonable fear of firearms or an agenda promoted by those who do not trust their fellow citizens. We do appreciate Lieutenant Colonel Bateman's honesty in stating that he desires law enforcement and the military to confiscate firearms from law-abiding citizens of this country. Too often those who wish such actions refuse to openly state it. For that, we thank him and are on notice: He has indicated his intent, appears to possess the ability, and is only awaiting the opportunity to violate our constitutional rights. We remain vigilant.

Whenever a politician, police officer, or other government representative starts an argument with "Why do you need _____?" (fill in the blank: an assault rifle, a pistol that holds more than 10 rounds, etc.), be afraid. Why do Americans need 500-horsepower Ford Mustangs? Or, why do they need motorcycles capable of reaching speeds in excess of 190 miles per hour? The gun control issue is a shibboleth that transfers responsibility for individual behavior from the person to an inanimate object.

During a discussion with a police patrol sergeant and Special Weapons and Tactics (SWAT) trainer in the greater Philadelphia metropolitan area on this topic, he wisely observed the following bad trend among his rookies. Pennsylvania is a right-to-carry state: Law-abiding citizens can obtain a concealed carry permit if they have no history of violent behavior and pass a criminal background check. When a young rookie officer would conduct a car stop for a minor traffic violation and the operator of the vehicle politely advised the officer that he is a concealed carry holder and has a weapon on his hip, the young officer would instantly revert to a felony car stop, dragging the hapless citizen out of the car and placing him facedown on the pavement. How's that for improving community relations? Take a law-abiding citizen and taxpayer and treat him like a felon simply because he lawfully possesses a firearm and dutifully told the officer that.

It took a great deal of patience for our friend to retrain his officers in the following points: (1) If someone tells you about and shows you his CCW permit, that person is probably not a threat, so (2) simply ask him, "Where is the gun right now?" and when told ("It's on my hip" or "In the center console"), simply ask him not to access the weapon or make sudden moves toward it during the duration of the car stop. This is a mature, experienced SWAT sergeant speaking words of wisdom, virtue, and justice.

Lastly, there is a huge misperception concerning the firearms proficiency (or lack thereof) of most law enforcement officers. Other than dedicated SWAT/ERT (emergency response team) officers, or those that understand that firearms skills are tough to master and are perishable, the majority of American police officers train and shoot their firearms less than two hours a year. Why, then, do Americans believe and trust that law enforcement officers are the only ones possessing some magic power to safely and effectively defend themselves and others against violent, determined criminals? This Hollywood or television myth must be understood and exposed before any serious discussion can ensue on the rights of Americans to possess and bear firearms.

As so clearly presented by Professor Papachristos of Yale (see the footnote on p. 165), the overwhelming number of unlawful gun-related shootings and deaths (85%) occur among a very small criminal element. The remaining 15% are the result of social violence, such as domestic disputes, but these have occurred throughout history and long before firearms were invented.

The manner by which police view their population (hopefully as colleagues and peaceable citizens, except for the dangerous few felons) and the population views the police (hopefully as friends and fellow citizens within the greater community) will shape America's future for better or worse. The core framework of that relationship must remain the Constitution of the United States, rather than the whims, fancies, and trends of a rudderless modernity. The founding fathers were not a bunch of "Old Dead White Men,"* but rather visionary geniuses who intimately understood human nature and the coercive nature of oppressive government. If we lose both the rudder (the Constitution) and the North Star (our cardinal virtues), the American ship of state will surely crash upon the rocks of history.

The police–populace relationship is key to maintaining both adherence to the Constitution and respect for the cardinal virtues in good order—hence the importance of remembering our citizens' natural rights to remain free from unreasonable searches made without probable cause and presumption of innocence. Exigencies are the times when such freedoms are tried, but most sorely needed. Look at Boston after the 2013 marathon bombing or New Orleans after Hurricane Katrina for a glimpse of what a coercive police state gone wild can look like. That vision is not a pretty one; yet, too many Americans accept it, even laud it, in their illusory belief in safety.

The legal standard by which the law demands the government to prove its case is sometimes frustrating to law enforcement and the public alike. As so pithily stated by renowned criminal defense attorney and Harvard law school professor Alan Dershowitz,†

> That is why a criminal trial is not a search for truth. Scientists search for truth. Philosophers search for morality. A criminal trial searches for only one result: proof beyond a reasonable doubt.

---

* One contemporary rap song—"Old Dead White Men"—chronicles the alleged shortcomings of the early leaders in the United States. Of President James Monroe's tenure, the rap says: "White men getting richer than Enron/They stepping on Indians, women, and blacks/Era of Good Feeling doesn't come with the facts." Unbelievably, such tripe is taught in at least one school district in the United States. Known as Flocabulary, its founder said the lyrics are meant to be "provocative and humorous." What about factually and historically correct? This "thinking out of time" error, that is, seeing historical decisions through the lens of today's pop culture, is just plain ignorant and unproductive in creating a just and virtuous society.

† One of the nation's foremost civil liberties lawyers and distinguished defenders of individual rights, Dershowitz is a vocal critic of those on both sides of the political aisle who wish to infringe upon our citizens' liberties and rights. Most police officers have a knee-jerk, sometimes visceral, reaction to the mention of his name. A more thoughtful response is due, as he would be the first to come to their aid if falsely accused in a use-of-force incident. While we may disagree with some of Professor Dershowitz's political stances, abortion being one in particular, we respect and laud his career and contributions to the freedoms we all enjoy. We also wholeheartedly support Dershowitz's stance on Israel's inherent right of self-defense.

The beyond a reasonable doubt standard is an important bulwark against convicting the innocent in the court of public opinion or by police officers' mere suspicions or confabulations. Police are human and make mistakes, but never should a citizen go to prison based on weak or false evidence—no matter the crime alleged.

16

How the Lack of Virtue
Undermines Society Itself

We have served our country with over 90 years of collective military and law enforcement service. When we began that service to our nation, Richard Nixon was president. With the exception of the eight years under Ronald Reagan, the United States has been headed in the wrong direction politically, socially, and spiritually. While George W. Bush is a fine man, personally, as president he created an unnecessary bureaucracy in the Department of Homeland Security, signed onto the mass surveillance of the American people, and spent money almost as fast as his successor.

The United States was founded on the principles of individual freedom, private property rights, and a quiet, yet fundamental, belief in the Judeo-Christian faith of our forefathers. These tenacious, dedicated men, mostly from Ireland, England, and Europe, created the greatest bastion of freedom ever witnessed in the history of mankind. Those that now denigrate that history and model have been deceiving our populace and sowing the seeds of unhealthy dissent. Envy, racial discord, and mediocrity in the clothing of secular humanism are the tools of their trade. This needed to be said right up front lest anyone accuse us of being passive-aggressive, as is the practice of those bent on destroying all that is good and pure about this great nation. An immoral, secular, ignorant, and envious population is not a good recipe for peace and harmony. It plays hell for those charged with keeping order.

THE DEATH OF PRIVATE PROPERTY RIGHTS AND AMERICA'S FUTURE

Human freedoms and individual wealth are not derived from reliance on a sovereign. Freedom only truly flourishes in the presence of laws that protect private property rights and intellectual freedoms, and allow minimal governmental interference. Two of the biggest lies told by modernity are that capitalism is evil and successful people have not earned their wealth, but have somehow screwed the rest of society out of their share of the pie.

Envy is a powerful weapon. In fact, industrious people typically have worked very hard for what they have earned and often pay taxes at a confiscatory rate. The top 10% of taxpayers paid over 70% of the total amount of taxes collected. The remaining 90% bore just under 30% of the tax burden. And, as Mitt Romney got excoriated for truthfully pointing out, 47% of all Americans now pay hardly anything at all. This populace is most susceptible to class envy and the lies of socialism.

William F. Buckley Jr. wisely observed of the coercive power of the mob and the envy on which it thrives:

> I will hoard my power like a miser, resisting every effort to drain it away from me. I will then use my power, as I see fit. I mean to live my life an obedient man, but obedient to God, subservient to the wisdom of my ancestors; never to the authority of political truths arrived at yesterday at the voting booth.[*]

In the early 1950s, William F. Buckley Jr. wrote his first book, *God and Man at Yale*[†]:

> Buckley charged that Yale's values were agnostic as to religion, "interventionist" and Keynesian as to economics, and collectivist as regards the relationship of the individual to society and government. While conceding the validity of academic freedom for a professor's research, Buckley insisted that a professor did not have the right to inseminate into the minds of his students values that were counter to the values of the parents paying his salary. He urged parents, alumni, and trustees to resist this aberrant form

---

[*] Buckley Jr., William F., *Up From Liberalism* (New York: McDowell, 1959).
[†] Buckley Jr., William F., *God and Man at Yale: The Superstitions of Academic Freedom* (New York: Regnery Publishing, 1951).

of academic freedom. Drawing upon his university experience, Buckley submitted that Yale had abandoned Christianity, free enterprise, and what he called "individualism." (He described himself in these early days as an "individualist" rather than as a conservative.) He said that the faculty members who favored atheism and socialism ought to be fired because the primary goal of education is to familiarize students with an existing body of truth, of which Christianity and free enterprise are the foundation. "Individualism is dying at Yale," he declared, "and without a fight."[*]

The notion that those that are wealthy somehow steal their wealth from the rest of society is a falsehood not only in political theory, but also in reality. A colleague of ours recently had the opportunity to spend a workweek with one of Apple's real vice presidents. He observed a man who worked 24/7. He would work nonstop from 6:30 a.m. until midnight, eating meals on the run and barely taking a moment's rest. He would then often be awakened at 2:00 a.m. to answer critical emails from China or participate in a brainstorming session during his "off time." This notion that rich people do nothing but play golf, vacation, and hang out with their buddies is pure fantasy. The only ones that indulge in that behavior appear to be high-level politicians, who think nothing of wasting millions of taxpayers' dollars to fly their families, security details, and straphangers to exotic golfing locales.

The concept of property rights is essential to a well-functioning republic. However, it is always tempting for a government to take from its people what it wants. The more powerful the government, the more likely it will take what it wants with little input from those who own what it wants. This is a natural progression, and can be seen throughout history. As governments grow and become more powerful, they, like all of us, want to increase their power even more. More is never enough. Money through taxation is the most common method for gaining control. This movement to consolidate power and money may be studied by watching the rise to power of the Nazis in Germany. Brutal pragmatism and egalitarianism are rapidly trumping individualism and private property rights.

To guard against such evils, our founding fathers recognized that a moral populace was a necessary vanguard against the lies of political hucksters and the evils governments are capable of doing. But, if Americans believe that only the two-dimensional Nazis, like those seen on black-and-white film clips from the 1930s and 1940s, are capable of barbaric pragmatism, they

---

[*] Edwards, Lee, "William F. Buckley, Jr.: A Conservative Icon," *The Heritage Foundation*, December 18, 2012.

need only read the writings of Peter Singer and other modern philosophers who support infanticide and animal rights* over human life itself. Singer, whose writings are sometimes given as reading assignments to our college students, wrote that "human babies are not born self-aware, or capable of grasping that they exist over time. They are not persons ... [therefore] the life of a newborn is of less value than the life of a pig, a dog, or a chimpanzee."†

While studying and assessing diverse points of view may be important to a well-rounded education, absent the critical thinking skills that a firm grounding in the cardinal virtues and the natural law provides, a student may very well become desensitized to, or even accept, such violent, strange, and evil ideologies. The step to actual infanticide or forced euthanasia is very small indeed. Absent virtue's footholds, which provide humankind the abilities to cope with life's vicissitudes, the slide toward a throwaway society is short and steep.

Even the lives of postpartum human beings are now denigrated below those of animals. Witness the silence of Americans when confronted with mass murders in Rwanda, contrasted with their screaming outrage when a professional footballer engages in dogfighting and a small number of Staffordshire Terriers are maimed or killed. Or, in 2007, the months of media coverage over the death by drug overdose of Anna Nicole Smith, who married a multimillionaire 60 years her senior, while a living saint, Mother Teresa of Calcutta, died with relatively little fanfare.

All of this occurs under the false banner of reproductive rights or other contrived gibberish that modernity invents in an attempt to silence the voices of its individual and collective conscience. To do otherwise would make people feel bad or sad. Modernity and progressivism seek fleeting happiness and assiduously avoid personal responsibility. On the other hand, those living maturely and virtuously seek joy in the face of sacrifice and suffering. Consequently, modernity is an easy sell to Americans not raised in virtuous households and used to immediate gratification. That, in a nutshell, is why virtuous leadership and its lifestyles are so important to the continued strength and health of our great republic. It is the last counterweight to the excesses of progressivism's social, economic, and moral failures.

---

* This is not to say that those engaged in efforts to stop animal cruelty are not cognizant or sympathetic toward human sufferings, but there is a peculiar correlation between the numbers in extreme animal rights groups (like PETA) and those that aggressively promote late-term abortion mills.

† Singer, Peter, *Practical Ethics*, 1st ed. (Cambridge: Cambridge University Press, 1979).

There will be those crass, cynical, and nihilistic news hosts and editors that will scoff at this as being too evangelical or out of touch with the average American. Perhaps so, but if we continue to believe in the fundamental truths as set forth by our creator, and follow that course of right reason, we will prevail. But, it will be no easier today than it was for Thomas Jefferson, Thomas Paine, John Adams, and George Washington.

All of this *directly* impacts the police–populace relationship. If the majority of the populace believes in the importance of private property rights and individual freedoms and civic responsibilities, then their relationship with the police will be one of mutual respect and esteem—so long as the police operate with integrity and within the bounds of the U.S. Constitution. This would be the optimal end state: a virtuous populace and police department. On the other hand, if a large segment of the populace is ignorant, overly reliant on government, and spitefully envious of those that have made good on the American dream, they will be mistrustful of the police and the police will revert to simply being the thin blue line. More dangerously, if our government begins to ignore the private property rights of its citizens, and the police become a coercive foe to otherwise good citizens, then we can quickly spiral into near-civil-war-like chaos.

17

The Power of Link Analysis

In the early 1990s, the Defense Advanced Research Projects Agency (DARPA) began studying methods of using the then-new supercomputers, like the Cray systems, to perform link analysis of telephone numbers dialed by suspected foreign threats (in the vernacular, spies) and terrorists. Link analysis identifies association among known and unknown individuals and then creates a link chart for the user's easy visualization and comprehension. Intelligence analysts can then review network charts to discern patterns of interest (Figure 17.1).

This method requires extensive domain knowledge and information. Consequently, it would be extremely time-consuming if an analyst were manually reviewing such vast amounts of data. But, the use of the supercomputers to quickly sort and analyze data brought an exciting and effective tool to the intelligence community (IC). Such social network analysis diagrams have been highly effective tools that can be used in discerning, tracking, and locating bad actors. Now, the power of supercomputers of the 1990s can be found in portable laptop units. Accordingly, U.S. and coalition military intelligence units can use this technology at the tactical level to identify, track, and locate terrorist cells around the world. This is a perfectly lawful, reasonable, and expected activity.

Remember, though, that such systems require sources of data to analyze. It was the revelation by Edward Snowden (and other leakers)* that National Security Agency (NSA) and other members of the IC were obtaining *all*

---

* The authors condemn Snowden for violating the nondisclosure agreement he signed when agreeing to work within the IC. The harm he has done to our republic is incalculable. None of the information contained within these pages discloses classified information. Rather, we have relied on open-source news reports and information commonly found on the Internet. We stand by our nation's authority and obligation to conduct intelligence activities necessary to be forewarned against attacks by foreign governments, nonstate actors, or individual "lone wolf" terrorists. The tools available to the IC, however, may not be appropriate for domestic law enforcement's use.

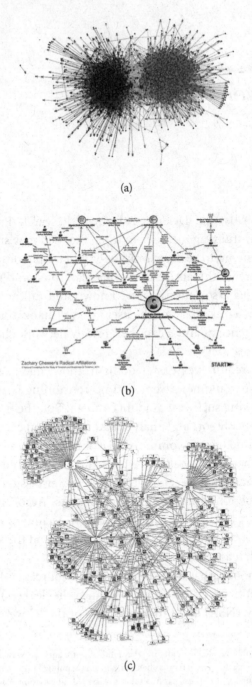

(a)

(b)

(c)

FIGURE 17.1

The Gordian knot depicted above is a graph showing how computer-driven link analysis works. Modern algorithms can take huge amounts of seemingly unrelated data—like telephone call records—and find common nodes or related suspects.

telephone-dialed number data that alarmed most Americans. Without a warrant, probable cause, or even articulable reasonable suspicion (the lowest threshold of suspicion required for law enforcement to temporally detain or begin a search process), intelligence agencies are acquiring all telephone data from all of the nation's common carriers, such as AT&T, Verizon, and T-Mobile. Now, if such information was cordoned off, kept private, and used only to identify terrorists or foreign intelligence agents and sources, most Americans would be pleased—in other words, who doesn't expect that our intelligence community is doing this?

The more serious question is, who else within the administrative branches of our government is doing this type of data mining? The answer is out there in the wide open and is probably constitutionally permissible, but no one is asking the right questions and understanding the depth of the constitutional concerns that should be self-evident.

For instance, starting well before 9/11, diverse law enforcement agencies within the Department of Justice began experimenting with supercomputers, data, and link analysis algorithms. These programs collected an almost *unlimited* number of toll call data records from nearly all telephone service providers in the United States using the administrative subpoena process. Such subpoenas are not judicially reviewed. Rather, they are simply letters written on agency letterhead declaring that the information or records sought have a nexus to suspected illicit narcotics or other criminal activity. The obvious problem is that no such suspicion or nexus existed for the *all* of the information sought! Conceivably, like us all being six degrees from Kevin Bacon, everyone has a nexus to drug dealers. But, the reality was (and is) that law enforcement was simply sucking in all metadata regardless of any criminal nexus.

These near-daily "takes" of all phone calls made to and within the United States were processed by the supercomputers, which performed complex link analysis algorithms that "connected the dots" among suspected drug lords and underlings. None of this was done with the requisite probable cause under the Fourth Amendment to the Constitution. Now here is the concern. Instead of openly providing the results of the analysis to agents in the field, the agencies involved set up an elaborate shell game, whereby intelligence analysts would "pass over the fence" so-called tips and leads to the supervisors within regional investigative offices. In turn, the supervisors would tell teams of agents working for them, "You may want to take a look at person of interest X based on reliable information that he is involved in the drug trade." The agents, knowing that they had a proven source of information, would reverse-engineer a case against a defendant. None of these activities were ever provided to defense counsel as required under *Brady v. United States*. Of perhaps more concern, none were being provided to the prosecuting attorneys.

As reported by *Forbes* magazine, accordingly to a former federal agent, the tip system works as follows:

> "You'd be told only, 'Be at a certain truck stop at a certain time and look for a certain vehicle.' And so we'd alert the state police to find an excuse to stop that vehicle, and then have a drug dog search it."
>
> When the … tip leads to an arrest, the agents then *pretend* that the drug bust was the surprise result of pulling the vehicle over as a routine traffic stop.
>
> So secretive is the program, (it) requires that agents lie to the judges, prosecuting attorneys and defense attorneys involved in a trial of a defendant busted as a result of (the) surveillance—a complete and clear violation of every American's right to due process, even when that American is a low-life drug dealer.
>
> Every criminal defendant is entitled to the legitimate data and facts surrounding their arrest so that their counsel can examine the propriety of the arrest and attack procedures that may be improper and illegal under the law in defense of their client. When sensitive, classified data is involved in such a case (data possibly collected in surveillance of a foreign national that reveals incriminating evidence involving an American), it is the prerogative of the judge to decide what should and should not be admitted into evidence.[*]

So, for decades it appears that law enforcement has been doing domestically what NSA has recently been accused of doing against foreign adversaries and governments. They have vacuumed up nearly all of the domestic telephone call record data—every phone call, cellular or landline, you may have made—and used it to crunch data and perform link analysis.

If you thought your records were private absent probable cause, think again. In 1978, the U.S. Supreme Court established a concept known as third-party doctrine. That doctrine holds that records held by a third party, such as the call records held by a phone company, are *not* covered by the Fourth Amendment.[†] Such a ruling, made in 1979 when wiretaps were manually installed and officers collected call records via pen registers,

---

[*] Ungar, Rick, "More Surveillance Abuse Exposed! Special DEA Unit Is Spying on Americans and Covering It Up," *Forbes*, August 5, 2013.

[†] *Smith v. Maryland*, 442 U.S. 735 (1979).

could never have anticipated the invasive and powerful nature of the Internet and supercomputers. Moreover, despite what the consensus of judges may rule, the authors seriously doubt that the average, reasonable American believes that the Fourth Amendment should protect whom and when she calls another private citizen. And the "What do you have to hide?" argument is specious, circular, and very dangerous. People would be well served to remember that the greatest threat to their personal safety, security, and lives has been governments, not criminals. That is why our founding fathers drafted and ratified our Bill of Rights.

Our adversarial system of justice requires that the government (prosecution) and defense work on a level playing field. Courtroom drama—the "surprise" witness—is a Hollywood plot device. The U.S. Supreme Court, as well as every state's highest courts of appeal, has required full disclosure of potentially exculpatory evidence to a defendant:

> The American criminal justice system prides itself as being based on fundamental fairness. Although adversarial by nature, the system includes protections and practices intended to even the playing field between prosecutor and defendant, including such constitutional safeguards as the presumption of innocence and proof beyond a reasonable doubt. The Founders' grave concern with protecting the accused against abuses by the government can be seen in the very structure of the Bill of Rights, in which four of the ten amendments are devoted to guaranteeing the criminally accused fair process and proceedings. In 1963, the Supreme Court pronounced another constitutional tenet designed to equalize opportunity between prosecutor and defendant. In the landmark case of *Brady v. Maryland*, the Court found that criminal defendants have a due process right to receive materially exculpatory evidence in the prosecution's possession. In its opinion, the Court ardently invoked the principles of fairness and justice, and the *Brady* Court's directive seems clear: If the prosecution has evidence that is material to the defendant's innocence, the prosecution, in the interest of fairness, must give it to the defendant.[*]

The only exceptions to this are legitimate cases where disclosure of a source is not material to the guilt or innocence of the defendant and would endanger an innocent source. For instance, when a "concerned citizen" tips off the police as to suspected criminal activity, in order to protect the safety and security of law-abiding citizens, courts have ruled that the

---

[*] Dodds, Emily Jane, "I'll Make You a Deal: How Repeat Informants Are Corrupting the Criminal Justice System and What to Do About It," *William & Mary Law Review, 50*(3), 2008.

government does not have to expose or identify that concerned citizen. But, *Brady* material or evidence the prosecutor is required to disclose under this rule includes any evidence favorable to the accused, evidence that goes toward negating a defendant's guilt, evidence that would reduce a defendant's potential sentence, or evidence going to the credibility of a witness. Thousands of defendants are imprisoned without their or, more importantly, their defense counsel's knowledge of the source or veracity of the government's case against them. More disturbingly, it appears that some special agents involved in these operations lied and deceived the assistant U.S. attorneys (AUSAs) responsible for prosecuting the cases. So, even if the AUSAs wanted to comply with *Brady* and other procedural rules of disclosure, they couldn't have because they too were completely in the dark about the program.

This is not a case whereby there was a giant government conspiracy to spy on Americans. Rather, it was a case of false assumptions by many, combined with a lack of integrity by a few, that transformed a valuable tool into one that possibly tarnished the agency. But, overarching all of these details is a basic question that should have been asked by many: Regardless of the relative lawfulness of the act, how would the average American feel knowing that a domestic law enforcement agency was obtaining, compiling, and retaining everyone's individual phone records?

This book is about the trust and bond between the police and populace that must exist if we are to live in a free, safe, and secure society. Secret activities, no matter how well intentioned, create a level of mistrust that is not healthy for our republic. Such activities are necessary to protect us from our foreign enemies, but they are inherently wrong to use against U.S. citizens in the regular course of law enforcement business. "But, we are locking up dirtbag drug dealers!" is the hue and cry that we hear from some of our closest colleagues in law enforcement. That is generally true, but how do we know that the asset forfeiture divisions of these agencies are lawfully, fairly, and in accordance with due process seizing monies and properties that are truly fruits of the drug trade? The need to find sources of funding in fiscally austere environments can make otherwise good, decent persons get overly creative in order to feed the beast.

If everything is not transparent, we are simply left with the option of "Trust us. We are the government!" This, from a government that has recently brought us Lois Lerner's Internal Revenue Service (IRS) that was fiscally targeting Americans because of their political beliefs. Or, former White House chief of staff Rahm Emanuel's infamous statement,

"You never want a serious crisis to go to waste. And what I mean by that is an opportunity to do things you think you could not do before."* Then, using armed Department of Homeland Security tactical teams to raid a citizen for allegedly importing a Land Rover Defender SUV that was not Environmental Protection Agency (EPA) compliant! Such hubris is exactly what our founding fathers warned against:

> Our governments seem the most susceptible to the disease of too easily writing and passing an excessive number of new laws.
>
> *Publius*†

Power always sincerely, conscientiously, *de très bon foi*, believes itself right. Power always thinks it has a great soul and vast views, beyond the comprehension of the weak.

John Adams, letter to Thomas Jefferson, February 2, 1816

Such hubris, recklessness, and power must be reined in by the other branches of government, or the populace will rein it in by civil disobedience, black market sales, and potential violence of action. If the average citizen believes that he or she is being unlawfully screened, prodded, processed, or surveyed—barely tolerable at airports—the likelihood of him or her seeking redress through other than political means is heightened. We do not want to see this happen in our sacred republic. But, law enforcement agencies cannot turn a deaf ear to such concerns by trying to marginalize voices of dissent and reason. They must now take a virtuous, contemplative look in the mirror or risk being marginalized.

Do not misread this chapter. The authors wholeheartedly support law enforcement in general and the many brave special agents of the Drug Enforcement Administration (DEA) with whom we have fought shoulder to shoulder in Afghanistan and other wretched places on earth. Our critique and commentary is not directed at such fine individuals. Rather, this chapter is written as a bellwether and safety valve, warning of a larger system gone awry. The very essence of integrity, exemplified by former FBI director Louis Freeh or former DEA director Jack Lawn, is being worn thin. Absent the guiding internal moral compass afforded by the cardinal

---

* Motley, Seton, "Rahm Emanuel: Don't waste a 'Serious Crisis,'" MRCTV News, November 21, 2008. See also McQueary, Kristen, "If Only Chicago Were in Crisis," *Chicago Tribune*, April 2, 2015.

† As the anonymous authors of *The Federalist Papers* were called, now known to be Alexander Hamilton, James Madison, and John Jay. They too were worried about this contingency.

virtues, a coercive and all-knowing government is not a recipe for freedom. Despite all the great intentions and results, there are simply some things a government does *not* need to know. Absent probable cause, those with whom we communicate, and from where we initiate and receive such calls, should remain invisible.

Where does the appetite for information stop? Our health records, income tax filings, property records—everything about us—are now digitized and easily accessed by law enforcement, as well as other less benign state and nonstate actors. We are not advocating building Faraday cages and wearing tinfoil hats, but too many Americans have fought and died to preserve our fundamental liberties. Political or law enforcement expediency is not a reason to surrender them.

18

The Ugly and the Good in Police Reformation

Reforms in American policing need to be driven by factual, peer-reviewed science and led by virtuous leaders. This chapter primarily examines the good practices of the New Haven, Connecticut, Police Department, as it properly uses both scientific advances, like comparative statistics (COMSTAT), and virtuous leadership to lessen crime and heal wounds in its neighborhoods. New Haven is to be applauded in its efforts to bring about a healthy police–populace relationship. Using race-neutral methodologies to police and heal some of its neighborhoods facing higher rates of crime, it is a model of success in a truly diverse city.

But, before we get to the good of this chapter, we wish to address an egregious ugly example of both junk science and impious leadership by no less than America's attorney general and the Department of Justice (DOJ). We are hesitant to fire this salvo for fear of immediately alienating potential readers who are supporters of the current administration, but the mistakes the current attorney general has made have set police–populace relations in America back by two decades. And this is a shame, as we believe that a crucial opportunity for healing race relations at this stage of America's history was squandered. The failure in this regard is the 800-pound gorilla in the room that hardly anyone in mainstream academia wants to address.

But, former New York City mayor Rudy Giuliani recognized this failure implicitly in the following statement:

> "We've had four months of propaganda starting with the president that everybody should hate the police," Giuliani said during an appearance on Fox News early Sunday. "The protests are being embraced, the protests are being encouraged. The protests, even the ones that don't lead to violence,

a lot of them lead to violence, all of them lead to a conclusion: The police are bad, the police are racist. That is completely wrong."[*]

Entire books could be written examining his biases and examples of poor leadership at the Department of Justice, but the following story concerning its investigations and studies of local and state agencies alleging racial bias are nothing short of Orwellian in their scope and nature. Instead of encouraging cultural assimilation, unity, and any notions of personal responsibility within all of America's communities, the DOJ has flamed the fires of racial hatred and mistrust, resulting in more tribalism and racial fault lines.

While every hen believes she has laid the best egg, the authors believe that there are fundamental rights and wrongs that truly civilized societies must follow. These truths are founded in the natural law and rights of man. Efforts to unravel America's constitutional unity by highlighting individuals' immutable characteristics are intrinsically evil and ugly.

THE UGLY

In New York City, just as he had done to departments in Seattle, St. Louis, and New Orleans (and dozens of other agencies), Attorney General Eric Holder is mandating that cops be subjected to "de-biasing" training. In these cases, federal trainers—at heaven knows what costs to the American taxpayer—attempt to teach cops to think twice about stopping or questioning suspects of color, potentially ignoring signs of criminal behavior and preassaultive threat indicators the police have learned from years of street experience. Not only does such hesitation place the officers' lives in greater danger—as suspects are already ahead of the action-reaction power curve—but it also increases risks to the safety and sanctity of society.

Under the current attorney general, the Justice Department's Civil Rights Division shifted its attention from prosecuting *intentional* discrimination to investigating such concepts such as unconscious or implicit bias. It is all part of the attorney general's efforts to reform the criminal justice system to fit a particular set of prejudices and biases. According to open-source

---

[*] Sink, Justin, "Obama's 'Propaganda' Pushed People to 'Hate the Police,' Giuliani Says," *The Hill*, December 21, 2014.

information, including the DOJ's own records, the department has more than doubled the number of police department probes that were conducted in the previous administration. Since 2009, the Department of Justice has opened more than 20 sweeping investigations of entire departments, resulting in 15 of those agencies having to submit to consent orders to stop "biased policing" and other alleged violations. Therein lies the problem. The only evidence of bias was raw data: data that simply showed that police stopped or investigated proportionally more Black suspects than White. The data did not note whether there was underlying criminal behavior that may have prompted this disparity. In other words, the investigations make an unsupported assumption that Black citizens are disproportionately stopped, relative to the Black crime rate. While it is true, as we argued earlier, that officers can learn from their experiences, and that sometimes this learning can be biased, it is not at all clear that the Black crime rate, which is much higher than the non-Black crime rate, is not the appropriate cause of this disparity.

What's truly striking about these federally mandated consent orders is the total lack of evidence or peer-reviewed science that would show that these agencies stopped and arrested Black people simply because of such bias. The investigators simply assumed that the raw numbers themselves demonstrated bias rather than the very real possibility that the minority suspects actually committed crimes. In other words, the investigators came into the study with a preconceived belief that officers were engaging in a "pattern and practice" of discrimination toward Blacks. This, in fact, is a very real source of bias against police.

DOJ based its findings on its dogged belief in implicit bias, which argues that cops subconsciously discriminate in making disproportionate stops of non-Whites. Stated plainly, the DOJ and the attorney general were projecting their own bias onto the officers they were supposed to be objectively investigating!

"Biased policing," the DOJ explained in its findings letter to the Seattle PD, "is not primarily about the ill-intentioned officer but rather the officer who engages in discriminatory practices subconsciously," adding that even a well-meaning cop can violate the civil rights of Black suspects by operating "on implicit biases that impact that officer's behavior or perceptions." The letter went on to say "many in the community perceive that pedestrian stops are overused and target minorities." While this may be the perception of the community, the facts underlying this perception were never challenged. DOJ admits it couldn't verify the accuracy of the complaints and never even bothered to get the officers' side of the story. So, the U.S. Department of Justice based its entire report on the subjective perceptions of an unruly populace rather than the results of an objective finding of fact based on evidence. This scandalous activity by DOJ is detailed by writer Paul Sperry in his *New York Post* article of December 7, 2014. In relevant parts it says:

> Some of the directives are bizarre. In Las Vegas, police have banned patrol officers from touching African-American suspects during foot chases. Only partners uninvolved in the chase can step in and use force to arrest the fleeing perp.
>
> In Fayetteville, NC, where Justice started retraining cops in October, searches of black suspects are no longer allowed—even when the suspect gives consent. "Hot-spot" policing in high-crime neighborhoods is also considered biased against blacks.
>
> Social psychologist Lorie Fridell is credited with pioneering the "unconscious bias" theory in policing. She developed her "Fair and Impartial Policing" program with generous grants from Holder's department and has trained officers in more than 250 precincts and agencies across the country, including Seattle's.
>
> Like Holder, Fridell wants to ban all criminal profiling that takes a suspect's race into account. She believes legal definitions of unlawful discrimination are "outdated" and should be broadened to include even unquantifiable prejudice against people of color that occurs "outside our conscious awareness."
>
> While Fridell admits the link between blacks and crime is statistically strong—African Americans commit 53% of all murders and are 10 times more likely to commit violent crimes than whites—she trains cops to resist that "stereotype."
>
> By retraining cops' minds to perceive blacks as less of a threat, Fridell hopes they'll be less likely to use lethal force against black suspects.
>
> An inherent problem with her theory is that she has never produced empirical results to prove her theories actually work to reduce actual discriminatory policing. She admits it's impossible to look at the actions of an individual cop and know for certain they were influenced by prejudice.
>
> Some local black law enforcement officials say the notion cops target blacks out of bigotry is wrong. "Every complaint I've ever gotten that suggests that an officer is out there making stops and making law-enforcement decisions based solely on race has turned [out] not to be true," said Milwaukee County Sheriff David Clarke, a Democrat.[*]

* Sperry, Paul, "Eric Holder Believes All Cops Are Racists, Targets 'Unconscious Bias,'" *New York Post*, December 7, 2014.

Until proven, such junk science has no place in modern police reforms *unless* subjected to peer-reviewed analysis and backed up by hard evidence. But, "never let the facts get in the way of political agenda" appears to be the watchword for today's DOJ, where the inmates appear to have taken over the asylum. In the meantime, Fridell's consulting services are in high demand, as chiefs of police throughout America scurry to appease their sometimes well-intentioned but often factually ignorant political bosses and populaces. The effect of such orders on the police who are entrusted with serving the population is apparently not of concern to the DOJ.

Here are some of those facts that society, as a whole, must address if there are to be any meaningful improvements to police–populace relationships and crime rates in our communities. Otherwise, solutions such as Fridell's are akin to giving a glass of sweet iced tea to someone with a sucking chest wound. These problems require society at large and departments specifically to return to the cardinal virtues as anchor points for a better world that is based on the principles of the natural law, not vacillating laws and whims of man.

- *Disintegration of the nuclear family as the root cause of African American poverty and crime.* When LBJ initiated his Great Society and "war on poverty" in the 1960s, the out-of-wedlock birth rate for Black Americans was 25%. Fifty years later, after the passage of the Civil Rights Act, $15 trillion spent on welfare programs, and the election of America's first non-White president, over 70% of Black children are born out of wedlock. Consequently, unemployment and poverty remain far higher for Blacks than for the rest of America.
- *High crime rate among young Black males.* While most violent crime is intraracial (e.g., Black-on-Black or White-on-White), in interracial (e.g., Black-on-White or White-on-Black) circumstances—homicides against strangers—Blacks (24.7 offenders per 100,000) are seven times more likely to be offenders than are Whites (3.4 offenders per 100,000). Stated more simply: Whites are simply far more likely to be victims of interracial crime than Blacks. That, of course, didn't stop Jesse Jackson from telling the *Los Angeles Times* at the height of the Trayvon Martin frenzy that "targeting, arresting, convicting blacks and ultimately killing us is big business."* Why is this? Society needs to turn down such hateful and false rhetoric and start talking

---

* Lynch, Renee, "Trayvon Martin Case: 'Blacks Are Under Attack,' Says Jesse Jackson," *The Los Angeles Times*, March 23, 2012.

facts instead of fictions. News outlets repeatedly state words such as "White officer shoots unarmed Black male" when there are no indicia that racial animus played a role in these cases. But, hatred sells news and the truth be damned.

- *Media bias in underreporting Black-on-White crime.* One reason that the George Zimmerman–Trayvon Martin case garnered so much attention was the unusual nature of a White man allegedly accosting a Black teen (as a "man bites dog" story). Sadly, when it comes to interracial crime, the reverse is anything but rare. But, mainstream media outlets are loath to report the suspects' race in cases of Black-on-White violence. It is because such cases are so rampant as not to be newsworthy (as "dog bites man" stories) that they are ordinarily totally ignored by the press.

For example, the DOJ was silent when the following officers were killed in the line of duty:

- Detective Melvin Santiago, a Jersey City police officer who was shot to death on July 13, 2014. Santiago was White. His killer, Lawrence Campbell, was Black. Does anyone recall any national figure appearing before national television and calling for justice for Officer Santiago's family? Does anyone recall the attorney general rushing to Jersey City to see that justice was done?
- Officer Jeffrey Westerfield of Gary, Indiana, who was shot to death on July 6, 2014. Officer Westerfield was White, while his killer, Carl LeEllis Blount Jr., was Black.
- Officer Perry Renn was an Indianapolis, Indiana, police officer who was shot to death on July 5, 2014. Officer Renn was White. His killer, Major Davis, was Black.
- Two men gunned down Deputy Sheriff Allen Bares of Vermilion Parish, Louisiana, on June 23, 2014. Deputy Bares was White. His two killers, Quintlan Richard and Baylon Taylor, were Black.
- Detective Charles Dinwiddie of the Killeen, Texas, Police Department Special Weapons and Tactics (SWAT) team was murdered on May 11, 2014, by Marvin Lewis Guy, a Black male. Officer Dinwiddie was White.

These are just a few of the many law enforcement officers—of all races—killed in the line of duty by Black suspects in only 2014. Did anyone bother to appear on national television to express condolences or concern over these deaths? Or how about when 13-month-old Antonio West was shot in the face at point-blank range by two Black teens who were attempting to rob the child's mother: Where was President Obama, Attorney General Holder, or Reverend Al Sharpton in this case? One can hardly believe that their silence was emblematic of anything but their own racial bias. This must stop. It causes enormous damage to the social contract between our police and the people they serve by so selectively ignoring deaths caused by Black criminals, and only attending to those deaths of Black persons. Even those are ignored if they are committed by Black criminals.

Unspeakable acts of violence perpetrated by Black offenders on White victims rarely get much media attention. While poverty is still a significant problem in urban America, and a failed war on drugs does have a disproportionate impact on those poorer communities, neither of these factors can fully explain the troubling spike in Black criminal behavior that only genuine leadership and self-examination can eventually solve.

We uniformly condemn individuals, even a president, who project their overt racism and inflammatory rhetoric into every use-of-force incident where they can insinuate themselves. Their actions incite rioting, looting, and violence; the police and firefighters and communities are left to deal with these problems, while the Sharptons fly off to their next campaign of ignorance. Society should stop giving a voice to these parasites and start listening to voices of character within their communities. Otherwise, problems like Ferguson will become self-licking ice cream cones of violence, resentment, and ignorance.

America must tone down its rhetoric and ramp up factually based investigations. Truth and time salve most wounds, but in the meantime, those that spew racial hatred and lies must be called out for the charlatans they are. Race of either a suspect or an officer should remain an irrelevancy absent some clear evidence of malice aforethought.

Recommendation: Instead of reacting to a mob or agenda-driven personalities like Sharpton, police leaders and policy advisors need to get ahead of the information cycle of the news: in essence, beat the hate mongers to the punch by making fact-based and confidence-inducing statements that are grounded in truth. And, then they should follow up initial statements with any new facts as soon as possible. It is reasonable to do so, and communities expect it. We believe, in accordance with the cardinal virtues of courage, competency, self-control, and justice, that law enforcement leadership should not shrink away from the press and public and speak factually when addressing officer-involved shooting (OIS) cases within their jurisdictions. Truth does set people free, bad news does not get better with age, and the overwhelming majority of the public will rightly give officers the benefit of ·

the doubt. As explained by Brian Willis, a former Calgary police officer and an internationally recognized expert on police training, "no comment" is not an option in today's world of information wars:

"No comment."

Those are the "two most dangerous words" a law enforcement administrator or spokesperson can utter these days after an officer-involved shooting, Refusal to provide information on a major force event "will be interpreted as a cover-up," Willis explains, "and often becomes the tipping point for determining how an incident plays out in a community."

On other types of incidents, "police give the facts as they know them and talk about the ongoing investigation," Willis says. When they refuse to do that after an OIS, it "opens the door for self-appointed and alleged experts, politicians, and special interest groups to comment. And their comments are often based on rumor, innuendo, speculation—always based on emotion, rarely based on facts."

"Within the law enforcement community, 'no comment' should no longer be acceptable," Willis declares. Police executives "need to have the courage to give the facts as they know them," with the assurance that corrections will be made if necessary as the investigation progresses.[*]

Tolerance, freedom from racial prejudice, and understanding are a two-way street. Police officers nationwide are deeply incredulous of intolerant leaders who pander to racial interests instead of the freedom of the truth. The New York Police Department's police union publicly denounced Mayor Bill de Blasio, who openly claimed that his biracial children were at risk of being shot by law enforcement officers. The authors applaud the courage of the union members for rebuking such nonsense. Martin Luther King famously and virtuously proclaimed that people should be judged "by the content of their character, not the color of their skin." How is it that, 50 years later, society's leaders have failed to grasp and communicate this sane and righteous message?

Race-focused pronouncements by public officials lend credence and give a passive imprimatur to those persons bent on violence. The cold-blooded, premeditated murder of two NYPD officers, Rafael Ramos and Wenjian Liu, on December 20, 2014, was the indirect result of how many of America's so-called leaders responded to the earlier events in Ferguson and New York City, where two criminal suspects died while resisting

---

[*] Remsberg, Chuck, "Law Enforcement's '2 Most Dangerous Words' in Today's Tense Times," *Force Science News* #271, Mankato, MN: Force Science Institute, December 17, 2015.

arrest. Instead of immediately coming out as a voice of reason and calm, these three public officials made lukewarm pronouncements that vilified police officers and inflamed an already bad situation.

It is unclear exactly what federal laws were at stake in either Ferguson or New York to provoke statements by either the president or the attorney general. But, if they felt the need to say anything, they should have simply stated, "We will examine the facts, as they become known, under the light of applicable law. If violations of federal law appear to have occurred, we will support appropriate prosecutions. In the meantime, law enforcement will not tolerate violent protests, looting, or rioting: Such acts will be met with the quick and overwhelming force necessary to protect innocent life, limb, and property." Instead, they equivocated to such a degree that their statements were interpreted as critical of the officers involved and the rule of law itself.

This, in turn, gave impetus to Ramos and Liu's killer, 28-year-old Ismaaiyl Brinsley, to vow in an Instagram post to put "wings on pigs" as retaliation for the deaths of Black men at the hands of White police. Brinsley is a classic failure of our criminal justice system. He had at least 19 arrests in Georgia and Ohio, spent two years in prison for gun possession, and had a troubled childhood so violent that his mother was afraid of him, police said. He ranted online about authority figures and expressed "self-despair and anger at himself and where his life was." His killings of Officers Rafael Ramos and Wenjian Liu heightened fears about the safety of law enforcement officials nationwide that are unabated as of this writing.

Brinsley shot the two cops dead as they sat in a patrol car in Bedford-Stuyvesant, allegedly to avenge the deaths of Michael Brown in Ferguson and Eric Garner in New York City. Earlier the same day, he also shot his former girlfriend at her home in a Northwest Baltimore suburb.* The cold-blooded cop hater is suspected of being a member of a notorious prison gang, the Black Guerrilla Family (BGF), which has declared open season on the NYPD.

One source said that Baltimore police were already investigating Brinsley's connection to the BGF gang, which started in California's San Quentin Prison in the 1960s by Black Panther member George Jackson. BGF has been talking about getting back at cops for the Eric Garner and Michael Brown killings, according to law enforcement intelligence intercepted in Baltimore area prisons. Brinsley boasted on social media about wanting to kill cops

---

* Coincidentally, that shooting was only blocks from where author Bolgiano, when serving as a police officer, shot a robbery suspect at a McDonald's restaurant.

hours before ambushing two police officers on a Saturday afternoon as they sat in their patrol car outside the Tompkins Houses in Bedford-Stuyvesant.

All of this comes full circle, as the BGF also supported the Nation of Islam and its leader, Louis Farrakhan. This is the same Farrakhan who incited his audience to kill "two for one" during his state-funded speech at Morgan State University in Baltimore.

Following the murders of Officers Ramos and Liu, Attorney General Holder said something the authors agree with:

> "Our nation must always honor the valor—and the sacrifices—of all law enforcement officers with a steadfast commitment to keeping them safe," Holder said. "This means forging closer bonds between officers and the communities they serve, so that public safety is not a cause that is served by a courageous few, but a promise that's fulfilled by police officials and citizens working side by side."

We are afraid it is too little, too late.

In response to the murderous actions of the cop killer in New York City, many otherwise good officers have become indignant and even bellicose. Some suggested pulling back all police support for a few weeks of cooling off. Conversely, others suggested an all-out war on these neighborhoods. It is hard for the police to remember, given all the animus put forth by senior political leaders, that most of the citizens, even in these areas, are good people, not rioters or murderers. An experienced former SWAT commander[*] and shift lieutenant from the Baltimore Police Department offered the following sage advice:

> Well it's not that bad, these areas can easily be controlled by competent aggressive police work. Unfortunately, there are many factors that prevent this in the new era:
>
> 1. Politicians who love to second-guess cops
> 2. Lack of competent police to do the aggressive work (10% do 90% of the work)
> 3. Lack of support from command
> 4. A half-ass criminal justice system that will actually give a violent offender low or no bail

---

[*] This officer, retired from municipal police work, is still working for the government in an important counterterror position. As such, he will remain anonymous, but he is a dear friend of all three of the authors. More police commanders should possess his vision and temperament.

An aggressively run shift, one whose supervisors go out and *actively* participate in policing the area, can put a serious hurting on all open-air drug activity and violent crime.

Too many people are on police forces just for a job and not to do police work anymore.

We could think of no better introduction to the following good news out of New Haven, Connecticut, where Chief Esserman is doing much of what our friend from Baltimore suggests.

THE GOOD

Our friend Gary, who related the story about his grandfather's experiences with Babe Ruth as a peace officer in New Jersey, first told us about New Haven's police department and the innovative leadership of Dean Esserman. A retired soldier and senior executive service leader at the Defense Intelligence Agency (DIA), Gary is one of our republic's finest warriors and leaders in the field of counterterrorism and intelligence "field craft." Almost by happenstance, during a conversation about policing in modern America, Gary related that he recently had the opportunity to sit in on a COMSTAT briefing in New Haven. He was so upbeat about what he saw that had it come from a lesser source, we would have been incredulous. But, Gary's word is his bond, so we followed up and secured an invitation to travel to New Haven and meet the chief of police, Dean Esserman. It was time well spent, for finally we can report some good news as a counterweight to Ferguson and its collateral events.

The New Haven Police Department seems to have "cracked the code" on integrating technologies like COMSTAT with the human performance dynamics of community policing.

New Haven, Connecticut, with a population of 129,779 people, is the second-largest city in Connecticut after Bridgeport. With 47,094 households and 25,854 families, its population density is 6,859.8 people per square mile (2,648.6 per square kilometer). The racial makeup of the city is 42.6% White, 35.4% Black, 27.4% Hispanic or Latino, 0.5% Native American, 4.6% Asian, 0.1% Pacific Islander, 12.9% from other races, and 3.9% from two or more races. Chief Esserman speaks with virtue and calm to the whole of that community in his message on the department's website:

> We are dedicated to ensuring a safe and inclusive environment throughout the city of New Haven by reinitiating and revitalizing its community-based policing strategies throughout each of the city's neighborhoods.
>
> These strategies are built upon our commitment to professionalism, fairness, integrity and community partnerships, and this web site will be used to facilitate increased collaboration and communication between the New Haven Police Department and our community. The New Haven Police Department strives to reduce crime, increase safety, and create solutions to challenges affecting each of our city's diverse districts.

There is every reason to believe Dean Esserman's sincerity and methodology. He has brought the whole of government to bear on New Haven's crime problem and is also a strong proponent of true community policing. A visit to one of his weekly COMSTAT briefings is a clue that this leader understands how to use this statistical tool: not as a whipping post for subordinates, but as a measure of the landscape on which to overlay police, probation officers, federal agencies, child welfare case officers, prosecutors, and all of the other non-law enforcement solutions to a particular problem. Most police departments who have copied the COMSTAT model—of which Esserman was in on the ground floor of designing while serving in New York City under Commissioner Bratton—only convene monthly or quarterly. It is then that it often devolves into a toxic leadership tool where leaders are only looking at numbers, not correlations. New Haven's department meets weekly.

Chief Esserman has learned that a relatively small number of people in each community are actual "bad actors," and he focuses enforcement on managing those malefactors. Sometimes straightforward arrests and incarcerations are in order. Other times, just getting an addict into an effective treatment program kills the individual's need for a fix, consequently ending his need to steal in order to feed the beast of his addiction. The results have been not only a reduction in criminal activity, but also a healthier police–populace relationship.

But, New Haven's chief of police offers much more to his community than just a better way of reducing crime statistics. He brings a mature, introspective, and academic personality to bear on complex problems of society, both the internal society of the police department and the greater society they serve. Speaking as a guest speaker at the Yale School of Management's CEO Summit, he acknowledged to the crowd that there are always two narratives to any given problem. He reminded the audience that the victors tell one history, and another is whispered by the vanquished. That simple saying reminds us that the whole of society must make efforts to see what might be behind flashpoints like Ferguson, Rodney King, Amadou Diallo, or the death of Eric Garner in New York City. These flashpoints, Esserman points out, are merely symptoms of a larger problem. And, as long as we focus on the symptoms, we will never find a cure.

The primary problem is that America continues to define and shape discussions in terms of race—or tribalism, as we call it—instead of in terms of responsibilities as citizens. And, the disease itself is defined by historical legacies that are different for different peoples. Finding common ground for discussion and positive motivations that recognize the attendant duties and responsibilities of citizenship are a must for a unified, safe, and productive America.

Do not misread the authors here. Chief Esserman, no doubt, can be as hard as woodpecker lips when he needs to be as both a cop and a leader. He has no need to prove himself, however, by being a bully cop. Instead, he carries himself with the assuredness of a well-schooled commander. And this, as he notes, can be problematic in law enforcement circles, where rank often trumps knowledge. Law enforcement needs to be changed from leader-centric organizations, where rank trumps knowledge and big trumps small, into organizations where knowledge and success trump historically unsuccessful methods. One way to do this is through what the authors have experienced in special operations: Anyone, no matter the rank or experience, is able to bring new ideas to the table as possible solutions. Only then will true knowledge and critical thinking skills work to solve internal and external problems of policing. And, such an adult learning environment decreases battles between chiefs and cops.

For new recruits, New Haven is probably unique in that the chief requires all rookie officers to walk a beat in one neighborhood for a solid year before branching out into other areas of patrol or more specialized police work. He also tries to teach his commanders that their subordinates will respond better to positive affirmation and peer pressure than coercive leadership. "Catch your cops doing something good and praise them in public for it" was a lesson Esserman learned in New York. Or as we say in the military, "Praise in public, correct in private." He tries to make a point of doing exactly that at COMSTAT and other venues. "Knowledge follows love, not pain and fear," the chief teaches. What a breath of clean, true knowledge that statement in and of itself represents. America needs more of that not only within its police agencies, but also corporately and societally.

Rookies also devolve into the routine of their life as police. That can be bad if it leads to an imbalance where they start to see the world in an "us-versus-them" manner. Esserman realizes that the power of the badge can be intoxicating. He counters this by having each rookie class of officers meet once a month in the chief's conference room during their first year on the beat. They talk among themselves and to him about their trials and tribulations. Each officer has to tell a story from his beat. As the year progresses, the chief notices how the officers mature from inwardly focused individuals to community-focused officers. By the end of the year, they have shared their cell phone numbers with the citizens of their beat and have all become involved in the community as people, not problems. In so doing, they pierce the thin veil of race and color and understand their neighborhoods as fellow citizens.

Societally, Chief Esserman believes that America has suffered because of the lack of a draft. Not that he advocates compulsory military service for everyone, but he believes that programs such as Teach for America can restore the sense of societal "skin in the game" that is missing in many communities.

Police departments also need to stop rewarding mediocrity among their ranks, where seniority is the end state of many careers. He has instituted internal sabbaticals, learning and teaching opportunities, and ways for his officers to blossom into better citizens and cops. This is important, he notes, because the number one mishap is not police shootings, but problems with officers' mouths. The number one complaint, by far, is rudeness and discourteousness. These seemingly minor negative interactions with the public can cascade into a seething hatred and mistrust if left unchecked. This, most likely, is what went unchecked in Ferguson. And, when the officers needed the support of their community, those trust bridges had already been burnt. The social contract that relied on both sides was severely damaged, if not destroyed, in the years that led up to the particular incident that was a flashpoint.

Also, most police shootings occur within the first five years of an officer's career and in off-duty situations. He sadly notes that the number-one killer of police officers is themselves, via suicide. On duty, it is traffic accidents, not shootings. To attenuate these concerns, the chief highlights the importance of mental health and physical fitness among his officers. Fit and sound officers perform better, are less likely to be injured, and have lower suicide rates. The motional survival of his officers is critically important to this police leader. His methods and mindset should be emulated throughout our country.

He admits, however, that the difficulty in achieving such well-intentioned goals is hamstrung by the political realities of becoming and remaining a chief of police. Many chiefs on departments of all sizes go to bed worrying about whether they will be fired the next day due to the poor judgment or performance of one of their subordinates. This, in turn, can lead to an oppressive zero-defect micromanagement leadership model. In those cases, chiefs do not trust their officers and, consequently, do not allow the officers the degree of discretion and judgment to be good community police officers. Chief Esserman understands that it takes time for officers and leaders to blossom. While there are some natural leaders, he believes that leaders can be made as well.

Dean M. Esserman is a man who seamlessly weaves into conversation the wisdom of Sophocles's *Antigone* or Clausewitz's *On War*. He does so without sounding imperious or condescending; rather, he is a thoughtful, soulful individual who deeply cares about his officers, the department, and his community. America's police community could learn much from Dean Esserman in terms of both internal leadership of departments and proactive community peace officer relations. Whether politicians and departments have the courage to discard decades of leader-driven bureaucracy is the magic question. When they learn to do what they ought to do, not what they can do, America's streets will be safer and full of the liberty and freedoms our founding fathers envisioned for all citizens.

19

Some Solutions

> Everything that grows begins small. It is by constant and progressive feeding that it gradually grows big.
>
> —**St. Mark the Hermit,** *De lege spirituali*

DEVELOPING MAGNANIMITY WITHIN POLICE OFFICERS AND DEPARTMENTS

Fixing many of the problems set forth in this book will take patience, time, and dedication. But, as St. Mark the Hermit sets forth, taking such seemingly small daily steps can gradually build a department imbued with a sense of unit humility and selfless service. Internally, it can truly help transform an organization from a dour, miserable place to work into a magnanimous command where people are excited and proud to serve.

Police departments, like any organization, are comprised of people. Their job centrally revolves around dealing with people of all walks of life: hardened criminals and their pathetic, hurt victims, normally reasonable people who may become dangerously violent and unpredictable under the highly stressful circumstances in which they interact with police, alcoholics and drug addicts, introverts and extroverts, the sane and lunatics, bipolar housewives, and sanguine bankers. The more officers learn compassion and self-control when dealing with all those with whom they come in contact, typically the better the result with be for all parties involved. This requires trust between commanders and their officers: trust and authority to exercise judgment and discretion. In a world ever more controlled by body cameras, intelligence fusion centers, and comparative statistics (COMSTAT), it is increasingly more difficult for the human aspects of policing to remain paramount. But, they must, for good, holistic, and truly effective policing, involve managing people-to-people relationships.

Effective police departments and law enforcement agencies depend on people of good virtues to lead and man them. Herodotus's commentary that "Persians educate their boys to ride well, shoot straight, and speak the truth"* recognizes that there are absolute truths and an internal moral compass that good men should follow. It is time to reexamine the importance of these cardinal virtues as they might relate to healing the tensions and wounds that exist between police and our populace.

In his book *Virtuous Leadership*,† Alexandre Havard writes of the importance and relevance of the cardinal virtues—competency, courage, self-control, and justice—to both effective leaders and healthy organizations. Any person or group that lacks in one or more of these core character traits is doomed to failure. As William Penn, the founder and namesake of Pennsylvania, said:

> Governments, like clocks, go from the motion men give them; and as governments are made and moved by men, so by them they are ruined too.... Let men be good and the government cannot be bad.... But if men be bad, let the government be never so good, they will endeavor to warp and spoil it to their turn.‡

Police departments, like governments, must acknowledge fundamental truths to guide daily actions. Living pursuant to the cardinal virtues can inoculate officers from self-absorbed, licentious behaviors, such as one routinely observes in Hollywood and professional sports leagues. America's police departments must strive to remain above the fray of partisan politics and the gutter of licentiousness.

If our police forces are to remain effective guardians of our populace, they must not proceed under the false belief that aspiring to live virtuously is somehow an irrelevant modality for a postmodern world. The first obstacle often thrown out by those objecting to infusing virtue's lessons into policy is that doing so somehow violates the First Amendment's Establishment Clause,§ which proscribes a formal church–state

---

* Davis, William Stearns, *Readings in Ancient History: Illustrative Extracts from the Sources*, Vol. 2: *Greece and the East* (Boston: Allyn and Bacon, 1912), pp. 58–61.
† Harvard, Alexandre, *Virtuous Leadership: An Agenda for Personal Excellence*, Second Edition (New York: Scepter Publishers, Inc., 2014).
‡ Quoted in Thomas Clarkson, *Memoirs of the Private and Public Life of William Penn*, Vol. I (London: Richard Taylor and Co., 1813), p. 303.
§ U.S. Constitution, First Amendment.

relationship. Such an objection is a canard that is predicated on ignorance of history and the law.

Historically, the importance of the cardinal virtues is illustrated not only in all of the world's major religions, but also in classical literature and philosophy. Legally, those that bristle against any open religious activity, such as the presence of a chaplains' corps in the military or police departments, seem to ignore the Free Exercise Clause of that very same amendment. Sadly, these voices have found traction of late within executive, legislative, and judicial branches of government.

Our nation's founders, such as William Penn above, recognized the importance of the goodness and virtues engendered by the free exercise of religion. Accordingly, they never intended to cordon off such wisdom from polite and practical society. For these reasons, or if only to protect their subordinates' right to exercise their religious freedoms, senior civilian and police leaders need to remain vigilant against those who wish to diminish such rights.

Sadly, reality television shows like *Cops* and videos on YouTube often present a stage for officers lacking the cardinal virtues to showboat and treat citizens badly. The ubiquity of foul language and grandstanding by such "bully" cops should be disconcerting to any police leader who watches such shows. Unfortunately, however, such shows breed copycat behavior among police officers as well as criminal suspects. Police leadership, through promulgation of general orders and repetitive in-service training, need to make it clear to officers that such unprofessional behavior is to be strongly avoided. While cops are human and accordingly make mistakes under stress, recidivist complaints or activity should be grounds for suspension or termination.

Professionalism in Leadership

Contrary to popular belief, the etiology of leadership in police departments is not the military. Rather, police were formed out of citizenry night watches akin to volunteer fire departments. While they became more professionalized at the recommendations of Sir Robert Peel in England, their command structure actually flowed out of seniority and political appointments. As such, there exists an ingrained sense of "we do it that way because we have always done it that way" that is difficult to overcome. Take note that most of America views politicians as scoundrels. However, although they despise politicians, they like and continually reelect their scoundrels. Similarly, politics within departments and, to some extent, larger police organizations, such as the International Association of Chiefs of Police, has become a game of not promoting the better interests of society, but rather promoting self-interests. This needs to change. As noted by Chief Esserman, performance in departments is often trumped by rank and tradition. Departments that want to change and grow might consider ways to break these artificial glass ceilings.

Part of that change might come from how departments assess, select, and train their new recruits. From the beginning, police should *treat* themselves as professionals, not just *call* each other professionals. But, what are the attributes of a professional? Doctors, lawyers, accountants, and architects are considered professionals. Why? What is it about these jobs that make them professional? Is it that they work indoors and wear suits? Is it an honor-based concept, or something more? For the purposes of policing, we submit that being a professional is in the calling of the work. It is about serving others rather than self. It is striving for that unit humility and magnanimity to which Alexandre Havard speaks. It requires getting rid of the selfish "I want" and replacing it with "What can I do to help?" Police officers that come to the job with that expectation are more likely to have job satisfaction than those that come with false expectations. If recruits come with self-glorifying expectations derived from Hollywood or television, they will either quickly sour to the job or, worse, try to make the job fit their expectations. That is where we get the prototypical officers wearing sap gloves and a bad attitude. Serial killer Jeffrey Dahmer probably had a decent idea of who he was. But, the job is not about each of us individually being our very own "special snowflake." It is all about what officers can bring to the table as guardians of the whole society: caring, serving, and sacrificing. Departments must therefore recruit those that look outside of themselves and possess those attributes associated with selfless service as the baseline standard.

But, all of the best recruitment and training can quickly be lost if the leadership does not mirror, recognize, and promote these very same values. How many departments have a meaningful mission statement that serves as an inspirational model for who officers should be? Departments must model appropriate behavior and aspire to inculcate that behavior within each officer as they go about their daily duties. Again, as Aristotle showed, by modeling the professional, they will become professional. If departments and agencies inculcate themselves with moral and virtuous attributes, they will begin to act morally and virtuously. By acting morally, they will ingrain it as a practice. By ingraining it as a practice, it becomes habit. Habit will then become a habitual, subconscious behavior. Once ingrained or inculcated as an inherent, subconscious trait, officers will have achieved the desired affect: to ride, shoot straight, and tell the truth. When that plateau is reached, officers can then further refine their behavior and attention to other specialized endeavors required of the position, rather than seeking more selfish development of the person. Officers that are always looking for the next job as a mere stepping-stone for a promotion should be vilified, not rewarded.

Now more than ever, there is a thirst in our society for such virtuous policing. Society as a whole wants it, and surprisingly to some, the young seeking law enforcement careers want it too. Society owes it to the police to provide them an environment to train and grow such a virtuous force. We don't ask for or expect that same civilized behavior from the Snookis or Kim Kardshians; yet, we demand it from those expected to keep order. Since we do not reward our police financially, their reward must flow from the enduring sense of professionalism and service that a well-led department can offer.

We believe that our friend Alexandre Havard is pure genius in his observations and vision set forth in *Virtuous Leadership*; consequently, the discussion of the cardinal virtues in earlier pages bears review. But, so that they are succinctly preserved in this one easily accessible chapter, along with other steps and leadership principles that law enforcement leaders can reference in their quest for magnanimity, they are again listed, as follows:

Competency or prudence
Justice
Courage
Self-control or temperance

These cardinal virtues used as both the individual's and the organization's building blocks will lead to a magnanimous work environment. *Magnanimity* is an underutilized and not frequently understood word. It is that loftiness of spirit enabling one to bear trouble calmly, to disdain meanness and pettiness, and to display a noble generosity. It is the essence of chivalry. A magnanimous person is the opposite of a pusillanimous or small-minded person. Some vivid examples of magnanimity and pusillanimity in specific sports professions follow. The authors have no idea how these individuals behaved in their private lives, but one may have suspicions based on how they acted on the field or the stage of life:

Magnanimous	Pusillanimous
Cal Ripken Jr., Roberto Clemente	Alex Rodriguez, Barry Bonds
Muhammed Ali, George Foreman	Mike Tyson
Jason Kidd, Jerry West, Michael Jordan	LeBron James
Bobby Jones, Arnold Palmer	Tiger Woods
Tom Landry	Bobby Knight
Peggy Fleming	Tonya Harding

For younger readers who might be unfamiliar with the name Bobby Jones, a bit of background is in order. Not only was Bobby Jones one of the best golfers of the 20th century—some say of all time—but he also exemplified the principles of sportsmanship and fair play. By way of example, in the first round of the 1925 U.S. Open, Jones's approach shot to the 11th hole fell short and landed in the deep rough of an embankment. As he took his stance to pitch onto the green, the head of his club inadvertently brushed the grass and caused the slightest movement of the ball. He took the shot, and then informed his playing partner, Walter Hagen, and the U.S. Golf Association (USGA) official covering their match that he was calling a penalty on himself. Hagen and the official both tried to talk Jones out of it. After the round was complete, but before Jones signed his official scorecard, the officials again argued with Jones not to take the penalty. But, Jones insisted that he had violated golf's rule 18: moving a ball at rest after address. This self-correction gave Jones a score of 77 instead of 76 on that round, and eventually cost him winning the Open by a single stroke in regulation. Afterwards, many sportswriters praised him for his gesture. In response, Jones said, "You may as well praise a man for not robbing a bank." Such is the trait of a truly virtuous and magnanimous human being.

Every police leader, from squad supervisor to head of the agency, should strive to foster environments where such magnanimity flourishes. A police officer living a true and straight life has enough to worry about on the job. He or she should not have to worry about the virtue of peers, bosses, or subordinates. Having such a trustworthy team should be every leader's goal. Absent a deep understanding and practice of the cardinal virtues, however, such a goal is futile because that leader lacks the inherent capacity to foster unit humility and magnanimity. In other words, a person can be polite, politically correct, and yet still be pusillanimous and mean spirited.

WORDS OF CAUTION

The dangers for any police officer in not acknowledging and living pursuant to the cardinal virtues should be obvious. But, when one considers how to boil a frog,* the pitfalls may not be as obvious as they once might have been. Just consider the virtues generally practiced by the Greatest Generation. Ronald Reagan's speechwriter, Peggy Noonan, recently observed that things that were once vices are now government-funded or sanctioned activities. And, matters of personal liberty—private rights of firearms ownership, weekly exercise of one's faith, and voting obligations—are now at low ebb, if not under outright attack. These are just observations proffered in furtherance of the boiled frog analogy. America enjoys God's blessings, but must never forget that they are blessings.

If there are rational and moral concerns about any policy or course of action, voices expressing such concerns should be encouraged rather than quelled or shunned. Sadly and dangerously, this does not appear to be happening enough today.

Trends to muzzle virtuous voices must be reversed if our republic is to remain morally fit and strong. This is especially true among those given the authority to enforce laws and keep the peace. When an average citizen sees a police officer on the street or in their rearview mirror, he or she should feel relief, not fear or trepidation. If police departments are more concerned about filling the state's coffers with so-called asset forfeiture funds than keeping the peace, there will eventually be trouble in River City.

Police departments should never be a growth industry or a source of revenue for the state. Unfortunately, too many jurisdictions—some sold a bill of goods by red-light and speed camera manufacturers—have gotten hooked on the asset forfeiture crack pipe. It is this type of bureaucratic behavior that turns average, good citizens against the police. America cannot afford to trend toward such a gulf between police and populace. Mayberry can quickly turn into Ferguson, and this has nothing to do with race.

Another reason for dissonance between police and populace is the explosive growth of administrative laws and procedures. Government needs to contract rather than expand, but no U.S. president since Ronald Reagan

---

* If one places a bullfrog into a pan of boiling water, the frog will jump out. If, however, one puts the frog into a pot of cool water, and then gradually turns up the temperature, the frog will peacefully stay in the pot until cooked to death. It is the allegory that points out the dangers of incrementalism.

has pledged and succeeded in doing so. Accordingly, we are left with governments—local, state, and federal—being involved in every little aspect of our lives. In *Three Felonies a Day*,* author Harvey A. Silverglate reveals how federal criminal laws alone have become dangerously disconnected from the English common law traditions, and how prosecutors can pin arguable federal crimes on any one of us, for even the most seemingly innocuous behaviors. This must stop before the currently unacceptable imprisonment rate of 1 in 420 Americans grows to an even more unstable state. Prisons are prime breeding grounds for dangerous, antisocial behaviors, to include radical Islamic organizations and violent racial supremacy groups.

Not surprisingly, a 2004 study[†] showed that most prison gang leaders demonstrate behaviors that are the least virtuous or impious. For example, four character traits of these career criminals are

1. Disdain for authority, particularly legal authority, that when coupled with a propensity for violence can lead to sudden and unpredictable acts of aggression (lack of justice)
2. Acute awareness of their environment that can be used to take advantage of less savvy inmates
3. Criminal versatility that allows habitual offenders to engage in assorted acts of misconduct with fluidity
4. Inflated sense of self that can contribute to attempts to intimidate, coerce, and prey upon other inmates

Not exactly the type of individuals to whom we want to expose more of our young. Yet, if we pass more and more laws and enforce them without discretion, we ought not be surprised if there are increased memberships in prison chapters of Al Qaeda, the Muslim Brotherhood, the Black Guerillas, or White supremacy groups.

Politicians probably believe they are doing something by passing more and more legislative agendas. But, sometimes doing nothing is the right choice. Voters should be cognizant of this when making electoral decisions. But, police leaders can also recognize that more laws are not necessarily the answer to criminal problems. Organizations such as the International

---

* Silvergate, Harvey, *Three Felonies a Day: How the Feds Target the Innocent* (New York: Encounter Books, 2009).
† DeLisi, Matt, Berg, Mark, and Hochstetler, Andy, "Gang Members, Career Criminals and Prison Violence: Further Specification of the Importation Model of Inmate Behavior," *Criminal Justice Studies*, 17(4), 369–383, 2004.

Association of Chiefs of Police (IACP), the National Sheriffs Association (NCA), and the National Tactical Officers Association (NTOA) have a voice in these matters. In fact, fewer, more clearly defined statutes may decrease the actual crime rate and stabilize our social order.

Repeating lies loudly and often enough does not make them true. Senior leaders must not simply parrot the opinions of their political masters. Sometimes, abiding by the cardinal virtues demands that they speak the truth. But, perhaps paralyzed by the fear of losing their jobs, most will remain silent.

Subordinates watch and learn from their leaders. If those leaders go into defilade instead of standing up for what is virtuous, what lessons will be passed down to the next generation of police officers? This is not a matter of arguing the value of one training system over another or the efficacy of Tasers. This is about retaining core virtuous principles that spawn courage, truth, and selflessness.

Citizens expect high standards from their police officers. Officers must forfeit many of their erstwhile civilian idiosyncrasies—faddish haircuts, sleeping late, using or associating with those who use illegal drugs, and being couch potatoes—in order to become part of a greater whole. Ideally, our police forces should be a corps of moral, disciplined, compassionate, and fit individuals that can close in on and capture or kill dangerous felons in one hour, and then help an elderly person change a flat tire on the side of a rainy road in the next. Hence, they must never forget to ride, shoot straight, and speak the truth—even if doing so ruffles some political feathers. Our officers and citizens deserve nothing less.

Internally, not only will departments that acknowledge and reward officers possessing and practicing the cardinal virtues become better places to work, but their interactions with the society they serve will also be more positive in nature. Citizens who do not feel that they are on the receiving end of a need to feed and pad arrest numbers or the agency's budget will be more receptive to getting stopped for a moving violation—even if a ticket results. Physicians have long known that if they take an extra five minutes to talk with their patients and listen to their complaints (in essence showing compassion), they are much less likely to be sued, even if they act negligently.

So, understanding and practicing the cardinal virtues on a daily basis can form the cornerstone of a magnanimous department, inwardly and outwardly. Once a department's leadership plumbs and levels itself internally upon the solid foundation of these virtues, departments, big or small, will internally grow a healthy culture of unit humility and magnanimity. Soon after that happens, toxic leaders will either transform, quit, or be fired. More interestingly, magnanimous and creative leaders will quickly rise to the top, not out of greedy motivations or ambition, but out of a sense of duty and need. People naturally want to follow magnanimous leaders. Now, assuming a department is on that right path, what individual steps can leaders and officers take to become more competent, as well as to bridge the gulf to the populations they serve?

GETTING OUT OF THE OFFICE AND VEHICLES AND BACK INTO THE STREETS

Officers need to get out of the safe cocoon of their patrol cars and interact with the public. This sounds like a tired mantra of community policing, but that makes it no less true. An officer that does not know by face and name the business owners and prominent citizens on his or her post is doomed to failure. Not only will this help socialize the departments with the citizenry—making the first contact with their police a positive one rather than a negative traffic ticket or crime report—but it will also help officers stay fit. As discussed in previous chapters, an out-of-shape officer will quickly start to lose in a physical altercation, making it more likely that he will need to revert to deadly force. Officers that are not fit are also much more likely to become injured on the job, contract diabetes and heart ailments, and become spiritually and psychologically depressed. The studies on all of this are settled science.

So, why do so many police departments not have an annual or biannual physical fitness test? Other than Special Weapons and Tactics (SWAT) and emergency response team (ERT) officers, too many—even many 1811 series special agents in the federal government—never take a PT test after they graduate from their basic training academy. This is slowly changing, but one of the authors remembers that other officers in his squad ridiculed him and his squad supervisor for coming to work early in order to lift weights and run. A quick scan of many of our co-workers' bellies answered that question in our mind. Unfortunately, a quick scan of many young officers today shows no higher degree of fitness.

How many minutes in a flat-out fight can an overweight officer last before exhausting his cardiovascular capability to process oxygen? The results of many studies are enlightening: Most out-of-shape officers last less than a minute in a fight against a determined adversary. What good would that young officer be to his side partner if totally winded so soon into the battle? We hear time and again from senior police leaders, "We can't force them to exercise or take PT tests because they will sue us or file EO or ADA volition complaints against us." To that we say, "Let them." If we are in the right and acting virtuously, there is nothing to worry about. In reality, what they are worried about is another incident clouding the matter. A superior was playing footsies with a young officer in her patrol car one night, and now the young officer is holding that over the supervisor's head as retaliation for his trying to enforce PT standards. The courageous fix would be to discipline them both for the separate and distinct violations.

Additionally, physical fitness also cures one of the plagues of police work: depression. More cops are killed each year by suicide than assailants. But, how many departments undertake programs to improve their officers' mental health?

Departments need to find means, motivation, time, and incentives for police to come in to use the exercise room. So, the first step might be to get an exercise room and stock it with simple, modern pieces of equipment that all levels of fitness are comfortable using: rowing machines, solid weight racks, kettle bells, and other core-strength-enhancing exercise programs. Encourage officers to come in to use it, too. If the exercise room turns into a supply closet, what message does that send the unit? And if supervisors themselves are grossly obese, what does that say about how seriously the organization takes fitness?

First-line supervisors need to get out of the station house in order to respond with and observe their subordinates in action. How else will they be able to mentor and train those under their supervision? If an officer is performing traffic stops in an unsafe manner or inadvertently being rude to citizens, a supervisor that never leaves the police station will only discover these matters when an accident occurs or a citizen complaint is filed. Or, the supervisor will be tempted to rely on grainy and out-of-focal plane lapel videos to assess officer performance. While technologically cool, this virtual leadership concept is no better than a general trying to play squad leader from the Pentagon's military command center or, worse, the White House.

Higher levels of command need to break away from their desks, computers, and statistical tools, so they can get out into the public to speak with

citizens' groups, churches, business leaders, and other communal touch-
stones within their jurisdictions. There is a truism in the medical-legal
community: patients who like their physicians are much less likely to sue
them, even when that physician has committed a clear breach of the standard of care. This is because people are inherently forgiving of those with
whom they already have a personal relationship.

Think of how we might be tempted to act in incidents of road rage. It is
very easy to flip off an unknown driver in the other car: Conversely, we
would rarely do the same to even a casual acquaintance in the other vehicle.
Similarly, if a police department has taken the time to build personal relationships with the community it serves, should a traumatic incident occur,
even a seemingly questionable officer-involved shooting (OIS), that community will be much more resilient and forgiving. This is just one more
way to break down the barrier of the "us-versus-them" mindset. This is
difficult to do after the fact, so the sooner the better is our advice.

Departments can also use such community outreach programs to
educate the populace about some of the immutable truths of policing in
general. For instance, as explained by David Blake of Blake Consulting
and Training Group:

> The truth is there are about 700K police in this country who make about
> 40 million arrests and yet we use force less than 2 percent of the time
> during those arrests. It's well known within the blue line that police often
> don't use force when they could/should and sometimes they themselves
> become injured as a result. Police are viewed through a "Hollywood" lens
> that shows us shooting guns out of suspect's hands as we let the cigarette
> dangle from our lips. Yet, in all truth; we are poorly trained, sometimes
> overworked, tired, and just as afraid as any normal human might be under
> similar frightening conditions, and we are fallible—just like everyone else.
> Our image; however, says otherwise.*

This one paragraph says a lot, but mostly it says that police are more
human and fragile than the public might otherwise believe. So, that
message needs to be communicated to the public in real and effective
ways. If a district or precinct commander in a large city police department, or an assistant chief of a smaller department, visited community
groups and churches and simply communicated, in person, what Blake

* Blake, David, *Ferguson Police, Michael Brown and "The Vilification of Police"* (St. Helena, CA:
Blake Consulting & Training Group, 2014).

sets forth above, this would greatly help humanize the department and its officers. Unfortunately, much of the public forms its opinion about how the police can and should act by what Hollywood portrays. If a TV cop can shoot to wound or talk a knife-wielding suspect into surrendering without a shot being fired, then why can't real police? Community outreach and education can go a long way toward preventing a Ferguson, Missouri, incident from going viral in the community.

The Federal Bureau of Investigation (FBI) routinely invites attorneys from the Department of Justice's (DOJ) Civil Rights Division to the FBI Academy at Quantico in order to expose them to the use-of-force training that special agents receive. At the end of the day, some people are simply uneducable (due to either deeply ingrained prejudices or plain stupidity*), but most are open and receptive to being educated on these otherwise arcane topics. There is nothing wrong with inviting members of civic groups or church elders into training academies so that they, too, can both observe and participate in such training. Often, once they viscerally experience the stress of even very simple force-on-force situational training exercises, such groups are much more understanding of officers' actions, even mistakes, in the clear vision of 20/20 hindsight. These exercises most often utilize either nonlethal training aids such at Ultimate Training Munitions™ or Simunitions™ or video-based training devices such as Milo™, VirTra™, or FATS™ interactive judgment simulators.

The nonlethal training aids are typically marking paint-filled plastic rounds instead of bullets. These are then fired out of modified versions of actual duty weapons. They not only show hits and misses, but also sting like the dickens when they hit. They are the closest thing one can experience to an actual gunfight without suffering permanent injury. Participants use appropriate eye, face, and groin protection, but the rounds do sting when they hit unprotected portions of the body. They are supposed to, as the sting punishes bad tactical behavior.

The video devices use laser rounds and a light-sensitive projection screen to present scenarios to which a trainee can assess and respond. In addition to being great fun, especially for the uninitiated, the lessons learned by using them help better educate a civilian review board or civil rights group. Departments need to stop perceiving such groups as the enemy and take affirmative steps to integrate their concerns into a positive policing

---

* As our friend and author John C. Hall is fond of saying, "God struck some people stupid, but forgot to tell them!"

environment. Pick up the phone—do not email—and make a personal invitation. Emails are impersonal and subject to miscommunication, as they can't adequately capture the tone and sincerity of the sender's voice.

INFORMATION OPERATIONS

Contrary to being a negative application of the art of psychological operations, information operations simply means a department getting out ahead of a news story before rumor, falsehoods, and those with antisocial agendas fuel it. Truth must form the foundation of all news conferences and discussions. If news media or the public feels deceived, it is nearly impossible to regain that trust. "We simply do not know all the facts yet, but are diligently working with all of our resources to fairly and accurately assess what occurred" is much better than an assumption or guess that is later proved incorrect. In this age of information ubiquity, a "No comment" or "We can't discuss matters under investigation" will no longer suffice. A simple, truthful statement reassuring the public that a neutral fact-finding investigation is underway and that the rule of law will then be applied to the results of that investigation is much better than nothing or stonewalling.

Rare for Hollywood and television, a recent episode of *Blue Bloods* ended with Tom Selleck's character as commissioner of the NYPD coming out and doing what David Blake recommends: personalizing the officers, explaining the facts as they were known at the time, and assuring that his officers would be held to the standards of reasonableness as set forth by the U.S. Supreme Court in *Graham v. Connor* and its progeny. It was a rare instance where Hollywood got it mostly right. We suspect that Tom Selleck, personally, had much to do with the writing of this episode, as he is more knowledgeable on firearms and their use than most in the industry.

KEEPING UP WITH THE STATE-OF-THE-ART KNOWLEDGE: COMPETENCY IN PRACTICE

Officers need to receive relevant, up-to-date in-service training after their initial certification training at the academy. Most police departments provide a 12- to 26-week initial training at a central academy, followed by at least a month of field training with an experienced and trusted veteran officer. This training sets the initial tone for how officers will behave and act throughout their career. But, the time spent with a field training officer and his or her initial assignment is critically important to shaping a new officer's professional ethos. If the first assignment is with a squad that plays fast and loose with ethical boundaries or treats the populace as a burden to be mistrusted or feared, that can irrevocably contaminate a young officer for the rest of his or her career.

In-service (or annual follow-on professional education) must be vibrant and relevant to the officers' beats. Departments that send their best and brightest to teach at their in-service academies and spend the money to appropriately train the trainers will both better inoculate themselves from lawsuits and better create truly magnanimous workplaces. Police officers have a very low tolerance for incompetent instructors. But, this does not mean that officers cannot learn "new tricks" or better ways of doing their jobs. Instructors should not be passing on inaccurate old wives' tales such as the following we have heard at diverse academies: "All you need to say if you use deadly force is 'I was in fear of my life' and then just keep repeating that phrase." In reality, whether an officer is in fear of his or her life is a legal irrelevancy, for a coward might be in fear of his life without reasonable provocation, and a fool might not be in fear of his life when he reasonably should be! What is relevant is to train officers on recognizing real preassaultive behaviors, and then provide them with competent counsel to help them articulate why a suspect demonstrated those behaviors, if extant.

FITNESS FOR DUTY

We have all seen the stereotypical donut-eating cop: rolls of fats drooping over his equipment belt, sweating butter, and breathless after the most minor of physical exertions. Departments that do not maintain a physical fitness standard after initial training are doing themselves and their officers a severe disservice. Not only are the out-of-shape officers a liability to themselves, the public, and other officers—who wants a grossly obese or 90-pound weakling arriving as backup or attempting to stop an assault in progress or armed robbery?—but they also become fiscal albatrosses by incurring repetitive line-of-duty injuries and mental illnesses due to stress.

Departmentally, it takes an up-front commitment by both the officers and their departments to agree to implement a fitness program. Older officers will need to do this on their own, as they will most likely be exempt from newly written rules by grandfather clauses. It is simple, however, to write employment contracts for all new accessions that require their passing a biannual physical fitness test. But, veteran officers can be offered this as a voluntary incentive for promotion and to maintain their personal health. Some might claim that police unions or collective bargaining agreements make this impractical or impossible. But again, communication is the key to success. When officers see the benefits of a paid physical fitness program, all but the stubbornly or willfully ignorant will sign up for these opportunities.

Individually, officers should find a training buddy. It is far more difficult to blow off a PT session if you know your friend is counting on you to be there. And, always try to work out with someone who has the moral courage or fortitude to stick it out. The rewards physically and mentally of even a moderate PT program will improve one's social and family life—yes, that includes a healthier sex life—but, it will drastically improve one's chances of surviving mortal combat.

SOME IMPORTANT COURSES AND TEXTS

Courses

Force Science Institute Courses

For nearly 30 years, Dr. Bill Lewinski and his professional colleagues at Force Science Institute have been at the forefront of producing peer-reviewed research and application of *unbiased* scientific principles and processes to determine the true nature of human behavior in high-stress and deadly force encounters. This is extremely important for anyone seeking to bypass the hyperbole and falsehoods surrounding many officer-involved shootings with a view toward factually discerning a just resolution. The institute's groundbreaking studies address real problems encountered by law enforcement officers on the street and are meticulously documented.

Any prosecuting attorney, civil rights division counsel, homicide or internal affairs investigator, or law enforcement leader would be well served by attending a Force Science Institute course. At a minimum, reading and comprehending the institute's readily available reports and studies is required to maintain a reasonable degree of competency in this field. Being articulate in the facts and science behind use-of-force dynamics helps police leadership to better articulate why an officer chose a course of action. In fact, departments would also be well served by inviting political leadership to these types of courses so that the policy makers and funding sources have a better understanding of the dynamics of deadly force encounters.

We sincerely believe that most people, once properly educated, will then support officers who act in good faith—even if they make a decisional error under stress. Moreover, once educated, municipalities, states, and federal entities will be less likely to pay out ridiculous settlements to criminal plaintiffs in civil suits alleging excessive force or a civil rights violation. Do not misread us: If an officer willfully violates a citizen's civil rights and causes actual harm, then there should be consequences for both the agency and the individual officer. But, when jurisdictions pay out millions of dollars out of fear or ignorance of the law, then shame on them. Unfortunately, however, innocent officers often pay the price for such ignorance.

The Force Science Institute is the umbrella organization for three subordinate divisions: the Force Science Research Center, the Force Science Consultation Division, and the Force Science Training Division. Their website is www.forcescience.org, from which the following is gleaned:

> Force Science Research Center: Dedicated to scientifically determining and fully understanding the true physical and psychological dynamics of force encounters by conducting groundbreaking research into officer and suspect behaviors during rapidly unfolding, high-stress confrontations.
>
> Force Science Consultation Division: Provides expert support that will help attorneys, judges, jurors, review board members, investigators and others responsible for determining the appropriateness of officers' behavior during force encounters to better understand the scientific realities surrounding these events as revealed by Force Science studies.
>
> Force Science Training Division: Provides training that will educate administrators, trainers, investigators, attorneys, officers and other legal professionals on Force Science findings and will help facilitate the application of Force Science concepts during their investigations, training and work in the field. There are one-day, two-day and a full weeklong Certification course, the latter universally recognized as being the "gold standard" for experts in this field of study.

Often, many regional agencies pool their resources to fill a Force Science Institute class. The Force Science training team will then bring the program to that geographic region, cutting down on travel and lodging costs for officers and their agencies. In addition to receiving the unparalleled training from Force Science, departments that are otherwise too busy to communicate with one another in person are socialized. Many cases have been resolved and training methodologies shared via this route. Their weeklong certification course is the best academic week one can find: Meeting other officers from different departments is just icing on that cake.

Federal Bureau of Investigation

In addition to teaching its special agents, the FBI also offers many courses and training resources to departments and agencies worldwide. Some require nominations and travel to Quantico, Virginia, while others are accessible locally and online.

The National Academy

The FBI National Academy is a professional course of study for U.S. and international law enforcement leaders that serves to improve the administration of·justice in police departments and agencies at home and abroad and to raise law enforcement standards, knowledge, and cooperation worldwide. Its mission is "to support, promote, and enhance the personal and professional development of law enforcement leaders by preparing them for complex, dynamic, and contemporary challenges through innovative techniques, facilitating excellence in education and research, and forging partnerships throughout the world."[*]

Each class is comprised of leaders of state and local police, sheriffs' departments, military police organizations, and federal law enforcement agencies. Participation is by invitation only, through a nomination process. Participants are drawn from every state in the union, from U.S. territories, and from over 160 international partner nations.

National Executive Institute

The NEI was established in August 1975 when then FBI director Clarence Kelley tasked the FBI Academy with developing a proposal for a law enforcement executive training program. Topical areas selected for the program, which now trains domestic and international law enforcement

---

[*] See http://www.fbi.gov/about-us/training/national-academy.

leaders, included national and international political, economic, and social trends affecting the policing function; ethics and integrity; the effects of affirmative action on hiring and promotional policies; media relations; labor relations; the future structure of police organizations; financing of police operations; training and legal issues; labor relations; and the impact of criminal activity on policing. The training division, through local FBI offices and overseas legal attaché offices, solicits nominations for new participants.

Law Enforcement Executive Development Seminars (LEEDS)

A two-week program designed for chief executive officers of the nation's midsized law enforcement agencies—those having between 50 and 499 sworn officers and serving a population of 50,000 or more. Executives are provided instruction and facilitation in the areas of leadership, strategic planning, legal issues, labor relations, media relations, social issues, and police programs. Participants have the opportunity to exchange plans, problems, and solutions with their peers, develop new thoughts and ideas, and share successes.

Law Enforcement Instructor School (LEIS)

An intense 40-hour practical, skill-oriented course designed to provide fundamentals in adult instruction and curriculum design. State and local law enforcement partner participants learn and practice a variety of teaching strategies to deliver effective instruction. Participants incorporate different instructional methodologies for effective delivery to a variety of audiences in different learning environments, and engage in public speaking exercises to hone their presentation skills. The LEIS has been aligned to meet Police Officer Standards and Training (POST) Commission instructor certification requirements in many states throughout the United States.

Leadership Fellows Program

Senior police managers and executives from around the world are offered the opportunity to enhance their leadership skills by teaching, networking with staff and students, addressing leadership issues in their sponsoring agency, attending a variety of courses, and developing a blueprint for personal growth. The first six months of the program is in full residency, where fellows work closely with Center for Police Leadership and Ethics (CPLE) instructors to develop and instruct leadership curricula, address challenges or prospective issues in their host agency, having a beneficial impact upon their return, and attend leadership development courses in accordance with their individual development plans. The second six months consists of fellows continuing to support the CPLE instructional mission domestically and internationally while serving as adjunct instructors and providing instruction in accordance with CPLE needs.

Active Shooter Program

After the Newtown shooting in December 2012, a White House working group specifically tasked the DOJ and the FBI with training law enforcement and other first responders to ensure that protocols for responding to active shooter initiatives are consistent across the country.

Firearms Training

The training division delivers a comprehensive and consistent firearms training curriculum that provides new agent trainees, special agents, and police officers the skills needed to safely and effectively use firearms, if necessary, while performing their duties. The experienced firearms training instructors assigned to the division also offer certification and recertification training to all FBI firearms instructors who provide training to agents in the field and support state and local law enforcement partners.

Sabbaticals and Educational Incentives

America needs to change police careers from being entry-level, trade school positions (where young police officers are simply taught the requisite elements of their state's POST* certification) to a graduate-level profession (where officers are clinically taught the arts of communication and persuasion). Many officer-involved acts of violence—to include their own suicide rates—might be precluded if officers where trained and treated as professional clinicians. Very few, if any, departments offer such a professional career path for their officers. They are working off of training modalities developed in the 1960s or earlier: how to affect an arrest, firearms qualifications, which forms to fill out, and tactical vehicle emergency operation courses. They think and work in terms of shift work and

---

* Peace Officers Standards and Training (POST) Councils are state entities that attempt to ensure uniform training within police jurisdictions throughout each state. Typically, a state's POST has voting members and a number of advisory members who meet quarterly. Members of the council are appointed from state, county, and local law enforcement agencies, professional associations, and the peace officer population. Therein lies part of the problem: They are too insular.

paid court overtime, and promotions are often based on rote examinations rather than leadership skills.

Law enforcement's own internal structure is treating officers as blue-collar manufacturers rather than the clinicians that society expects and needs them to be. We submit that departments should assume a more modern approach that trains officers to focus on how humans interact, rather than on merely enforcing laws. This must be a concerted, educated effort among politicians, law enforcement leadership, and police unions. Departments should encourage assessment and selection from institutes of higher learning and encourage continuing education among its veterans.

Texts and Professional Reading Materials

In Defense of Self and Others: Issues, Facts & Fallacies—The Realities of Law Enforcement's Use of Deadly Force, 2nd edition, by Urey W. Patrick and John C. Hall. This book, written by two retired supervisory special agents of the FBI, is the holy grail of books concerning the law and dynamics of deadly force encounters. Now in the midst of its third rewrite (Carolina Academic Press should publish the 3rd edition by 2016), it is too important a text not to buy the edition currently available.

FBI Law Enforcement Bulletin (LEB). A Department of Justice publication available for free on the FBI's public website, it is a scholarly forum for the exchange of information on law enforcement-related topics. The *LEB* solicits articles written by nationally recognized authors and experts in the criminal justice field and delivers relevant, contemporary information on a broad range of law enforcement issues. Its audience includes criminal justice professionals, primarily law enforcement managers, but it is also widely considered a valuable training tool at all levels.[*]

Unintended Consequences by John Ross. This book, first published in 1996, should be a must-read for any serious student of the relationship between governments and the people. A work of fiction, it nevertheless accurately sets forth the conditions by which free peoples, pushed to their limits by an overzealous law enforcement-centric government, fight back. It should serve as a stern warning to those who believe people are nothing more than statistics to be managed. Many readers might find our endorsement of this book to be disconcerting, as the protagonist of the fictional plot commits some

---

[*] See http://leb.fbi.gov.

graphic and violent acts against fictional law enforcement agents. But, we feel it is important to see the book for what it is—a stark warning against those who wish to widen the gulf between police and populace. A flashpoint almost occurred recently when a cattle rancher's use of Bureau of Land Management (BLM) land to graze his cattle almost became the cause of violence. Federal officers began to confiscate his cattle from BLM land, based on his nonpayment of leasing fees. Over several days, numerous armed citizens began to congregate around the area. Many of these citizens were better armed than the federal officers, having long-range hunting rifles. Luckily, confrontation was averted. The authors adamantly stand against any acts of violence against our law enforcement brethren. Understanding the risk, though, we must stop the breakdown of trust that is essential between citizens and our government.

Men in Black: How the Supreme Court Is Destroying America by Mark R. Levin. This book articulately and in lay terms examines how activist courts are subverting our constitutional freedoms and fundamental liberties. Well-educated police need to understand the source and limits of their authority, and this book is a fun, delightful read that will probably never be taught in the average police academy or undergraduate institution.

Serpico by Peter Maas. Most may be familiar with the screen version of this story starring a young Al Pacino. As good as the movie is, the book is better, detailing the small missteps toward corruption that otherwise good cops take. Our dear friend and colleague Colonel Steven "Randy" Watt (Army Special Forces soldier and former assistant chief of police of the Ogden Police Department) rightly points out to his subordinates that corruption rarely starts big. It begins by taking an inconsequential piece of property from a suspect's car or turning a blind eye to your partner's persistent bad behavior. *Serpico* marvelously tells of how this happened in the colorful background of the NYPD in the late 1960s and early 1970s. It is a timeless police morality tale.

Interestingly, Frank Serpico wrote a recent article in *Politico*, where, among other observations, he wrote the following:

In some ways, matters have gotten even worse. *The gulf between the police and the communities they serve has grown wider.* Mind you, I don't want to say that police shouldn't protect themselves and have access to the best equipment. Police officers have the right to defend themselves with maximum

force, in cases where, say, they are taking on a barricaded felon armed with an assault weapon. But when you are dealing every day with civilians walking the streets, and you bring in armored vehicles and automatic weapons, it's all out of proportion. It makes you feel like you're dealing with some kind of subversive enemy. The automatic weapons and bulletproof vest may protect the officer, but they also insulate him from the very society he's sworn to protect. All that firepower and armor puts an even greater wall between the police and society, and solidifies that "us-versus-them" feeling.*
(Emphasis added)

And, while Serpico is no more an expert on law enforcement leadership because of his experiences than John McCain is on torture because he was a POW in the Hanoi Hilton, in that same *Politico* article Serpico does make the following prescient observations about how to diminish the police–populace gulf and restore trust in our communities:

1. **Strengthen the selection process and psychological screening process for police recruits.** Police departments are simply a microcosm of the greater society. If your screening standards encourage corrupt and forceful tendencies, you will end up with a larger concentration of these types of individuals;
2. **Provide ongoing, examples-based training and simulations.** Not only telling but *showing* police officers how they are expected to behave and react is critical;
3. **Require community involvement from police officers** so they know the districts and the individuals they are policing. This will encourage empathy and understanding;
4. **Enforce the laws against everyone, including police officers.** When police officers do wrong, use those individuals as examples of what not to do—so that others know that this behavior will not be tolerated. And tell the police unions and detective endowment associations they need to keep their noses out of the justice system;
5. **Support the good guys.** Honest cops who tell the truth and behave in exemplary fashion should be honored, promoted and held up as strong positive examples of what it means to be a cop;
6. **Last but not least, police cannot police themselves.** Develop permanent, independent boards to review incidents of police corruption and brutality—and then fund them well and support them publicly. Only this can change a culture that has existed since the beginnings of the modern police department.

---

* Serpico, Frank, "The Police Are Still Out of Control: I Should Know," *Politico*, October 23, 2014.

The modern police community needs to take advantage of all the technical tools and procedures available to them. We believe that our police should never be outgunned, outmaneuvered, or otherwise circumvented by wily criminals or rich cartels. And, they should never be overwhelmed in any manner by terror groups, foreign or domestic. But, in so equipping and arming themselves, they must *never* forget their roots and part in their communities. And, they should never feel the necessity to circumvent the constitutional protections that they themselves and the citizens they serve so richly deserve.

We believe that it is possible to be a competent, savvy modern-day peace officer. We have served with and taught many such officers and agents, so we know this is not a pipe dream or unrealistic expectation. Any arguments that we are trying to turn back the clock to the days of Andy Griffith's *Mayberry RFD* or *Adam-12* miss the point. We expect our officers to be technically savvy, tactically capable, and vigilant. But, we demand that they should be virtuous and caring—not bullies on one side of the us versus them dichotomy. Both society and its officers will be truly magnanimous as a result. It is our hope and realistic dream that all can scale life's cliffs to reach for such a summit. It is for these officers, and the virtuous members of our greater society, that we have written this book.

Index

Printed in the United States
by Baker & Taylor Publisher Services